Language Development

Language Development

LouAnn Gerken

PLURAL
PUBLISHING
INC.

SAN DIEGO
OXFORD
BRISBANE

5521 Ruffin Road
San Diego, CA 92123

e-mail: info@pluralpublishing.com
Web site: http://www.pluralpublishing.com

49 Bath Street
Abingdon, Oxfordshire OX14 1EA
United Kingdom

Typeset in 11/13 Garamond by Flanagan's Publishing Services, Inc.
Printed in the United States of America by McNaughton and Gunn, Inc.

Library of Congress Cataloging-in-Publication Data

Gerken, LouAnn.
  Language development / LouAnn Gerken.
      p. ; cm.
  Includes bibliographical references and index.
  ISBN-13: 978-1-59756-263-8 (alk. paper)
  ISBN-10: 1-59756-263-7 (alk. paper)
  1. Language acquisition. I. Title.
  P118.G38 2008
  401'.93—dc22
                        2008036173

■ Contents

■ Preface

Language is an inextricable part of almost every human life. Indeed, language is so interwoven with our humanity that just deciding which thread to pull first to unravel its mysteries is a daunting challenge. Should we study it as part of culture, as part of biology, as part of social psychology, as part of the cognition of individuals, as a complex pattern, or in some other way entirely? Writing this book has amplified my awareness of all the different perspectives on language and its development in human infants and children that I could have taken, but did not. Let me explain why I took the perspective that I did and therefore what you can expect to find if you choose to read beyond this preface.

The perspective most clearly represented in this book is that of cognitive science, the interdisciplinary study of the mind. Cognitive science is a mix of several traditional fields, including psychology, philosophy, computer science, neuroscience, artificial intelligence, and linguistics. I have chosen this perspective for two reasons. The first is that cognitive science is the discipline with which I am most closely affiliated. As an undergraduate, I took courses in psychology, linguistics, philosophy, and computer science. I have continued to pursue some mixture of these fields throughout my career, and currently am the Head of the Cognitive Science Interdisciplinary Program at the University of Arizona.

The second reason for employing a cognitive science perspective is that I wanted to write a book about language development that is theoretically coherent. Rather than following language learners from birth to some point at which we might say they have adultlike language abilities, I have organized this book around a set of contrasting theories. Throughout, I have tried to show how research in different areas of language is driven by researchers' attempts to tease apart these theories and their predictions. Therefore, this book has the potential to provide an understanding of competing accounts of language development, as well as a substantial sampling of the research that these accounts motivate.

Alas, good news seldom comes unaccompanied, and there is a cost to theoretical coherence. With some important exceptions, cognitive science as a field has tended to focus on individual minds and the computational processes used by these minds to make sense of their environments. Many of the enduring controversies about how young humans learn language have construed them in this way—as individual minds trying to extract and generalize the linguistic patterns of their community. This way of viewing language development is certainly missing some central properties of infants and children, such as the emotional factors that motivate them to learn in the first place, what they use language to communicate about and with whom, and how language develops at the same time as many other abilities. Therefore, in striving to paint a coherent picture, I have left out myriad studies and a few areas of research that on their own are priceless gems, but that I found difficult to place into the framework used to organize this book.

For the reader who is already familiar with the field of language development, I apologize if the studies or areas I have left out are some of your favorites. For the reader who is just learning about this field, you will find enough material to keep you occupied for some time, and you will learn about how theoretical debates drive research—certainly a good start. Whatever your reason for reading this book, I hope that you will be able to appreciate the mystery of how young humans come to exhibit a defining characteristic of our species—language.

LouAnn Gerken

This book is dedicated to:

My friend and colleague, the late Peter Jusczyk, who planted the seeds for this book over a decade ago. I wish we had been able to write it together.

My husband, Patrick Neher, who has been unconditionally supportive and encouraging of this and all of my many projects.

The former and current students in my Language Development Lab and in my Language Development courses, whose questions and insights have allowed me to see my field in new ways.

LouAnn Gerken

1 Introduction

■ Why Study Language Development?

Our ability to communicate with each other through language, either spoken, written, or signed, is one that many of us seldom consider. However, if you have ever spent several days, or even several hours, in a foreign language environment, you know the feeling of relief and pleasure that comes when you are again able to use your own language. Language is so much a part of most of our lives that losing its use, even for a short time, can feel like the social equivalent of oxygen deprivation. Although we can also communicate without language, using eye contact, gesture, and so forth; these alternatives are crude tools when compared with linguistic forms of communication.

Nevertheless, the state of being unable to produce or comprehend the language of our social environment is the way we all begin our lives. Like adults in a foreign language environment, infants and young children can communicate with the world around them in non-linguistic ways. However, language becomes the main tool of communication for most children within the first few years of life. What is the nature of human language that makes it the powerful and pervasive communicative tool that it is? How do human infants and children develop language so quickly and with such apparent ease? These two questions, and the research that they stimulate, compose the scientific core of the study of language development, which is the central focus of this book.

But studying language development also has a number of practical, or applied, benefits. For example, many people might want to know the answers to the following questions:

1. Is it good or bad for a child's linguistic development to be raised as a bilingual?

2. What is the best way to teach reading skills?
3. What are the likely outcomes of hearing impairment on language development?
4. How can we build a computer that comprehends and produces language as well as a 3-year-old child?

One group of people who might want answers to such questions is current and future parents. For a parent, the first indication that his or her infant understands a word or phrase is a joy and a relief because it signals the end of a period in which the infant's needs and desires must be guessed from nonverbal cues. Even more momentous is the child's first word. In many cultures, the first word signals the transition from infancy into childhood. For example, some cultures view infants as unintelligent beings until first word production. Indeed, our own English word *infant* comes from a Latin phrase meaning *unable to speak*. For parents, knowing what to expect about the course of language development can make observing the process more interesting. It may be especially interesting to know that, even before your child shows signs of understanding or producing language, he or she is making enormous progress toward joining you as a fellow language user. Knowing what to expect may also allow for better decisions about what to do when language development seems disrupted in some way.

Studying language development can also benefit people who are preparing for a career involving children, including those in daycare centers, schools, hospitals, or clinics for children with speech, language, or hearing disorders. Understanding the normal course of development is useful in these settings in order to identify children who may not follow the typical path. Even more importantly perhaps, people working with children in professional settings should understand the many components of a language system that must develop, and stay updated on the variety of tools being created to assess the separate components of language development. People working with children in professional settings also stand to benefit as our understanding of developing language abilities, such as word comprehension or sentence production, is increasingly paralleled by our understanding of brain development. Some careers in organizations that serve infants and young children also entail making policy decisions, and people who make such decisions should be aware of the likely consequences. For example, the policy that all newborns must be screened for hearing status that many states have implemented is a direct result of policy makers' understanding the role of intact hearing at the very earliest stages of spoken language development.

Careers in the information technology fields can also benefit from the study of human development in general and language development in particular. For us to create computers that are maximally interactive with humans, understanding how our impressive human abilities developed is invaluable. Conversely, different hypotheses about how language learning works can be implemented in different computer programs in order to determine how well the computer performs in comparison to real human learners. The **computational models** of learning that perform best are taken to be closer approximations to the way infants and children learn. These models of language learning can, in turn, help language development researchers design experiments to ask more fine-grained questions about the language learning process.

In addition to introducing you to the scientific study of language development, one of the goals of this book is to demonstrate some of the currently available tools that might be used to answer practical questions like 1 through 4, above, and to provide basic background to people who interact regularly with infants and children.

◼ The Nature of Language

Many organisms, in addition to humans, communicate with each other, but human language has two properties that, as far as researchers can tell, no other communication system has. First, language has the ability to combine **meaning units** such as words, and different combinations of the same words result in different meanings. For example, *Venetian blind* means something entirely different from *blind Venetian*. Second, the meaning units (e.g., words) of language are not atomic or indivisible units, but are themselves composed from a limited inventory of smaller parts, which we can call **submeaning units**. For example, the words *apt, pat*, and *tap* are all composed of the same submeaning units. Similarly, the signs used in American Sign Language (ASL) are composed of smaller components, including the location in which the sign is made and the shape of the hand. (For a more in-depth overview of the material described in this section see Akmajian,

Demers, Farmer, & Harnish, 2001). Although some other animals produce meaning units or meaning unit combinations, and others combine submeaning units, no animal other than humans, as far as we currently know, combines both meaning and submeaning units as part of their communication system. To better understand what the combinatorial ability of language can do, let's consider three systems used by nonhuman animals.

■ Meaning Units

Vervet monkeys make three danger calls: one for snakes, one for eagles, and one for leopards (Cheney & Seyfarth, 1990). Each call has a particular meaning or referent, and therefore is something like a word in human language. However, there is no way within the call system of the vervets to indicate that the snake that has just appeared is particularly large, or that there is an eagle in the distance that is not a strong threat at the moment. For example, the first message might be conveyed by making the snake-call twice. However, there is no evidence that vervets engage in such call combinations. In contrast, human language allows us to combine meaningful units to produce an utterance with a new meaning. For example, we can say *big snake* and *nonthreatening eagle*.

Combinable Meaning Units

Although there are a few other species that appear to be able to combine calls, the way in which they do so importantly is different from human language. One such species is a New World marmoset monkey called a cotton-top tamarin (Cleveland & Snowdon, 1982). Cotton-tops can make a chirp to indicate alarm and a squeak to indicate alertness. They can combine these calls, always with the chirp preceding the squeak, to indicate vigilance in the presence of danger. At first glance, this system seems very similar to the human ability to combine words. The signals are combined in a particular order, and the combination yields a meaning distinct from the meanings of either signal alone.

However, there appear to be two differences between the cotton-top's call combinations and the combinations of meaning units used by human language. First, different orders of the same two calls do not appear to have different meanings in the way that *Venetian blind* and *blind Venetian* do. Therefore, although call combinations allow cotton-tops to express a larger number of meanings than they could express by single calls alone, this species does not appear to take advantage of the full communicative power that call combinations can yield. The fact that cotton-tops do not use the full power of a call combination system is probably related to the second difference between their call combinations and those used by human language. Cotton-tops' call combinatons are like their single calls in that they refer to the internal alertness state of the animal making the call. Similarly, the vervet monkey's danger calls refer to a predator present in the environment. Contrast this **referential** use of signals with the English sentence *the eagle is eating the leopard*. This sentence describes a relation between a **predicate** (*eat*) and two **arguments** (*eagle* and *leopard*). The difference between referential and predicative utterances is most obvious when the meaning to be communicated is not about the moment in time at which the signal is produced. For example, it is possible in a predicative system, but not in a referential system, to convey meanings like *I saw an eagle yesterday* or *watch out for eagles*. The ability to use combinations of meaningful units to express predicative relations is a crucial property of human language and appears to have no counterpart in animal communication systems.

Combinable Submeaning Units

A property of human language that appears to have no counterpart in any other communication system is that meaningful units (e.g., words) are made up of combinations of submeaning units that are themselves meaningless (recall *apt, pat,* and *tap*). This ability to combine submeaning units into meaningful units gives human language the power to create a very large number of words. (The number of words could be infinite if there weren't a limit on the length of words we could perceive and produce.) Some species do combine meaningless units into larger sequences. For example, male gibbons (a type of ape) create elaborate songs from a set of acoustically distinct elements, or notes (Mitani & Marler, 1989). The notes are combined according to rules that limit the number of possible combinations. The fact that some combinations are "illegal" in the gibbon communication system might be seen as similar to human language. For example, recombining the sounds in *apt* to make *pta* is not allowed in English. However, unlike humans combining sounds to make words, one gibbon song with a particular combination of notes does not appear to have a distinct meaning from another gibbon song with a different combination of notes. Therefore, although other species do combine sounds in nonrandom ways, humans appear to be the only species that combines submeaning units into meaning units.

■ The Combinatorial System Used in Human Language

To fully understand the linguistic system that children develop, we need to consider the combinatorial system of language in more detail. As we have discussed in comparing human language to the communication systems of some other species, language is organized **hierarchically**, with larger units composed of smaller ones. The components of the hierarchy are called **linguistic levels**. In this book, we consider the data on how children master different levels of the hierarchy, with the largest unit under consideration being the sentence. Although adult humans communicate in connected sentences, or **discourses**, which have a structure of their own, we consider children's mastery of discourse only as it relates to their mastery of other levels. The levels in the hierarchy that we discuss in depth are described below.

Phonology (Submeaning Units)

Beginning with the smallest units in the language hierarchy, we have already noted that the meaningful units of language are made up of submeaning units. The submeaning units that are used by a particular language are called the **phonemes** of the language. The inventory of phonemes used in each language and the ways that they can be combined are topics studied in the field of phonology. We discuss how infants and children acquire the **phonology** of their native language in Chapters 2 through 4.

Lexical Semantics (Meaning Units)

Using the principles of phonology, phonemes are combined to make meaningful units, the most familiar of which are **words**. The words a person knows are thought to be stored in a mental **lexicon**, and the study of word meanings is part of the field of **lexical semantics**. We discuss how children acquire the meanings of words and build a mental lexicon in Chapter 5.

Morphology and Syntax

Meaningful units of language can be combined in two ways. One type of combination entails forming new words by combining meaningful units called **morphemes**. A morpheme can be a word itself, like *dog*, or a part of a word like the plural markers on *dogs*. The ways in which morphemes can be combined to make words is called **morphology**. The second way that meaningful units can be combined entails putting words together to make phrases (e.g., *Venetian blind*) and sentences (e.g., *I saw an eagle yesterday*) using principles of **syntax**. We discuss the acquisition of morphology and syntax in Chapters 6 through 8.

Grammar

The entire linguistic system comprising phonology, semantics, morphology, and syntax is called a **grammar**. The notion of grammar that is used in this book refers to a concise description of the patterns of a language that can be found at each level in the linguistic hierarchy. In the field of linguistics, this concise description is called a **descriptive grammar**. This notion of grammar is different from a **prescriptive grammar**, which you may have learned in grade school, in which rules specify the standard ways that language is used among educated people. For example, you may have learned a rule of a prescriptive grammar that tells you not to end a phrase with a preposition, which makes the following sentence **ungrammatical**: *This is the movie I want to go to*. According to such a grammar, the sentence *This is the movie to which I want to go* is **grammatical**. However, people, in fact, use sentences like the former, especially in casual speech; therefore, the sentence would be grammatical in a descriptive grammar of English. The goal of the study of language development is to determine how learners come to comprehend and produce sentences that are part of the descriptive grammar of their community.

■ Theories of Language Development

Children enter the world with no obvious linguistic ability. Within less than a year, they can recognize a few words, and a few months later produce words. After only two years, they are able to understand much of what is said to them and produce some simple word combinations of their own. All of this says that there are clear and rapid developmental changes in infants' and children's language abilities. How can we explain those changes? This section outlines four theoretical approaches to language development. Before we consider the four approaches, however, let's consider what we are trying to explain and why theories are important.

What Are We Trying to Explain?

For children to be able to speak or sign like the people in their community, they need to be able to perceive the physical signal that constitutes the utterances produced by others and to move their own articulators (mouth or hands) to make similar signals. Although these are daunting tasks, most theories of language development do not take accomplishing these tasks as their focus. Rather, what is taken to be the central puzzle in language development is how children **generalize** from the utterances that they encounter (the **input**) to new utterances. In other words, it is the ability to use language to convey any thought that might come into the child's mind, even if she has never heard that thought expressed before, that is, the focus of theorizing.

To understand this focus, consider a parent who points to a bear and says, *That's a bear*. Imagine that the child is able to produce some credible imitation of the sentence. Shortly afterward, the parent looks at a carton of orange juice and says *I want some juice*. Imagine that the child is able to produce a version of that utterance as well.

How far along in the process of language development is the child? To ask that question, let's further imagine that the parent never says in the child's hearing *I want a bear*. Now we can ask whether the child, who wants a toy bear, is able to utter *I want a bear*. If the child is able to produce this novel utterance that reflects a novel intended meaning, she is well on her way to becoming a full participant in her linguistic community. For you to find the remainder of this chapter, or for that matter, the remainder of this book, of any interest, you have to believe that children say things that they have never heard before. Although generalizing beyond her input isn't the only task for the child, it is at the heart of the mystery of language development.

Do humans generalize in other domains besides language? Do nonhumans also generalize beyond their experiences? The answer to both questions is *yes*. Let's consider an example of nonlinguistic generalization that we can use as a basis for considering what develops in language development. In the three examples shown in Figures 1-1A through E, Figures 1-2A through E, and Figures 1-3A through E, you will see three bars in a black rectangle. The A through D examples are your input. You need to decide whether the E example is a valid generalization from that input.

The answers to the questions posed in Figures 1-1E, 1-2E, and 1-3E are *no, yes, no*, respectively. In Figures 1-1A through D, the principle used to create the examples was that the three bars together needed to cover more than 50% of the area of the rectangle. This generalization is not particularly natural for humans, although pigeons can learn it over many trials. In Figures 1-2A through D, the principle used to create the examples was that the three bars had to differ in height. This generalization is relatively natural for humans, and even if you didn't get the correct answer from just four input examples, it is likely that you would have made the intended generalization with a few more examples. Pigeons, on the other hand, don't seem to be able to learn this generalization. Finally, the principle used to create Figures 1-3A through D was again that the three bars had to differ in height. However, many people are likely to have made a more narrow generalization—that the three bars had to decrease in height from left to right. Example 1-3E violated that generalization. Note that if you had seen, as part of the input examples, just one example of bars of different heights, but not decreasing in height from left to right, you would have abandoned the generalization about bars decreasing in height from the left.

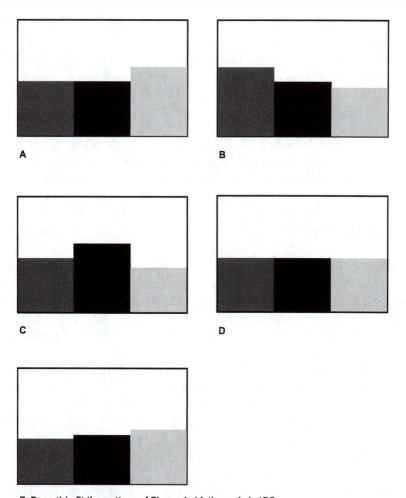

E. Does this fit the pattern of Figure 1–1A through 1–1D?

Figure 1-1. Example of a generalization that pigeons can learn but humans cannot learn.

The preceding examples tell us at least three things about generalization that a theory would need to explain. First, as the discussion of pigeon learning reflects, all animals generalize beyond the specific input they receive. Second, you need to be able to notice the right dimensions of generalization in the first place. When encountering stimuli like those in the examples you just saw, pigeons are more likely

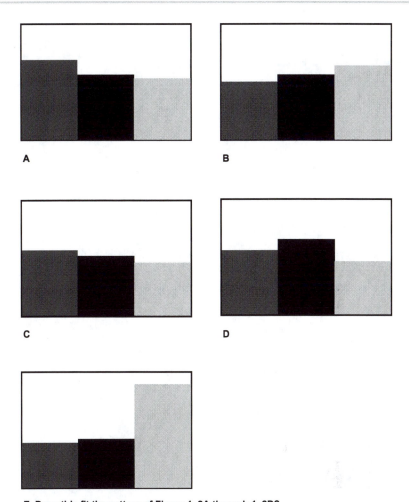

E. Does this fit the pattern of Figure 1–2A through 1–2D?

Figure 1–2. Example of a generalization that humans can learn but pigeons cannot learn.

to attend to area, whereas humans, without verbal instruction, are more likely to attend to the relations among bar heights. If you do not attend to area in Figures 1–1A through D, you are not able to recover the principle of generalization used to create the stimuli. Third, every set of input data allows for multiple generalizations. This observation is at the heart of the **induction problem**, which is what each of the

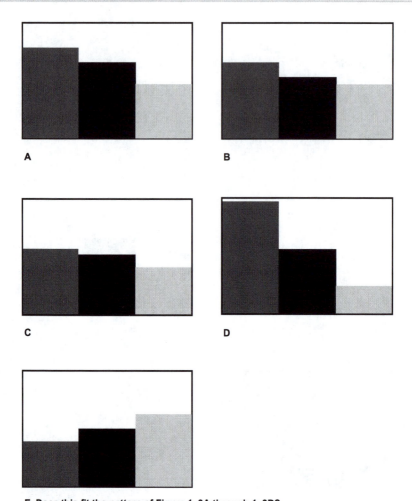

A

B

C

D

E. Does this fit the pattern of Figure 1–3A through 1–3D?

Figure 1–3. Example demonstrating that any input allows multiple possible generalizations.

four theories we discuss is attempting to solve. We discuss the induction problem in greater detail below. You can get a sense for the nature of the problem in the comparison of Figures 1-2A through D and 1-3A through D, which both conform to a generalization that the bars have to differ in height. However, Figures 1-3A through D support another generalization as well. Let's now turn to the question of why we need theories at all.

Why Are Theories Important?

In studying language development, why do we need theories? Why isn't data collection sufficient? If all you want to know is the "normal" course of language development, then data collection is probably sufficient. But if you want the answers to any "why" questions, such as why infants and children are such amazing learners, why it is difficult to learn a second language as you get older, why only humans have language, or why some children have greater difficulty learning language than others, you will have to do more. You will have to (1) come up with competing hypotheses (tentative explanations) for the phenomenon you want to understand, (2) collect new data that eliminate one or more of those hypotheses, and (3) refine the remaining hypotheses and begin the cycle again. Virtually none of the dozens of studies of language development that are described in this book were done because the researcher was just curious about the age at which a typical child knows a particular word or how an infant would respond to a particular linguistic stimulus. Rather, most of the studies were done to compare different hypotheses, and these hypotheses are ultimately part of larger theories of how language is learned by infants and children. Understanding what drove the researchers to do the particular studies they did can help in understanding the stimuli and methods they used, as well as their conclusions.

Overview of the Theories

Figure 1–4 illustrates a continuum of language development theories. The dimension represented by the horizontal line is the degree to which language learners are constrained by their biology to learn language, with the theory on the far left being most constrained and the one on the far right being least constrained. The vertical line divides the continuum into two halves. Theories to the left of the vertical line propose that infants are born with a set of constraints specific to the job of language development, or **innate linguistic constraints**. In contrast, theories to the right of the vertical line propose that a set of **general purpose learning abilities** can give rise to successful language development, as well as successful learning in other domains such as math and music. Much of the research presented

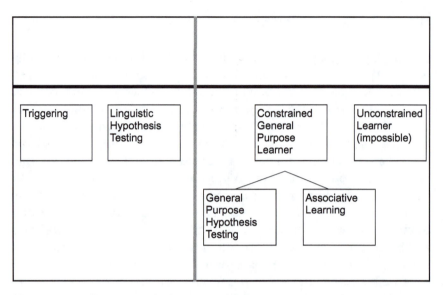

Figure 1–4. Theories of language development on a continuum from most constrained by human genetics (*left*) to least constrained (*right*).

in this book reflects an attempt to determine if language development is better characterized as falling to the left or the right of the vertical line.

In this section, we explore four of the theories shown in Figure 1-4: Associative Learning, General Purpose Hypothesis Testing, Linguistic Hypothesis Testing, and Triggering. The two hypotheses testing theories are discussed together. As briefly mentioned, all of the theories reflect different solutions to the induction problem—the observation that any set of input data is consistent with multiple possible generalizations. Before exploring these theories, however, let's rule out a theory shown in Figure 1-4 that we will not discuss further—Unconstrained Learner.

Ruling Out an Unconstrained Learner

We need to rule out the theory that a learner could be completely unconstrained in her approach to the input, because such a theory flies in the face of the induction problem. To get a better sense of the scope of the induction problem, consider the examples in Figures 1-1, 1-2, and 1-3 (the three bars), above. An unconstrained learner would come up with an infinite number of possible generalizations for each input, including area covered by the bars and bar height, as well as generalizations that might seem "crazy," such as bar height on Tuesdays, area covered by the first bar alone, light reflectance of the display, and so forth. In order to rule out each of these possible generalizations, or hypotheses, the learner would have to wait for new data, and given that there are an infinite number of hypotheses, the learner could never narrow down the set of generalizations to one. That is, the learner could never be guaranteed of making the right generalization. This scenario is the induction problem in its worst form. Because all organisms are able to generalize in ways that allow them to survive in their environments, we have very good reason to believe that they cannot consider an infinite number of hypotheses about how to generalize from their input. Therefore, all of the theories that we entertain assume that learners are constrained to consider some generalizations and not others. Our observation that pigeons do not consider bar height as a possible basis of generalization, whereas humans do not consider overall area, is consistent with the view that generalization is constrained within each species. The following three sections explore the ways that learners might be constrained.

Associative Learning—Making Connections Among Experiences

In the 13th century, St. Thomas Aquinas proposed that there is "nothing in the intellect which was not previously in the senses." Four centuries later, the empiricist philosopher John Locke discussed the connection of simple ideas or sensations (e.g., the color, shape, and taste of an apple). He noted that sometimes these associations can be incorrect. For example, if you eat an apple just before having symptoms of the flu, you might be inclined to avoid apples in the future because you associate them with illness. It is important to note that Associative Learning is different from the sort of hypothesis testing that we do as scientists. The associative learner has no "guess" about why the world is the way that it is, only a set of associations among experiences. One way to illustrate this point is to consider how associations can conflict with hypotheses. In a well-known example from social psychology (Banaji & Hardin, 1996), experiment participants saw words related to gender, such as *mother, father, nurse, doctor* immediately followed by target words that were either gendered pronouns like *she* or *he* or nonpronouns. The participants needed to respond as quickly as possible whether the target word was a pronoun or not. They were faster when target gender (e.g., *she*) matched the prime gender (e.g., *nurse*) than when it mismatched (e.g., *doctor*). That is, despite the fact that many people know women doctors and may believe that people of either gender can be doctors, their associations between males and doctors are much stronger than between women and doctors. Why might learning achieved via associations be different from other types of learning? One reason is **input frequency**. We encounter many more images of men than women doctors, and for generalization by associations, numbers matter. We contrast this type of learning with learning by hypothesis testing in the next section.

The previous example demonstrates that highly frequent associations are learned better (are stronger) than lower frequency associations. Is frequency the only factor that governs Associative Learning? No. Associations that are followed by **reinforcement** are also more likely to be learned than unreinforced associations. If you have taken an introduction to psychology course, you will know that B. F. Skinner did much of the research showing that any association between a stimulus and a subsequent behavior (response) could be strengthened through a positive outcome (reinforcement). For example, imagine that you want to train a pigeon to turn in a clockwise circle to get food. You might begin by rewarding the pigeon with food if it turns slightly to the right. On subsequent trials, the pigeon has to turn farther and farther in order to receive its reward. After many such trials, you can shape the initially random behavior of the pigeon into the behavior you initially had in mind. Skinner (1957) proposed that such shaping might account for how children learn language.

Such a view can be criticized based on the difficulty of identifying the external rewards that children might receive for making closer and closer approximations to adult language forms. However, a much more serious criticism can be found in children's production of distinctly nonadult forms (Chomsky, 1959). For example, you might have heard a child between the ages of 2 and 4 years produce past tense forms like *goed* instead of *went*, or *eated* instead of *ate*. If you think about it for a moment, these **overgeneralization** errors are hard to explain if the child is learning about associations that occur in the input, because neither *goed* nor *eated* is likely to have ever occurred in the child's input. However, the errors make intuitive sense, because they suggest that the child has learned something systematic about the relation between present tense and past tense forms, namely, that for most words, the past tense is created by adding something to the end of the present tense form.

The question is, how should we characterize the system that the child has learned? Two possibilities exist. One is that the child has learned a grammar, which we can say is a list of statements about the regularities in the language. Alternatively, maybe the way the input itself is stored and associated with other input is sufficient to account for generalization and overgeneralization, without there being a separate grammar. The latter view can be found in computational models of learning that emerged during the 1980s under the name **connectionism**. (For a more in-depth overview of connectionism, see Rumelhart & McClelland, 1986.) Connectionist models are computer instantiations of Associative Learning theory, in which the associations occur between inputs (e.g., *go*) and outputs (e.g., *went*). For example, the inputs might be a set of verbs in the present tense (e.g., *talk, sing, jump*, etc.). The outputs might be the same words in the past tense (e.g., *talked, sang, jumped*, etc.). More detail about the connectionist model of past tense learning is provided in Chapter 8. For present purposes, however, what is important is that the models overgeneralize, resulting in a temporary association between *go* and *goed*.

What does Associative Learning predict about language development? In this book, we consider four predictions: (1) Because the Associative Learning view can be applied to any domain, learning associations between linguistic inputs and outputs should closely resemble the learning of other abilities, such as music, mathematics, visual object recognition, etc. (2) Infants and children should also be able to learn language-like patterns that do not in fact occur in a human language as long as enough evidence is provided about the input-output associations of the pseudolanguage; (3) Learning should be gradual, and generalization should only occur after a relatively large number of input-output associations have been made; and (4) Errors should reflect the statistics (e.g., frequency) of the input as well as any reinforcement that might occur.

The Associative Learning theory depends on the learner keeping track of large amounts of information about the input over time to constrain the generalizations that she makes. That is, the constraints in this theory come largely from the sheer bulk of information in the environment, with fewer constraints coming with the learner herself.

The theories described in the next section entail tighter constraints on the learner and propose that the learner develops a grammar, rather than simply a network of associations among experiences.

Hypothesis Testing—The Learner as Scientist

Imagine that you are driving in your car at night. Ahead of you on the right you see the two small lights rise from near the ground to about two feet above the ground. When one light is up, the other is down and vice versa. What are you looking at? It may take you a moment of puzzlement before you infer that there is a nighttime jogger running along the wrong side of the road. We have all experienced scenarios such as this one, in which we realize that we cannot perceive some aspect of our world directly, but rather use the available cues to infer the event that might have given rise to a puzzling experience. That is, we can come up with a **hypothesis** about the cause of the experience.

Intuitively at least, many people feel as though they are engaging in hypothesis testing in the bar height task in Figures 1-1 through 1-3. Indeed, in the third example (Figure 1-3A through D), you may have even said "The bars are decreasing in height from left to right." That statement constitutes an explicit hypothesis about the nature of the generalization. In this case, the hypothesis took the form of a **rule**. How do you know whether or not your hypothesis is correct? One possibility is that you encounter disconfirming data. For example, if you hypothesize that all input should have three bars decreasing in height from left to right, and you encounter a contradictory example in which the middle bar is taller than the first, you immediately know that your hypothesis is incorrect and that you need to try out another one. Similarly, if you hypothesize that only men can be doctors and encounter a woman who is a doctor, you can rule out your original hypothesis. (Comparing the latter example to the study by Benaji and Hardin discussed under Associative Learning makes it clear that both learning by hypothesis testing and learning by association are possible within the same individual.) Unfortunately, much of the time, different generalizations are supported by the same data, and it is difficult or impossible to find new data to eliminate one generalization or another. For example, consider this variant of bar height example in Figure 1-3A through D. If the correct generalization is really that the bars are decreasing in height from left to right, all instances of this generalization will also be instances of the broader generalization that the bars just need to differ in height. That is, the data that you have been given do not reflect the full range of possible data. If you make the broader (different heights) generalization, there is no absolute way to rule it out if you keep seeing bars that decrease in height from right to left.

Consider a similar problem: I give you a set of numbers (e.g., 8, 400, 16, 96, 120, etc.), and I ask you what they have in common (what is the generalization?). One possible answer is that they are all divisible by 4. Another possible answer is that they are divisible by 2. Because any number that is divisible by 4 is also divisible by 2, you cannot be sure which of these generalizations is the one I intended, unless I give you a number that is divisible by 2 but not by 4. This lack of an absolute way to determine the correct generalization is part of the induction problem. There are ways of narrowing down the choices, especially if the sample of input you get is randomly selected (not biased to be of a certain type). For example, if you encounter 10 numbers divisible by 4 and none that are divisible by 2 and not by 4, and if your input is unbiased, you can make a reasonably safe bet that "divisible by 4" is a better hypothesis than "divisible by 2" (e.g., Tenenbaum & Griffiths, 2001). We return to this point in Chapters 5 and 8. Nevertheless, there is no guarantee that everyone who encounters the problem will come to the same solution. Therefore, both versions of hypothesis testing theories entail the possibility that different language learners might have somewhat different grammars.

How do General Purpose Hypothesis Testing and Linguistic Hypothesis Testing differ? General Purpose Hypothesis Testing, like Associative Learning, proposes that language development can be achieved by a general purpose learning mechanism, which can also be applied to other learning domains. Therefore, two of the predictions made by the Associative Learning theory of language development are also made by the General Purpose Hypothesis Testing theory: (1) Learning language should resemble the learning of other abilities, and (2) Infants and children should be able to learn languagelike patterns that do not, in fact, occur in a human language. However, hypothesis testing theories propose that learning and generalization occur because learners use their input to make guesses about the state of the world that gave rise to that input (the grammar, in the case of language). Because a single example can rule out a hypothesis (e.g., getting the number 6 in the input set rules out the hypothesis "divisible by 4"), hypothesis testing accounts can often close in on a reasonable generalization faster than Associative Learning. Therefore, General Purpose Hypothesis Testing (like Linguistic Hypothesis Testing) predicts that: (3) Generalization can occur after a small number (greater than one) of input examples, and (4) Errors should reflect incorrect hypotheses about the grammar.

One potential problem with General Purpose Hypothesis Testing is that the nature of constraints on hypotheses is not clear. Obviously a learner cannot include in her hypothesis information that she cannot perceive with her senses or remember for sufficiently long amounts of time. However, we currently do not have very good ideas about other sorts of general purpose constraints on hypothesis testing. The nature of constraints on hypothesis testing is more clearly addressed by the Linguistic Hypothesis Testing theory, which shares properties with both General Purpose Hypothesis Testing and Triggering (discussed below). The main difference between Linguistic Hypothesis Testing and General Purpose Hypothesis Testing is that Linguistic Hypothesis Testing proposes that infants and children recognize language as a separate learning domain from other learning domains, such as math or music. Furthermore, they are born expecting language to be a particular kind of domain; for example, one in which information is conveyed via predicates and arguments (see section on Combinable Meaning Units). Therefore, the hypotheses they come up with to explain the linguistic input that they encounter are linguistic in nature. In contrast, a learner using the mechanism of General Purpose Hypothesis Testing might attempt to explain linguistic input with nonlinguistic hypotheses.

For example, consider the sentences in 1a and 1b, below. A learner encountering the statement-question pair in 1a and 1b could either conclude that, to make a question from a statement, you move the main verb to the front of the sentence, or you move the first *is* you see to the front of the sentence. A learner who has the first hypothesis would make the correct question from the statement in 2a (2b); whereas, a learner who has the second hypothesis would make an ungrammatical question (2c, an asterisk in front of an utterance indicates ungrammaticality). The first hypothesis, because it involves the linguistic concept of "main verb" is a linguistic hypothesis, whereas the second hypothesis is nonlinguistic and just involves the serial order of a particular word in a sentence. A learner using a General Purpose Hypothesis testing mechanism could consider either hypothesis, whereas a learner using a Linguistic Hypothesis Testing mechanism would only consider the main verb hypothesis. Therefore, the Linguistic Hypothesis Testing theory is more constrained, and therefore closer to Triggering theory, than General Purpose Hypothesis Testing.

1a. The man is short.
1b. Is the man short?
2a. The man who is jolly is short.
2b. Is the man who is jolly short?
2c. *Is the man who jolly is short?

The Linguistic Hypothesis Testing theory, like the Triggering theory discussed below, predicts that: (1) Language learning is distinct from learning in other cognitive domains. Linguistic Hypothesis Testing and Triggering are also alike in that they use the grammars of actual human languages as the main source of information about what children can learn. Therefore, both predict that: (2) Children should not be able to learn languagelike patterns that do not occur in human languages. Finally, as we already noted, Linguistic Hypothesis Testing, like General Purpose Hypothesis Testing, also predicts that: (3) Generalization can occur after a small number (greater than one) of input examples, and (4) Errors should reflect incorrect hypotheses about the grammar.

One potential problem with both hypothesis testing theories is that, because of the induction problem, they cannot guarantee that a learner will ever arrive at the correct hypothesis. Linguistic Hypothesis Testing theory provides better odds of arriving at the correct hypothesis because learners only consider a restricted range of hypotheses. Furthermore, as noted above, a learner who encounters a representative sample of her input also has quite good odds of arriving at the correct hypothesis. However, the lack of a guarantee strikes many language development researchers as problematic because language is clearly very important to our species, and arriving at an incorrect grammar might be a very serious problem. Therefore, the final theory we consider leaves language learners no possibility of arriving at the wrong grammar.

Triggering—A Minimal Role for Experience

The main motivation for the Triggering theory is the proposal that learners do not receive a representative set of input, which, as noted above, puts both hypothesis testing theories at a disadvantage. The idea that learners do not receive representative input is called the **poverty of the stimulus** argument. It can be thought of as a special, extreme case of the induction problem. On the assumption that the input to language learners is, in fact, impoverished, a number of theorists came to consider the possibility that the human infant comes to the world with a robust biological endowment for language. This proposal would be easy to understand if all humans had the same language and grammar, but because this is not the case, a mechanism is needed by which a child can learn the particular grammar of her community but at the same time be guaranteed of the correct grammar. On the Triggering theory, all of the world's languages share a certain set of properties. For example, all languages have a hierarchical, not a flat, structure (see examples 1a and 1b and 2a through 2c above and Chapter 6). Differences among languages actually reflect variations on another set of properties, called **parameters**. For example, some languages, like English, require that there be a subject on every statement (e.g., *I want ice cream*), whereas other languages, like Spanish, allow subjects to be dropped under a variety of conditions (*Quiero helado = want ice cream*). Whether or not a sentence must have a subject is a linguistic parameter. The set of fully universal linguistic properties plus the set of parameterized properties make up a **Universal Grammar (UG)**.

In this view, each language learner has available to her at birth all of the possible grammars of human languages. For each parameter, she is able to use very limited information from her input, called a **trigger**, to rule out an incorrect parameter setting. On this view, language development uses **deduction**, not induction: All of the possible grammars are given to the child in advance, and the input is used only to rule out some grammars in favor of others. For example, the parameter concerning sentence subjects just described is called the **pro-drop parameter** (Chapter 8). It has been proposed that all children begin life with the pro-drop parameter set to allow sentences without subjects and that children exposed to a non-pro-drop language like English need to encounter a trigger in the form of a sentence with a subject that doesn't refer to anything (e.g., *It is raining*) in order to reset their pro-drop parameter to the correct setting for their language.

On triggering accounts of language development, children really do not learn language in any normal meaning of "learn." Rather, they make their way through a series of possible grammars by using triggers to rule out any parameters settings determined to be incorrect. Therefore, when children appear not to know the correct generalizations of their own language, they just haven't encountered (or encoded) the appropriate trigger yet. Nevertheless, the parameter setting that they are using is grammatical in some languages of the world. What are the predictions of the Triggering theory? (1) Language learning should not resemble the learning of other abilities, (2) Infants and children should not be able to learn language-like patterns that do not, in fact, occur in a human language, (3) Children can potentially master some aspects of language with no input and generalize other aspects based on a single input example (a trigger), and (4) Children's errors should reflect only the patterns observed in languages of the world.

Summary of Theories

The four theories that we discuss in this book, along with their predictions, are shown in Table 1-1. You learned in previous sections that four theories overlap in different ways, and these areas of overlap are illustrated in Table 1-1. As was mentioned in the discussion of Figure 1-4, much of the research on language development has been directed at asking whether humans are born with genetically based constraints to learn language, as predicted by Triggering and Linguistic Hypothesis Testing theories, or whether we can account for language development data by assuming more general purpose learning mechanisms. More recently, some studies have also attempted to pit Triggering against some version of hypothesis testing, or Associative Learning against hypothesis testing. As you make your way through the dozens of studies of language development described in this book, remember to ask yourself how each study fits into the theoretical framework illustrated in Table 1-1. Before leaving the discussion of theories, it is important to note that all researchers would agree that language development reflects an intricate dance of genetics and behavior.

Table 1–1. Four Theories of Language Development and Their Predictions for Observed Language Development Data. (Shading is used to highlight commonalities between pairs of theories.)

Theories	Predictions			
	Specificity of Domain	What Can Be Learned	Learning Speed	Errors
Associative Learning	Language learning should resemble learning in other cognitive domains	Children can learn languagelike patterns that do not occur in human languages	Learning should be gradual and based on input	Errors should reflect statistics of the input
General Purpose Hypothesis Testing	Language learning should resemble learning in other cognitive domains	Children can learn languagelike patterns that do not occur in human languages	Learning can be rapid, but based on input	Errors should reflect incorrect hypotheses about the input
Linguistic Hypothesis Testing	Language learning is distinct from learning in other cognitive domains	Children should not be able to learn languagelike pattern that do not occur in human languages	Learning can be rapid, but based on input	Errors should reflect incorrect hypotheses about the input
Triggering	Language learning is distinct from learning in other cognitive domains	Children should not be able to learn languagelike pattern that do not occur in human languages	Some properties of language need not be learned, and others can potentially be learned from a single piece of input	Errors should reflect possible human languages

The issue under consideration when we compare the theories to the left and to the right of the vertical line in Figure 1-4 is whether the environment **selects** among alternatives that are offered by genetics, or whether the mind is **constructed** (or emerges, see Elman et al., 1996; MacWhinney, 1999) from the interaction of genetics and environment. These are importantly different views of organisms and how they develop, and one of the broad goals of the study of language development, is to contribute to the scientific study of development more generally.

■ Organization of the Book

In addition to this Introduction, the book is organized into five topics. The first topic is phonology. Chapter 2 provides an overview of phonology, and Chapters 3 and 4 provide examples of research examining phonology in language perception and production, respectively. The second topic is the lexicon, or mental dictionary, and is covered in Chapter 5. The third topic is syntax. Chapter 6 provides an overview of syntax, and Chapters 7 and 8 provide examples of research on children's knowledge of the forms of sentences, their knowledge of how to link sentence forms to meanings, and controversies in the study of syntactic development. The fourth topic, found in Chapter 9, is issues in the biology of language, including disorders of language development, learning language at different ages, and developing language in the absence of normal input. This chapter sets up questions about the biology of language by providing a summary of the preceding chapters and makes a final assessment of the debate concerning the degree to which language development reflects our biological endowment for language learning. Finally, Chapter 10 is meant as a resource for the rest of the book and provides an overview of some methods used in language development research. In the six chapters that present data from language development research with infants and children (Chapters 3, 4, 5, 7, 8, and 9), you will find a set of thought questions that are designed to help you think more deeply about the logic behind the research, the research methods, and the interpretation of the data. By the end of the book, you should have a good sense of (1) our current knowledge of the path of language development, (2) the theoretical frameworks that motivate the research and help us to interpret the data, and (3) the tools that researchers use to collect the data.

Two final notes on word use before we begin: First, to avoid the sometimes annoying "s/he" and "him/her" pronoun use, feminine pronouns ("she" and "her") are used in referring to infants and children throughout the book. However, unless specified, the statements using these pronouns refer to both male and female language learners. Second, but equally arbitrarily, the term "infant" is used to refer to language learners up to the age of 12 months, and "child" will be used to refer to language learners older than 1 year.

■ References

Akmajian, A., Demers, R. A., Farmer, A. K., & Harnish, R. M. (2001). *Linguistics: An introduction to language and communication*. Cambridge, MA: MIT Press.

Banaji, M. R., & Hardin, C. D. (1996). Automatic stereotyping. *Psychological Science, 7*, 136-141.

Cheney, D. L., & Seyfarth, R. M. (1990). *How monkeys see the world: Inside the mind of another species*. Chicago: University of Chicago Press.

Chomsky, N. (1959). A review of Skinner's "Verbal Behavior." *Language, 35*, 26-58.

Cleveland, J., & Snowdon, C. (1982). The complex vocal repertoire of the adult cotton-top tamarin (Saguinus oedipus oedipus). *Zeitschrift für Tierpsychologie, 58*, 231-270.

Elman, J. L., Bates, E. A., Johnson, M. H., Karmiloff-Smith, A., Parisi, D., & Plunkett, K. (1996). *Rethinking innateness: A connectionist perspective on development*. Cambridge, MA: MIT Press.

MacWhinney, B. E. (1999). *The emergence of language*. Mahwah, NJ: Lawrence Erlbaum Associates.

Mitani, J., & Marler, P. (1989). A phonological analysis of male gibbon singing behavior. *Behaviour, 109*, 20-45.

Rumelhart, D. E., & McClelland, J. L. (1986). *Parallel distributed processing: Explorations in the microstructure of cognition*. Cambridge, MA: MIT Press.

Skinner, B. F. (1957). *Verbal behavior*. New York: Appleton-Century-Croft.

Tenenbaum, J. B., & Griffiths, T. L. (2001). Generalization, similarity, and Bayesian inference. *Behavioral and Brain Sciences, 24*, 629-640.

2 Overview of Phonology

■ What Is Phonology?

Phonology historically has been the study of the sound systems of languages. Recently, however, our concept of phonology has expanded as researchers have begun to consider the structure of signed languages like American Sign Language. Signed languages obviously do not have sound systems, but they do exhibit properties that are parallel to the phonology of spoken languages. Importantly, signed languages, like spoken languages, appear to create meaningful units (signs) from **submeaning units**. Thus, both signed languages and spoken languages can create a large number of signs or words from a limited number of submeaning units, or **phonemes**.

In both spoken and signed languages, the study of phonology can be thought of as having two major components. One of these is **segmental phonology**, which is the study of the phonemes that make up words or signs in a particular language and how the language allows them to combine. The other component of phonology is **prosody**, which is the study of such properties as pitch, stress, and rhythm. We discuss both of these components with respect to spoken language in this chapter.

■ Segmental Phonology

As discussed in Chapter 1 and above, the meaning units of language (words and signs) are composed of submeaning units called "phonemes." For example, the English word *bed* contains three phonemes.

Phonemes are also called **segments**, which is why the study of phonemes and how they are combined is called segmental phonology. What exactly is a phoneme?

Phones and Phonemes

Humans are capable of producing and perceiving a very large number of different speech sounds. For example, say the word *lip* in the usual way, with your tongue touching the alveolar ridge behind your teeth when you produce the first sound. Now move your tongue farther forward so that it touches your top teeth as you produce the first sound of *lip*. The two initial sounds are different, and if you asked other people to listen, they could probably hear the difference. As you can reliably produce these two forms of *lip*, and listeners can reliably perceive the two forms, it would seem reasonable that English could have two different words with two different meanings. One pronunciation could mean the part of your anatomy surrounding your mouth, and the other could mean the way the air smells after a rain. Why doesn't English allow such a pair of words? That is to say, why is the place that you put your tongue when saying the first sound of *lip* not treated as a meaningful distinction in English?

The answer is that, although humans are capable of producing and perceiving a large number of speech sounds or **phones**, communication is much more efficient if only a subset of the differences between pairs of sounds is used to make distinctions among meaning units. Therefore, each language "selects" a set of sound contrasts that is relevant to the creation of meaning units. The sounds that are used to distinguish among words in a particular language are called the **phonemes** of that language. For example, English speakers do not distinguish the two versions of the phoneme /l/ (see more below about notation) that you just made, but speakers of a language called Mid-Waghi, spoken in Papua New Guinea, do. Thus, the two versions of the first sound of *lip* that you made are different phones, but they are not different phonemes of English. Two phones that are variants of a single phoneme of a language are called **allophones** or **allophonic variants** of that language. The two sounds in questions *are* different phonemes of Mid-Waghi, as well as different phones. You can tell whether or not two speech sounds are different phonemes of a language if there are two words (a **minimal pair**) that differ by just that sound. Thus, *vase* and *base* form a minimal pair for English speakers, telling us that the initial sounds are different phonemes in English. But these two words are not different to speakers of various dialects of Spanish, telling us that the two initial sounds are not different phonemes in those dialects.

A Note About Notation

When we write about the speech sounds of a language, we cannot use the **orthographic alphabet** we are used to reading and writing. The problem with this alphabet is that a single letter can be used to indicate many different sounds, and a single sound can be indicated by several different letters. For example, the letter *a* can have the sound in *cat* or in *cake* or in *about*. The sound at the beginning of *cat* can be indicated by *c*, *k* (as in *kidney*), or *ch* (as in *chord*). Because the orthographic alphabet is so ambiguous, we use a special alphabet, called the **International Phonetic Alphabet** or **IPA**, when we want to be precise in writing speech sounds. IPA symbols needed for English are given in Tables 2-1 and 2-2. Another aspect of notation that you should know is that square brackets ([...]) are used to indicate phones, the actual speech sounds produced. Slashes (/.../) are used to indicate phonemes, the sounds that are distinctive for speakers of a particular language. Thus, the English phrase *the shining threads* would be written in IPA as /ðə ʃainɪŋ θrɛdz/. (Note that spaces were left between the words to help you match the sounds to the symbols, but such between-word spaces are not typically used in IPA notation.) There are several differences between the orthographic and IPA versions of the phrase that we should highlight. First, sounds that are made with two orthographic symbols (e.g., the, shining, threads) are made with a single IPA symbol (/ð/, /ʃ/, /ŋ/, and /θ/, respectively). Also notice that even though *the* and *thread* both begin with the same orthographic symbols (*th*), they actually sound different and therefore map onto two different IPA symbols (/ð/ and /θ/, respectively).

Articulatory Features

The set of phonemes selected for use by a language reflects a clear systematicity. The system is based on the ways in which sounds are produced, with only a few dimensions of variation. Consider the dimensions that are important for marking differences between speech sounds in English. We need to treat consonants and vowels separately.

Table 2–1. Articulatory Features of English Consonants

Manner of Articulation	Voicing	Place of Articulation						
		Bilabial	Labio-dental	Inter-dental	Alveolar	Palatal	Velar	Glottal
Stops	voiceless	p pill			t till		k kill	
	voiced	b bill			d dill		g gill	
Fricatives	voiceless		f fill	θ thin	s sill	ʃ ship		h
	voiced		v villain	ð the	z zillion	ʒ azure		
Affricates	voiceless					tʃ chip		
	voiced					dʒ jilt		
Nasals	voiced	m mill			n nill		ŋ sing	
Liquids	voiceless				r rail			
	voiced				l lip			
Glides	voiced					j yes	w witch	

30

Table 2-2. Distinctive Features for English Vowels; the Vowels
([ɨ, ə]) Only Appear in Unstressed Syllables

Tongue Height	Tense/ Lax	Tongue Position		
		Front	Central	Back
High	tense	i beat		u boot
	lax	ɪ bit	ɨ* chick<u>e</u>n	ʊ book
Mid	tense	e bait		o boat, ɔi boy
	lax	ɛ bet	ə* <u>a</u>bout	ʌ but, ɔ bought
Low	tense			au cow, ai thigh
	lax	æ bat		a box

Consonants are produced when air flowing from our lungs and vibrat-ing our vocal folds (also sometimes called **vocal cords**) is constricted before leaving our body. By comparison, vowels are produced when the air is allowed to flow with little constriction. There are three dimensions, or **articulatory features**, by which we distinguish among all English consonants. These are shown in Table 2-1. One fea-ture is **place of articulation**, which is the place in the mouth where the air is constricted. Use Figure 2-1 to help you understand the place of articulation feature. There are seven places of articulation used in English. In **bilabial** consonants (/p, b, m/), air is constricted with the two lips. In **labiodental** consonants (/f, v/), air is constricted with the lips and the teeth. In **interdental** consonants (/θ, ð)/), air is con-stricted with the tongue and the teeth. In **alveolar** consonants (/t, d, s, z, n, l, r/), air is constricted by the tongue against the alveolar ridge behind your teeth. In **palatal** consonants (/ʃ, ʒ, tʃ, dj, j/), air is con-stricted by the tongue against the hard palate. In **velar** consonants (/k, g, ŋ, w), air is constricted by the tongue against soft velum. Finally, in the **glottal** consonant /h/, air is constricted at the glottis.

Another articulatory feature used to distinguish among English consonants is **manner of articulation**, which is the way that the air is stopped or restricted. In **fricative** consonants (/f, v, θ, ð, s, z, ʃ, ʒ, h/), the airstream is restricted so as to cause friction. In **affricate** conso-nants (/tʃ, dj), air is first stopped and then restricted as in a fricative.

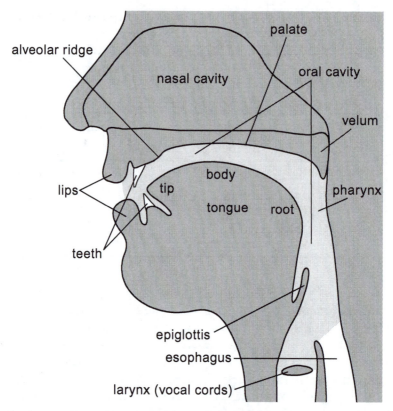

Figure 2–1. Cross-section of the human vocal tract. Courtesy of Michael Gasser, Indiana University (adaptation).

In **nasal** consonants (/m, n, ŋ/), air is channeled through the nose instead of the mouth. In **liquid** consonants (/l, r/), air is allowed to flow through the mouth without much constriction. In **glide** consonants (/j, w/), air is allowed to flow very freely, as in vowels. For this reason, glides are sometimes called **semivowels**.

The third articulatory feature used to distinguish among English consonants is **voicing**. Note that voicing is only an important feature for stops, fricatives, and affricates. In **voiced** consonants, the vocal folds vibrate at the same time that the air is released from the mouth. In **voiceless** consonants, there is a lag between when the air is released and when the vocal folds begin to vibrate.

Referring to Table 2-1, you can see that place of articulation is not used to distinguish among liquids (such as /l/) in English. This is why the two versions of *lip* that you produced earlier are not two different English words. Note that any English consonant can be described in a phrase using the two or three articulatory features used in producing it. Thus, /b/ is a voiced, bilabial stop, and /n/ is an alveolar nasal.

There are also three articulatory features by which we distinguish among all English vowels. These are shown in Table 2-2. One feature is **tongue height**, with the values high, mid, and low. A second articulatory feature used to distinguish English vowels is **tongue position**, referring to the location of the body of the tongue. The values of this feature are front, central and back. As indicated in Table 2-2, the central vowels /ɨ, ə/ are often called **reduced** and only appear in unstressed syllables. The third articulatory feature used to distinguish English vowels is the **tense/lax** dimension, which refers to the degree of muscular tension used to produce the vowel.

Acoustic Manifestations of Articulatory Features

The articulatory features described above are produced by talkers as an acoustic signal that listeners perceive. What acoustic information do listeners use to decide which articulatory features a talker is producing? Although a full description of the acoustics of speech is beyond the scope of this book, it is important to consider the nature of acoustic properties of the speech signal that learners hear.

As an example, consider the articulatory feature voicing. As noted above, voiced consonants are ones in which the vocal folds vibrate at the same time that the air is released from the mouth. In contrast, voiceless consonants exhibit a short lag between when the air is released and when the vocal folds begin to vibrate. For instance, for the English syllable [ba], vocal fold vibration and release of air happen more or less simultaneously, whereas for [pa], vocal fold vibration does not begin until at least 30 milliseconds after air is released. The relation between release burst and voicing is shown for /pa/ and /ba/ in Figure 2-2. Figure 2-2 is a **waveform**, in which the horizontal axis is time, and the vertical axis is amplitude (the acoustic dimension perceived as loudness).

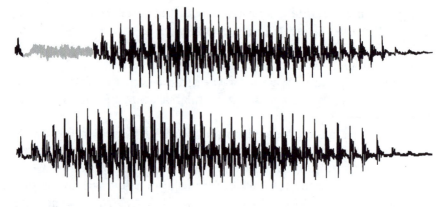

Figure 2–2. Waveforms of /pa/ (*top*) and /ba/ (*bottom*). The release burst on the left is in black, the voicing for the vowel in light gray, and the medium gray lag between release and voicing in the top waveform is the voice onset time (VOT) for /pa/. VOT for /ba/ in this figure is 0; thus, no medium gray appears.

From the listener's point of view, [ba] is an acoustic event characterized by a high-frequency sound corresponding to the air being released, occurring along with mid-frequency periodic (pulsing) sound corresponding to the vocal folds vibrating. In contrast, [pa] is characterized by the high-frequency sound and about a 30 millisecond lag before the periodic sound begins. The time between the high-frequency sound and the periodic sound is referred to as **voice onset time**, or **VOT**, and is an acoustic cue to voicing. Voiced consonants have a shorter VOT, whereas voiceless consonants have a longer VOT.

Variability in Acoustic Manifestations of Articulatory Features

There are numerous sources of variability that complicate the listener's task of deciding which articulatory features are manifest in the acoustic signal. One source of variability is natural variation in a talker's control over his or her articulators. Although, on average, the VOT of [ba] is 0, and the VOT of [pa] is 30 milliseconds, the timing of air release and vocal fold vibration is not exact. As a result, in producing [ba], the vocal folds might begin to vibrate 10 milliseconds before the air release in one case, and 10 milliseconds after the lip release on another occasion, and so on. Comparable variation occurs in the production of [pa]. Therefore, listeners must have sufficient perceptual capabilities to tolerate variability due to natural fluctuations in articulation.

Another source of variability comes from the contexts in which speech sounds are produced. For example, say the words *sloop* and *slip* to yourself and notice how your lips are positioned at the start of these words. Even though both words begin with [s], they differ in the way that they are produced from the outset. In the case of *sloop*, the lips are extended, but for *slip* they are spread apart. This difference in the positioning of the lips has to do with the nature of the vowels in these words, as you can verify by saying these vowels alone and attending to your lips. Even though the lip positioning relates to the vowels, the acoustic properties of the [s] are affected in both cases. **Coarticulation** occurs because speech production requires moving the articulators (vocal folds, tongue, lips, jaw, etc.) from one configuration to another in a very short time span. Because time is required to move the articulators into the correct position for each sound, speakers compensate by starting the gestures for one segment before finishing those for the preceding segment.

It is particularly important to understand that acoustic variation introduced by coarticulation in one language is often used to make a phonemic distinction in another language. To clarify this point, let's return to the two pronunciations of *lip* described above. Think about where your tongue is when you say the [l] in the phrase *zip lip*. You will probably find that your tongue is just behind you front teeth. Now think about where your tongue is when you say the [l] in *back lip*. Your tongue is probably somewhere behind your alveolar ridge. Due to coarticulation, you produce two different versions of [l] when you produce the word *lip* in different contexts. Nevertheless, anyone listening will treat your two versions of *lip* as the same word, not as a minimal pair. However, a native speaker of Mid-Waghi should treat the two versions of *lip* as different words (i.e., a minimal pair).

Yet another source of variability in speech sounds is due to the size and shape of size of the speaker's vocal tract and articulatory apparatus. On average, the vocal folds of adult males have greater mass than those of adult females. Consequently, the pitch, or **fundamental frequency**, of male voices is usually lower than that of females. Other features of the vocal tract such as the mass and flexibility of the tongue, the size and positioning of the teeth, the length of the jaw, and so forth, also influence the acoustic characteristics of speech sounds. As a result, the same speech sound produced by different talkers varies in its acoustic properties. Even within a single talker, the acoustic characteristics of a particular speech sound may vary considerably in different emotional states or at different speaking rates.

What all of this means is that there is no unique set of acoustic properties that will serve to identify a phoneme in all its possible speech contexts. This variability is a natural consequence of the way that speech is produced. Thus, listeners must have some means of compensating for factors such as differences in talkers' voices, speaking rates, phonetic contexts, and other sources of variability in order to identify phonemes in speech. In particular, some kinds of acoustic differences between speech sounds are irrelevant to determining which phoneme was produced, although they may be important indicators of the talker's identity or emotional state.

Given the amount of variability in the acoustic cues to phonemes, how do listeners succeed in understanding speech at all? One mechanism that apparently plays a role in compensating for the variability present in speech is **categorical perception**. Categorical perception is the psychological phenomenon of perceiving a continuous acoustic dimension (e.g., VOT) as having a distinct boundary (e.g., voiced vs. voiceless consonants). It has been observed for many consonantal contrasts, but not for vowel contrasts. Consider categorical perception of the voicing dimension. It is possible to use a speech synthesizing device to construct a continuum of sounds, ranging from [ba] to [pa], simply by varying VOT (e.g., 0 msec, 10 msec, 20 msec, etc.). When presented with successive sounds from this continuum, you might expect that listeners would report that they hear [ba] gradually being transformed into [pa]. Instead, when asked to **label** the individual sounds, most listeners report an abrupt change from [ba] to [pa] at some point in the series (Figure 2–3). Moreover, when their ability to **discriminate** successive members of the continuum (e.g., 0 msec vs. 20 msec) is tested, they tend to perform poorly, except for those pairs on the continuum where the labels changed from [ba] to [pa] (e.g., 20 msec vs. 40 msec). The discrimination data tell us that listeners don't just choose to impose categories on an acoustic continuum over which they actually perceive a gradual change. Rather, it appears

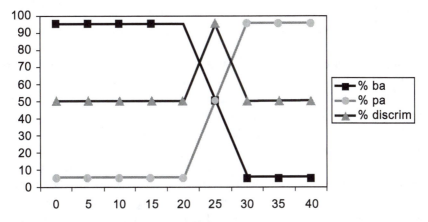

Figure 2–3. Labeling and discrimination functions for a VOT continuum.

that they truly perceive the continuum as made up of two categories. Categorical perception research suggests that listeners do not perceive the infinite variety that exists in the acoustic manifestations of speech. Rather, they are more likely to perceive those acoustic differences that are important for distinguishing one phoneme from another.

Orderings of Phonemes

Part of our knowledge of the segmental phonology of our language concerns the order in which phonemes are allowed to occur in a word, or the language's **phonotactics**. For example, an English-speaking adult who hears the utterance *blint* may treat this as an unknown word in the language. However, the same adult would be likely to treat the utterance *dva* as a foreign language word, because the phoneme combination /dv/ is not grammatical in English, but it is in Russian. Similarly, a Japanese speaker would know that that *McDonald's* is not a possible Japanese word, because syllables in Japanese must be composed of a consonant and a vowel (or a consonant + vowel + n). Thus, Japanese speakers adapt the word *McDonald's* to conform to Japanese phonotactics, resulting in [ma. ku. do. na. ru. do] (periods indicate the right edges of syllables).

■ Prosody

Prosody refers to the part of phonology that applies to units larger than the segment. One aspect of prosody entails marking the ends of phrases and clauses by lengthening the final word, dropping in pitch, and pausing. In examples (a) and (b) in Table 2–3, *cat* occurs at the end of a clause, which is a linguistic unit containing both a subject and a verb. In example (c), *cat* occurs at the end of the subject noun phrase of the sentence, but immediately before a parenthetical clause. In all three examples, the word *cat* is likely to be produced with a longer duration than it is in sentences (d) and (e). It is also likely that a speaker will pause after the word cat in these examples, and especially in examples (a) and (c). The word *cat* is also likely to be produced with a higher pitch than the following word in these examples, especially (a) and (c). Figure 2–4 shows waveforms of the sentences in a-e, demonstrating the different lengths of the word *cat*.

Another aspect of prosody is **lexical stress**. A **stressed** or **strong** syllable is one that is more prominent that an **unstressed** or **weak syllable**. Prominence is expressed by one or more of the following three properties: higher amplitude (perceptually louder), higher frequency (perceptually higher in pitch), longer in duration.

Table 2–3. Sentences with the Word "Cat" at the End of Different Linguistic Units

Sentence	*Linguistic Unit Ended by "Cat"*
a) After he chased the old yellow cat, my dog took a nap.	subordinate clause
b) My dog chased the old yellow cat before he took a nap.	main clause
c) The old yellow cat, I'm told, doesn't drink milk.	subject phrase before parenthetical clause
d) The old yellow cat doesn't drink milk.	subject phrase before verb phrase
e) The cat food is not very fresh	none

Figure 2-4. Waveforms of sentences a–e in Table 2–3, with the word *cat* in gray. The duration of *cat* in milliseconds is indicated next to each waveform.

39

Table 2–4 gives examples of some one- to three-syllable English words of different stress patterns. There are several things to note about the words in Table 2–4. First, all words have at least one stressed syllable, with the exception of those in row (b). These words are often referred to as **function words** and are described in more detail in Chapter 5. Although function words are not normally stressed, they can be given secondary stress in order to make a sentence more rhythmical, as described below. Another thing to note about the words in Table 2–4 is that some stress patterns are more common than others. The vast majority of English words begin with a strong syllable. Thus, if listeners noted the location of typical lexical stress in English, they would have a good chance of knowing they were hearing the beginning of a word when hearing a strong syllable. Other languages have other typical stress patterns. For example, many Spanish words exhibit the stress pattern seen in row (f) of Table 2–4. And, in Turkish, most words are stressed on the last syllable.

A third aspect of prosody is **rhythm**. The rhythm of language is related to lexical stress, but rather than focusing on the strong and weak syllables of words, rhythm refers to the pattern of strong and weak syllables across a sentence. For example, English speakers tend to produce sentences with an alternating rhythm of strong and weak

Table 2–4. Possible Stress Patterns in English 1- to 3-syllable Words

a) 1-syllable words that are stressed	*dog, house, run, think, red, nice, John, Ann*
b) 1-syllable words that are unstressed	*the, a, I, he, is, can, could, have, been*
c) 2-syllable words beginning with a strong syllable	*baby, tiger, cover, carry, yellow, Peter, Mary*
d) 2-syllable words beginning with a weak syllable	*giraffe, guitar, reply, insist, chartreuse, Jerome, Cecile*
e) 3-syllable words beginning with a strong syllable	*elephant, animal, octopus, Jeremy, Allyson*
f) 3-syllable words beginning with a weak syllable	*banana, pajamas, spaghetti, eraser, Rebecca*

Table 2–5. Rhythm in Some English Phrases and Sentences

a) Bread and butter   s   w   s w
b) Pay per view   s   w   s
c) Mary had a little lamb   s w s w s w s
d) I want a drink of water   w s w s w s w
e) He could have been a contender   w s   w   s w w s w

[s = strong (stressed) syllable, w = weak (unstressed) syllable.]

syllables, with at most two weak syllables between strong syllables. Consider the stress patterns in the sentences in Table 2-5. When examining Table 2-5, note the prevalence of strong syllables followed by weak syllables, which are underlined. These underlined strong-weak sequences are called **feet**. English-speaking adults tend to organize their utterances in terms of strong-weak, or **trochaic**, feet whenever possible. Sometimes, this means breaking up phrases, as in (d) in Table 2-4. Here, the phrase *a drink* is broken in the rhythm of the sentence, in order to allow the determiner to form a trochaic foot with the stressed verb *want*. Sometimes the goal of creating trochaic feet also means giving stress to words that normally are unstressed, such as the word *could* in (e).

▮ Summary

Chapter 2 provides an overview of the aspects of phonology that you will need in this book. In learning the phonology of their language, infants and children need to (1) perceive differences that are relevant in the target language(s), (2) ignore irrelevant differences (such as the two versions of /l/ in English), and (3) produce speech sounds like the members of their linguistic community. The first two tasks for the learner are discussed in Chapters 3 and the third in Chapter 4. The discussion of prosody also plays a role in Chapters 5 (Lexical Development), where you will learn how children might find individual words in the stream of speech, and in Chapter 7, where you will learn how children might decide what words in an utterance "go together" in a sentence.

3 Phonological Perception

■ Prenatal Speech Perception

From a historical viewpoint, the study of the development of speech perception began in the early 1970s. We examine these earliest studies, which focused on 1- and 4-month-old infants, in the next section. From a developmental viewpoint, we now know that speech perception begins even before 1 month of age. In fact, it begins even before birth. In this section, we review several studies that demonstrate the impressive speech perception abilities of newborn infants and what these studies tell us about prenatal language learning.

One of the earliest studies to suggest the possibility of prenatal learning was reported by DeCasper and Fifer (1980), who asked if newborn infants could discriminate the voice of their mother from the voice of another woman. Their study used a **Contingent Sucking Rate** procedure, which has two phases, a base rate phase and a test phase. In the base rate phase, 10 newborns were given a non-nutritive pacifier that was connected to a pressure transducer, and their median sucking rate was recorded. In the test phase, the stimulus that infants heard was contingent on their sucking rate relative to the base rate, with different groups of infants subject to different contingencies. Half of the infants were allowed to hear a recording of their mother reading a Dr. Seuss story if their sucking rate was equal to or greater than the base rate of sucking. These infants heard the same story read by another woman if their sucking rate was below the base rate. The other five infants heard their mother's voice if their sucking rate was below the base rate and another woman's voice if their sucking rate was equal to or greater than the base rate. The results showed that the majority of the infants (8 out of 10) modified their sucking rate from the base rate in order to hear their own mother's voice.

Thought Question

Why did the researchers divide infants into two groups so that half of the infants had to suck above the base rate and half below the base rate to hear their mother's voice?

The infants in this study had up to 12 hours of contact with their mothers (as well as with other women, such as nurses) before testing. Therefore, we cannot determine from this study whether infants hear enough of their mother's voice prenatally to recognize it after birth, or whether they learned to recognize their mother's voice over the short time they had been with her after birth. That question was addressed six years later by DeCasper and Spence (1986). In that study, women read one of three stories during the last six weeks of their pregnancy. They were asked to read their assigned story aloud "two times through each day when you feel that your baby (fetus) is awake" and to "read the story in a quiet place so that your voice is the only sound that your baby can hear." After infants were born, they were tested using the Contingent Sucking Rate procedure described above, in which half of the infants heard the familiar story when they sucked at or above the base rate and half heard the familiar story when they sucked below the base rate. Again, infants modified their sucking rate to hear the familiar stimulus. However, this time, the effect had to have been based on prenatal experience, because infants had never heard any of the stories between birth and testing. Before we consider the quality of the acoustic signal that infants might hear prenatally, let's consider one additional study of prenatal language learning.

Jacques Mehler and his colleagues (Mehler et al., 1988) asked whether newborns are able to generalize from their prenatal exposure to their mother's speech to properties of their mother's language (e.g., French, Russian, etc.). Forty 4-day-old infants from French monolingual homes listened to one of two speech samples as they sucked on a non-nutritive nipple. The speech samples were either in French or Russian, but recorded by the same French-Russian bilingual woman. The research method used is called the **High Amplitude Sucking** or **HAS** procedure. It is similar to the Contingent Sucking Rate procedure, described above, except that it has three phases: base rate, habituation, and test. During the habituation and test phases, infants hear a stimulus if their sucking rate is higher than their base rate. During the habituation phase, infants heard either Russian or French until their sucking rate declined to a predetermined criterion, at which point they had **habituated** to (lost interest in) the sound sample. During test, infants heard a new speech sample that was from the same language as the one they heard during habituation, or it came from the other language. The question was whether infants would **dishabituate** (show renewed interest) in the new stimulus. Table 3-1 shows the four groups of infants in the study and their responses to the test stimuli.

Thought Question

Why did the researchers use speech from a bilingual?

The fact that infants continued their lack of interest in the Russian-Russian and French-French conditions in Table 3-1 is not surprising. What is surprising is the asymmetry of responding in the two conditions in which test language differed from habituation language. The researchers attribute this asymmetry to the fact that in the French-Russian condition, the language at test was new, but it was a switch away from the infants' native, and therefore perhaps preferred language. In contrast, the test language in the Russian-French condition was different from habituation and also a switch to the native language.

Table 3-1. Summary of Newborns' Responses in Four Habituation-Test Conditions of a Study by Mehler et al. (1988)

Habituation Language	Test Language	Response to Test
Russian	Russian	Continued habituation
Russian	French	Dishabituation
French	Russian	Continued habituation
French	French	Continued habituation

If this interpretation is correct, we should find that a group of newborns whose mothers did not speak French when they were pregnant should dishabituate to both French-Russian and Russian-French habituation-test stimuli. The researchers found this pattern in a second study, in which mothers spoke a variety of languages other than French, suggesting that there was nothing about the stimuli per se that caused the asymmetry in Table 3-1, but rather the habituation and test stimuli, coupled with the infants' prenatal experience, gave rise to the pattern of results shown in Table 3-1.

Now we can turn to what it is about the mothers' speech that can be perceived prenatally. First, we have strong reason to believe that whatever sound is being transmitted to infants, it is transmitted through the mother's body, because infants show no evidence of recognizing their father's voice (DeCasper & Prescott, 1984). Because infants are surrounded by amniotic fluid, we have reason to think that the speech they hear is filtered in some way. You can begin to imagine what speech sounds like to infants if you have ever played a swimming game in which you say something to your friend under water, and your friend tries to guess what you said. Because water is denser than air, the sounds that are most likely to be transmitted through liquid have long wavelengths, and are therefore lower in frequency. That is, the speech that is transmitted is filtered to let only the lower frequencies pass through, or is **low-pass filtered**. Low-pass filtering allows through prosodic characteristics for speech (including rhythm, whether the utterance is rising or falling in pitch, etc.), but not those acoustic properties that allow us to discriminate one speech sound from another. To ask whether infants are able to recognize their mothers' language if the speech is low-pass filtered, Mehler and colleagues performed the same study schematized in Table 3-1, but now with the speech low-pass filtered. Their results are identical to the ones in Table 3-1, suggesting that it was the lower frequencies of the speech in their first experiment that caused infants' responses.

Interestingly, rats seem to be sensitive to acoustic properties of speech similar to the ones investigated in human infants (Toro, Trobalon, & Sebastián-Gallés, 2005). Rats were rewarded with food for either pressing a lever when Dutch or Japanese sentences were played. They were then tested with new Dutch and Japanese sentences, either played normally or played backward. Playing the sentences backward has a similar effect to low-pass filtering, removing information about consonants and vowels and leaving prosodic characteristics. The researchers found that rats were able to discriminate Dutch and Japanese under both circumstances, suggesting that some of the acoustic information used to break into language is not unique to language or perceivable only by our linguistic species.

The findings in this section suggest that humans are able to use the low frequencies of speech sounds that they hear in utero to learn something about their prenatal environment, including the specific prosodic patterns of their mothers' voices, the prosodic pattern of a particular story, and the more general prosodic pattern of their mothers' languages. We return to how infants might use their early sensitivity to prosody in Chapter 7. However, the next sections of the current chapter explore what infants are able to learn about the sounds of their language when they are able to hear the full range of frequencies, including those frequencies that allow them to differentiate one consonant or vowel from another.

■ Infant Speech Sound Discrimination

Studies of speech sound perception in infants have focused on their ability to discriminate pairs of similar sounds. By studying discrimination, how it changes over development, and how it differs based on the language(s) to which infants have been exposed, we can learn a great deal about the early development of phonological perception.

Early Exploration

Recall from Chapter 2 that one of the key properties of human speech perception is that it is categorical. That is, equal sized physical differences (e.g., differences in voice onset time or VOT) can give rise to unequal psychological detectability (adults are unable to hear the difference between two speech sounds within a phoneme category). In the 1960s, it was believed that categorical perception represented an innate, language-specific, mode of perception. Given this hypothesis about the nature of categorical perception, it was of great interest to psychologists and linguists to know whether infants also showed evidence of categorical perception. If they did, we would have evidence that categorical perception is an innate ability, and therefore, perhaps, that much of our linguistic ability, in general, is innate. That is, we would have evidence for a strongly constrained language learner.

The question was, how could we ask whether infants perceived speech categorically? Recall from Chapter 2 that categorical perception by adults has two parts: labeling speech sounds and discriminating pairs of sounds. Although it may be unreasonable to ask infants to label sounds, we might be able to ask about their ability to discriminate sounds that cross versus do not cross adult category boundaries. To ask that question, Peter Eimas and colleagues (Eimas, Siqueland, Jusczyk, & Vigorrito, 1971) used the then newly developed High Amplitude Sucking procedure. Recall that this procedure establishes a base sucking rate, then habituates infants to a stimulus, then tests for dishabituation to different stimuli. Infants in their study were 1- and 4-month-old infants from English-speaking homes and were habituated to the syllable /ba/ with a VOT of 20 msec (ba-20).

The question that the researchers wanted to answer was how infants would respond to different test stimuli. They hypothesized that if infants, like adults, engage in categorical perception, their sucking rate should increase (the infants should dishabituate) when the test stimulus was from a different category from the habituation stimulus. For example, they should dishabituate to a syllable perceived by adult English-speakers as /pa/ with a VOT of 40 msec (pa-40) if habituated to ba-20. Furthermore, if infants are like adults, they should not dishabituate to a stimulus that is 20 msec different in VOT, but comes from the same phoneme category as the habituation stimulus. For example, they should not dishabituate to ba-0 if they were habituated to ba-20. However, if infants are unlike adults and categorical perception is learned through experience, they should show equal dishabituation to any acoustic change, regardless of the phoneme category it reflects. A control condition in which the test syllable was acoustically identical to the habituation syllable (e.g., ba-20, ba-20) was included so that there could be one condition in which the investigators were sure of how infants would respond (no increase in sucking rate).

The results for the 4-month-olds are shown in Figure 3–1. The first panel shows infants' responses when the habituation and test stimuli came from different adult categories. The second panel illustrates the condition in which habituation and test stimuli are physically different, but from the same adult category. And the third panel shows the control condition. The first line within each panel shows sucking rate during habituation and second line shows sucking rate at test. Notice that only infants in the condition where habituation and

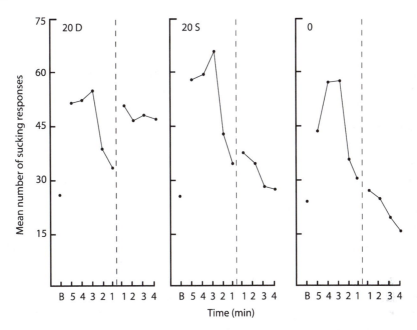

Figure 3–1. Sucking rate during habituation and test trials. From Eimas, P., Siqueland, E., Jusczyk, P. W., and Vigorrito, K. (1971). Speech perception in infants. *Science, 171,* 303–306. Adapted with permission from The American Association for the Advancement of Science.

test stimuli came from different adult phoneme categories showed significant dishabituation. Importantly, they did not show significant dishabituation for the same sized acoustic difference that did not also reflect a category difference. The research team concluded that 'The implication of these findings is that the means by which the categorical perception of speech, that is, *perception in a linguistic mode*, is accomplished may well be part of the biological makeup of the organism, and moreover, that these means must be operative at an unexpectedly early age (Eimas et al., 1971, p. 306, italics added).

Thought Question

What data might you want that are not depicted in Figure 3–1 to help you evaluate the claim of Eimas et al.?

Following the initial report by Eimas and colleagues, a number of other studies during the 1970s confirmed that infants could discriminate many speech contrasts that included the features voicing (as in Eimas et al. study), place of articulation, and manner of articulation (for a review, see Jusczyk, 1997). On the one hand, the data suggested that infants were indeed born with remarkable abilities to perceive speech. However, there were a few loose ends that ultimately caused a new look at the original claims that categorical perception represented innate abilities that are specifically linguistic.

Some Puzzling Findings Lead to a Reanalysis

What were those loose ends? First, not all languages use the same acoustic boundaries for phoneme discrimination. For example, the boundary between the sounds transcribed as Spanish /ba/ and Spanish /pa/ is not between 20 and 40 msec VOT, but rather around 0 msec, with a /ba/ and /pa/ having VOTs of approximately −20 msec and +20 msec, respectively. That is, Spanish /ba/ is produced with voicing occurring prior to the release of the /b/, which is called **prevoicing**. Lasky, Syrdal-Lasky, and Klein (1975) used a somewhat different procedure from Eimas et al. (1971), but similar in logic, to ask whether infants exposed to Spanish would show sensitivity to the English VOT boundary or the Spanish boundary. Four- to 6.5-month-old Panamanian infants heard a habituation syllable 80 times while their heart rates were measured. They then heard 20 new test syllables that were different from the habituation syllable. The habituation and test syllables either occurred in different Spanish /ba/~/pa/ categories but the same English category (−20 msec VOT, 20 msec VOT) or occurred in different English /ba/~/pa/ categories but the same Spanish one (+20, +60). The experimenters reasoned that infants' heart rates would decelerate if they perceived a difference between the habituation stimulus and the new stimulus. Infants for whom habituation and test stimuli came from different English categories showed a change in heart rate. Surprisingly, infants for whom habituation and test stimuli were in different categories for Spanish adults (−20, +20) failed to show evidence of discrimination.

What could be the basis of such a surprising result? Could it be a fluke? Results from another study suggest that the finding by Lasky et al. (1975) is probably meaningful. Streeter (1976) asked whether infants learning a language that has no voicing distinction at all for bilabial sounds show sensitivity to this distinction. She chose to study Kikuyu, which is a language from the Bantu family spoken in Kenya. She used the High Amplitude Sucking procedure to present 36 2-month-olds being raised in Kikuyu-speaking homes with a habituation stimulus followed by a new stimulus, using the following stimuli: (−30, 0), (+10, +40), (+50, +80), as well as a control condition in which the habituation and test stimuli were the same (e.g., +10, +10). She found that infants discriminated all three boundaries, even though their own language makes use of none of them. To account for her results, she proposed that 'this voicing distinction, due to its *psychoacoustic* properties, is naturally discriminable' (italics added). This suggestion, that categorical perception reflects acoustic, not linguistic, processing of speech stimuli, provided a new way to think about the phenomenon. The notion that categorical perception reflects acoustic processing was further confirmed by Patricia Kuhl and Joanne Miller (1975), who found that chinchillas also showed categorical perception for a /ba/~/pa/ continuum.

Aslin and Pisoni (1980) summarized the findings from the early to mid-1970s in a widely cited book chapter. In the chapter, they contrast three broad theoretical views of the development of speech perception. On the view they label "Universal Theory," infants are born able to perceive all speech contrasts and lose those contrasts that are not relevant in their native language. This view is called into question by the fact that Spanish learning infants are not sensitive to the VOT boundary used in adult Spanish. Another view is "Perceptual Learning Theory," in which infants learn only those contrasts to which they are exposed. This view is called into question by the fact that Spanish infants are sensitive to the English boundary and Kikuyu infants are sensitive to VOT boundaries at all, as voicing is not used in Kikuyu bilabials. A third view is "Attunement Theory," which was favored by the authors. On this view, infants are born able to make a set of auditory discriminations that map onto some contrasts of the world's languages. However, depending on their language community, infants might need to (1) stop attending to an auditory contrast not used in their language, (2) shift the boundary of a contrast to align better with their language community, or (3) sharpen or broaden the boundary to exclude or include the correct members of the category for the language community. Aslin and Pisoni and other researchers during the early 1980s came to view speech perception as a domain in which the auditory system of mammals (and perhaps other animals) provides areas of peak sensitivity, which are used and modified by spoken languages to maximize our remarkable human ability to recognize what the members of our speech community are saying. In short, because early speech perception abilities appear to reflect auditory and not linguistic processing, we probably cannot use these early abilities to determine whether humans are constrained by our biology to learn specifically language.

■ How Does Speech Perception Change Over Development?

At about the same time that Aslin and Pisoni were reassessing the possible basis of categorical perception and how it might change over development, Janet Werker and Richard Tees were also asking about the age at which language learners begin to lose their perception of speech contrasts that are not in their native language. For example, we know that it is very difficult for Japanese-speaking adults to perceive the difference between English /r/ and /l/. Similarly, it is difficult for English-speaking adults to discriminate the Swedish vowels /y/ and /i/. Presumably, if any child can learn any human language, there was a time when a Japanese-speaking adult *could* discriminate English /r/ and /l/ and a time when I, as native speaker of English, *could* discriminate the Swedish consonants. How old was I when I lost the ability?

Because it has long been observed that substantial changes in the ability to learn language occur in late childhood, just prior to puberty (see Chapter 9), Werker and Tees began their investigations comparing 4-, 8-, and 12-year-olds with adults. They were surprised to discover that all three groups of children, as well as the adults, found it difficult to discriminate a Hindi dental versus retroflex place of articulation contrast that 7-month-old infants were readily able to discriminate (Werker, Gilbert, Humphrey, & Tees, 1981; Werker & Tees, 1983). Given that the change in discrimination appeared to occur relatively early in life, Werker and Tees decided to focus on infants in their first year. They used a method called the **Conditioned Headturn** procedure, in which you can "tell" infants that you want them to notice changes in a series of stimuli by rewarding them with something they like (e.g., showing them a mechanical monkey playing symbols) if they turn their head just when the stimulus changes. Using this procedure, Werker and Tees (1984) exposed 6- to 8-month-olds, 8- to 10-month-olds, and 10-to 12-month-olds with two different contrasts that are not used to create different English words—the Hindi dental~retroflex contrast, and a glottalized velar~glottalized uvular contrast used in a Salish Native American language of the Northwest. They found that the percentage of English-learning infants able to make the two non-English discriminations dropped from near 100% in the 6- to 8-month-olds to near 0% in the 10- to 12-month-olds, with 8- to 10-month-olds somewhere in the middle (Figure 3–2). Importantly, infants learning Hindi and Salish continued to perceive the contrast used in their native language at 12 months of age, indicating that the loss in discrimination seen in English-learning infants must have been due to the lack of relevance of the two non-native contrasts for English. From these studies, we can conclude that infants begin to lose their ability to perceive those consonant contrasts not relevant for their native language some time during the period of 8 and 10 months of age, with the loss being nearly complete by 12 months. Subsequent studies with non-native vowel contrasts suggest that the process occurs even earlier (6 to 8 months of age, Polka & Werker, 1994).

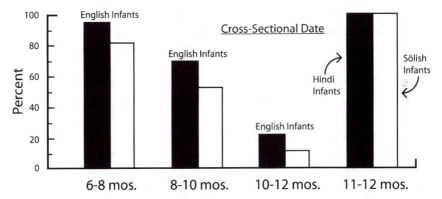

Figure 3–2. Percent of infants at each age that showed significant discrimination of Hindi (*black*) and Salish (*white*) contrast. Adapted from *Infant Behavior and Development, 7*, Werker, J. F., and Tees, R. C., Cross-language speech perception: Evidence for perceptual reorganization during the first year of life, pp. 49-63, Copyright (1984), with permission from Elsevier.

Thought Question

Notice in Figure 3–2 that the number of English-exposed infants who make the non-native contrasts decreases gradually over development. How might you determine if infants who lose their ability earlier in development are different from infants who lose their ability later in development?

The research of Werker and her colleagues provides compelling evidence about *when* infants lose sensitivity to speech contrasts not relevant for their native language. A remaining mystery is *how* infants come to ignore or lose their ability to perceive some contrasts. One possibility for the apparent loss in discrimination ability is sounds that infants do not hear in their environment. However, if you recall the example of English and Mid-Waghi /l/ from Chapter 2, you will realize that many sound differences that are not used to make a difference in meaning in a language nevertheless appear as allophonic variants in the language. Therefore, it seems that for at least some non-native sound contrasts, infants need to learn to ignore differences that occur in their input.

How do they decide what sound differences to ignore? Perhaps infants have begun to learn to pair auditory words with their referents, for example, learning that "pig" refers to a kind of animal and "big" refers to size (Throughout the rest of the chapter, "auditory word" is used to refer to just the sound of a word without regard to whether that sound is associated with meaning; whereas plain "word" refers to the sound of a word paired with its meaning.) They might use this information to determine which sounds are used contrastively (phonemically) in their language. However, infants begin ignoring non-native vowel contrasts earlier than they are likely to have acquired any/many words, suggesting that some other mechanism than learning minimal word pairs is required.

An alternative mechanism by which infants might come to ignore non-native sound contrasts has been explored by Jessica Maye and her colleagues (Maye, Werker, & Gerken, 2002). Maye noted that languages show different statistical distributions of sounds, depending on whether those sounds are being used phonemically (like Mid-Waghi l's) or allophonically (like English l's). In particular, she suggested that sounds that are used phonemically should show a bimodal distribution, where there are two frequent acoustic targets and some spread around each. In contrast, languages in which two sounds are allophonic variants should show a unimodal distribution, where there is one frequent central target and a wide spread around it. These two types of statistical distributions are show in Figure 3–3.

Can infants detect the difference in unimodal versus bimodal sound distributions? To ask this question, Maye and colleagues familiarized 6- and 8-month-olds with either unimodal or bimodal distributions of the acoustic continuum of syllables in which the consonant ranged between the one at the beginning of "day" to the consonant that you get when you splice the /s/ off the word "stay," resulting in the perceived syllable "day." The critical syllables, labeled at [da] and [ta] in Figure 3–3, were intermixed with filler syllables, so that the familiarization stimuli composed a string of varied syllables. At test, infants heard on different trials a string of syllables that alternated between the two endpoints of the continuum (stimuli 1 and 8) or stimuli composed of one syllable repeated (stimulus 1 or stimulus 8

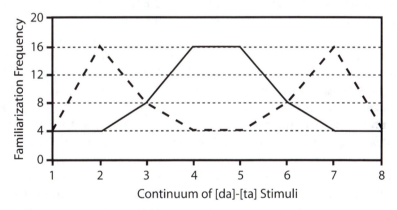

Figure 3–3. Frequency in familiarization stimuli of 8 acoustic tokens reflecting an acoustic continuum. Adapted from *Cognition*, *82*(3), Maye, J., Werker, J. F., and Gerken, L. A., Infant sensitivity to distributional information can affect phonetic discrimination, pp. B101–B111, Copyright (2002), with permission from Elsevier. Reprinted from *The Lancet, 83*, Maye, J., Weker, J. F., and Gerken, L. A. Infant sensitivity to distributional information can affect phonetic discrimination, pp. B101–B111, Copyright (2002), with permission from Elsevier.

over and over). If infants in the bimodal condition could use the bimodal distribution to infer that the continuum was made up of two phonemes, then they should perceive the difference in the two endpoints and therefore perceive a difference between the alternating and nonalternating test items. If infants in the unimodal condition could use the unimodal distribution to infer that the continuum was made up of a single phoneme, then the two endpoints should sound the same, and they should not perceive a difference between the alternating and nonalternating distributions. Infants were tested using a **Central Fixation Preferential Listening** procedure, such that they heard a test trial as long as they looked at a colorful bull's eye projected on a screen in front of them.

The question was whether infants in the two conditions would show differences in preference (looking time) for the alternating versus nonalternating test trials. The data supported Maye's predictions. Only infants in the bimodal familiarization condition showed differences in listening times to the alternating and nonalternating test items, listening longer to the latter. These data suggest that the loss of discrimination of non-native contrasts shown by Werker and her colleagues almost 20 years before might be due to infants' use of statistical information in their input. We discuss infants' apparent ability to make use of the statistics of their linguistic environment in several more places throughout this book. Recall that being able to keep track of input statistics is a prerequisite for less constrained theories of language development, particularly Associative Learning.

Interestingly, this view of the development of the role of language statistics on monolingual perception might also be relevant to explain some interesting data from infants learning two languages, Spanish and Catalan, simultaneously (Bosch & Sebastián-Gallés, 2003). Spanish and Catalan differ, among other ways, in the vowels they use. The difference that is relevant for this study is that Catalan uses both /e/ and /ɛ/ and Spanish uses only /e/. In terms of the acoustic properties of the vowels, Spanish /e/ is roughly between the two Catalan vowels. Spanish /e/ is also almost three times as frequent as Catalan /e/ and /ɛ/ combined. The researchers tested 4-, 8-, and 12-month-old infants who were exposed to both Spanish and Catalan in their homes on their ability to discriminate the two Catalan vowels. They used an auditory **Switch** procedure, in which infants listened to one of the two vowels as long as they attended to centrally projected picture. When they habituated (stopped looking), they heard new trials that were either the same vowel or the other vowel (the latter are the switch trials). If infants show more attention on switch trials than same trials, we can conclude that they discriminate the two vowels. The pattern of results was quite surprising: 4-month-olds and 12-month-olds discriminated the vowels, whereas 8-month-olds did not. The researchers attribute this pattern of results to the 8-month-olds treating the two Catalan vowels and Spanish /e/ as belonging to a single, unimodal, distribution of speech sounds. This misanalysis may be reinforced by the high frequency of Spanish /e/ and the fact that it is acoustically between the two Catalan vowels. However, by 12 months, infants may somehow have reanalyzed the acoustic input to treat the two Catalan vowels as belonging to their own bimodal distribution, and Spanish /e/ as belonging to its own unimodal distribution. What might have caused infants to reject the single language, unimodal analysis must be explored with future research.

■ Finding Phonological Patterns in Auditory Words

This section examines the types of sound patterns that infants are able to perceive in auditory words and how they generalize these patterns to new auditory words. One line of research asks whether infants notice what sounds typically occur next to what other sounds in a sequence. That is, do infants notice **phonotactic** regularities? Peter Jusczyk and his colleagues began this line of research by asking if infants can discriminate words composed of sequences of segments (consonants and vowels) that occur frequently in the their native language from less frequent (or entirely absent) sequences. In one study, American 6- and 9-month-olds were tested using the **Headturn Preference** procedure or **HPP**, in which the infants are allowed to listen to an auditory stimulus as long as they turn their heads toward a flashing light and speaker (Jusczyk, Friederici, Wessels, Svenkerud, & Jusczyk, 1993). The stimuli in this case were words of English and of Dutch. While English and Dutch are similar in terms of prosody and the consonants and vowels they contain, English allows some sound sequences not allowed by Dutch and vice versa. The words used in the study contained sound sequences that differed between the two languages. Whereas 6-month-olds showed no difference in listening time to English versus Dutch word lists, 9-month-old American infants listened longer to English words than to Dutch words. That is, they showed a preference for what is familiar, or a **familiarity preference**. The fact that infants were able to discriminate the two word lists suggests that they perceived differences among the phonotactic sequences.

Thought Question

Two explanations of the difference between the 6- and 9-month-olds are maturation (experience independent, age-related changes) and experience with the native language. Can you think of a study that could tease apart these two explanations?

One question that arises from this study is whether American infants knew that certain sequences were not allowed in English (which sequences were grammatical), or whether their preference for English over Dutch reflects a more graded sensitivity to what is statistically frequent in their language experience. To ask that question, researchers created new words that either contained sequences of sounds that are frequently occurring sequences in English or sequences that do occur in English, but not very frequently (Jusczyk, Luce, & Charles-Luce, 1994). American 9-month-olds who were tested using the HPP showed significantly longer listening times for words that contained frequent phonotactic sequences than infrequent sequences. This study was important because it marked the beginning of a period of growing interest in infants' knowledge of the statistical properties of their target language. Again, such abilities are required for less constrained theories of language development.

The two studies by Jusczyk and colleagues suggest that infants in the first year of life become sensitive to the typical (frequent) sequences of speech sounds in their language. Almost a decade later, other researchers began to wonder if infants are able to learn new patterns of speech sounds through a brief laboratory exposure. In one such study, Chambers, Onishi, and Fisher (2003) used the HPP to familiarize 16.5-month-old infants with consonant–vowel–consonant (CVC) syllables in which particular consonants were artificially restricted to either initial or final position (e.g., /bæp/ not /pæb/). During familiarization, infants simply sat on their parents' laps and listened to stimuli. During test, they listened significantly longer to new syllables that violated the familiarized phonotactic constraints than to new syllables that obeyed them. That is, they showed a listening preference for novel stimuli, or a **novelty preference**. This study suggests that infants are able to learn new phonotactic regularities in a short time. Other studies published at about the same time indicate that infants are able to learn new sound patterns in the laboratory by at least age 9 months (Saffran & Thiessen, 2003; Seidl & Buckley, 2005).

Thought Question

How does infants' listening preference in the Chambers et al. (2003) study differ from that seen by Jusczyk et al. (1994)? Can you think of a possible explanation for the difference?

Not only are 9-month-olds able to learn what sounds are likely to occur in sequence, but they are also able to learn which syllables in multisyllabic words should be stressed. The research addressing this question followed a similar path to the research on infants' sensitivity to phonotactics: Researchers began asking what infants know about the stress patterns of their *own* language and subsequently asked what they are able to learn about word stress in a brief laboratory exposure. The starting point for the research is the already noted observation that the vast majority of disyllabic (two syllable) words in English exhibit a strong-weak, or **trochaic** pattern, such as in the words *apple*, *teacher*, and *monkey* (Cutler & Carter, 1987). Jusczyk, Cutler, and Redanz (1993) used the HPP to ask whether 6- and 9-month-old American infants discriminate trochaic words from **iambic** (weak-strong, e.g., *giraffe*) words. They found that 9-month-olds exhibited significantly longer listening times to trochaic words, whereas 6-month-olds showed no significant difference in listening times. Thus, just as in the study of infants' sensitivity to English versus Dutch phonotactics, 9-month-olds, but not 6-month-olds, provide evidence for having extracted a frequent pattern in their target language.

Are 9-month-olds capable of learning a new word stress system in the laboratory? To ask that question, we need to consider the principles of stress assignment proposed by linguists. Two possible sets of principles are shown in Table 3–2.

Table 3–2. Stress Assignment Principles Used in Two Artificial
Languages by Gerken (2004)

Language 1 Principles	Language 2 Principles
Avoid two stressed syllables in sequence	Avoid two stressed syllables in sequence
Stress heavy (CVC) syllables	Stress heavy (CVC) syllables
Stress second to last syllables	Stress second syllables
Alternate stress from right to left	Alternate stress from left to right

Gerken (2004) asked whether 9-month-olds could learn a new
set of stress assignment principles from a set of invented words over
the course of a brief laboratory exposure. Using the HPP, infants were
familiarized with three- to five-syllable words from one of two artificial languages that differed in their stress assignment principles (see
Table 3–2). During test, infants heard new words with different stress
patterns than the ones heard during familiarization but based on the
same stress principles. That is, the particular patterns of strong and
weak syllables were new, but they were nevertheless consistent with
the principles of one of the languages. On some test trials, infants
heard words consistent with the stress assignment principles of Language 1, and on other trials, they heard words consistent with the stress
assignment principles of Language 2. Infants demonstrated a novelty
preference: those familiarized with Language 1 listened longer to Language 2 test words and vice versa. Consistent with the findings of
Jusczyk, Cutler, and Redanz, 6-month-olds did not discriminate the
test words.

The studies in this section suggest that, some time during the
second half of the first year of life, infants become experts at detect-
ing patterns in the auditory words they hear, both in their target language and in brief laboratory exposures. Is infants' impressive ability
to detect patterns and make generalizations restricted to linguistic
generalizations, that is, ones that occur in real languages? Several studies have begun to ask that question (e.g., Gerken & Bollt, 2008; Seidl
& Buckley, 2005). One study used linguistic stress principles like
those shown in Table 3–2, but the principle to stress syllables that end

in a consonant was replaced by a principle that does not occur in real languages: stress syllables beginning with /t/. Although 9-month-olds were not able to learn the language with the "unnatural" principle, 7.5-month-olds were. This apparent loss in perceiving certain sound patterns can be seen as a parallel to the finding that infants lose their ability to perceive sound contrasts that are not in their target language (e.g., Werker & Tees, 1984). Recall that both the General Purpose Hypothesis Testing and the Associative Learning theories predict that children should be able to learn patterns that do not occur in real languages. The data from the 7.5-month-olds are consistent with those theories and might be taken to suggest that infants become constrained to consider only linguistic generalizations as they have more linguistic experience. However, a proponent of innate linguistic constraints might counter that such constraints must mature over development. This example of data and competing interpretations illustrates the importance of looking at the outcomes of a range of studies when attempting to determine which theoretical framework best describes language development.

■ Phonological Perception of Words

So far, this chapter has focused on the perception of syllables and auditory words, without regard to meaning. This section focuses on the phonological perception of words—that is, auditory words associated with meanings. The starting point for this section is a surprising observation: The impressive perceptual abilities demonstrated by infants for syllables and auditory words do not appear to translate directly into the perception of meaningful words. The observation comes from studies in which young children are asked to identify referents of newly taught or previously known words. One of the earliest studies to examine children's ability to discriminate speech sounds used in words was done by the Russian psychologist, Shvachkin (1948/1973), who taught Russian-learning 10- to 24-month-olds nonsense words that referred to toys. Over a period of several months, each child learned a few minimal word pairs (two words differing by only a single phoneme or feature, e.g., *dax* vs. *bax*). Phoneme discrimination was tested by asking children to find the toy associated with one member of a minimal pair. Shvachkin found that, by the end of the study, approximately half of all of the children (mean age 22 months) were able to make all of the discriminations tested.

Shvachkin's technique of teaching new minimal pairs has been employed in a number of studies in the intervening decades. In the most recent studies, children between the ages of 14 and 18 months have been exposed to new words and tested in a procedure relatively better controlled than was available during the 1940s. In a referential version of the Switch procedure, described in the previous section, children see one of two new objects on each trial and hear the object's label (e.g., *lif* and *neem* or *dih* and *bih*). At test, children see one of the objects and either hear the correct label ("same" trials) or the opposite label ("switch") trials. Although 14-month-olds show longer looking on the switch than the same trials when the two words are phonetically dissimilar (*lif* and *neem*), they show no difference when the words are similar (*bih* vs. *dih*) (Stager & Werker, 1997). By 17 months, however, children show longer looking times on switch trials for similar sounding words (Werker, Fennell, Corcoran, & Stager, 2002). What is surprising about this finding is that infants and children of almost any age are able to distinguish the two similar sounding syllables when no referent is involved (e.g., using the Conditioned Headturn procedure).

There are at least two explanations for children's inability to distinguish similar sounding syllables when the syllables refer to objects, coupled with their ability to distinguish the same syllables with no referents. One possibility is that children change their focus of attention when they begin learning words, ignoring fine-grained phonetic details as they begin the task is associating sound patterns and referents. A second possibility is that children do not change how they perceive sounds, but tasks tapping their ability to associate sounds and meanings may be more difficult than tasks that measure sound discrimination alone. The more difficult tasks might prevent learners from showing their full abilities. Furthermore, in the Switch task used by Stager and Werker, the sound patterns, the referents, and the associations were newly learned and therefore perhaps not as readily accessed as more familiar sound-referent pairings.

Several findings support the task difficulty explanation of Stager and Werker's results. Swingley and Aslin (2002) used the **Looking While Listening** procedure and presented 14-month-olds with either correctly produced (e.g., *apple*) or mispronounced (*opple*) familiar words while the children looked at a display with two pictures (apple and car). Children spent less time looking at the relevant picture (in this case, at the apple) for mispronounced words, suggesting that were listening for sufficient detail for them to detect a mispronunciation of a familiar word. These findings suggest that the demands of learning two new words, two new referents, and two new word-referent pairings in the Stager and Werker (1997) study may have been responsible for children's failure to distinguish similar sounding words. This interpretation is supported by research in which experimenters gave parents of 12-month-olds a unique toy to take home for their children to play with (Fennell, Waxman, & Weisleder, 2007). The toy was not given a name at this point in the experiment. The children were brought back into the lab when they were 14 months old and participated in the Switch procedure. However, unlike in the original Switch procedure, the toy that the child played with at home was now given the label *din*. Unlike the 14-month-olds in the Stager and Werker study, these children looked longer at the object when it was given the incorrect label *gin* (with a hard /g/). The whole set of studies described so far in this section suggests that children are able to represent the sounds of words in fine phonetic detail, but that they have difficulty fully accessing words when the demands of the task are too high.

The preceding paragraph illustrates an important message about language development: Although we might construe the language learner's job as one of making generalizations about the sounds, words, and word combinations allowed in their language, we need to acknowledge that a big part of their task is also to comprehend and produce language quickly enough to be conversational partners. That is to say, in addition to learning the forms of language, infants and children must become efficient language processors. In keeping with the importance of language processing, a number of recent studies have begun to investigate the development of children's ability to access their mental lexicon. In one study, Swingley, Pinto, and Fernald (1999) used the Looking While Listening procedure described above to compare moment-by-moment, or **online**, speech processing in 24-month-olds and adults. Many accounts of adult word processing suggest that listeners begin to access a number of possible word candidates as they hear a word over time. For example, if an adult is hearing the word *doggie*, he might first access the words he knows that start with /d/, then narrow the set to words that contain /dɔ/, and so forth. If the adult needs to choose between a picture of a dog and a picture of a tree, he should be able to do so very early in hearing the word *dog*, because none of the activated word candidates could possibly be a match for a tree picture. But if the adult needs to choose between a picture of a dog and a picture of a doll, the words *dog* and *doll* should both be active at the beginning of the word "dog." Therefore, the adult should wait longer to decide which picture is correct.

The question asked by Swingley and colleagues was whether 24-month-olds show similar stages of partial access to spoken words. In their study, they played participants a word, such as *doggie*, in the presence of two pictures. The two pictures either had labels that either overlapped in their sounds *doggie* and *doll*) or no overlap (*doggie* and *tree*). Figure 3–4 shows that, although 24-month-olds took longer

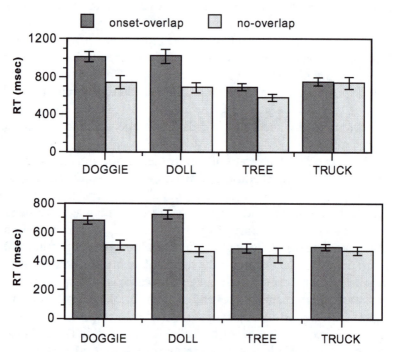

Figure 3–4. Reaction times of 24-month-olds (*top*) and adults (*bottom*) to look at the appropriate picture when the onset of the target word overlapped (doggie vs. doll) or did not overlap (doggie vs. tree) with the label of the incorrect picture. Adapted from *Cognition, 71*(2), Swingley, D., Pinto, J. P., and Fernald, A., Continuous processing in word recognition at 24 months, pp. 73–108, Copyright (1999), with permission from Elsevier. Reprinted from *The Lancet, 71*, Swingley, D., Pinto, J. P., and Fernald, A., Continuous processing in word recognition at 24 months, pp. 73–108, Copyright (1999), with permission from Elsevier.

to settle on the correct picture than adults did, both children and adults settled on the correct picture faster when in the no-overlap condition than in the overlap condition. These data suggest that children process words in a manner very similar to adults, but that they gain speed and efficiency over development. Subsequent studies using the Looking While Listening procedure demonstrate that children make rapid gains in the speed with which they access words between the middle of the second year and age two (Fernald, Perfors, & Marchman, 2006). Importantly, children's speed and accuracy of lexical access at age 25 months were related not only to their vocabulary at 25 months (as measured by parental report), but also to many earlier measures of language development that were taken from the age of 12 months. These findings reinforce the idea that we cannot study language development without also studying how young learners process language in real time.

■ Summary

At least three important themes are presented in this chapter. First, infants are sensitive to prosodic properties of language, including pitch rises and falls, pausing, and rhythm, before birth. Therefore, prosody appears to be infants' first entrée into their target language. We see other evidence of the importance of prosody in Chapter 7. Second, the work on early discrimination of speech segments (consonants and vowels) suggests that spoken languages make use of the auditory sensitivities of humans and that infants tune these sensitivities to their target language(s) over the first year of life. That is, infants do not arrive in the world prepared for the speech sounds of a particular language, but rather are shaped by their experiences. Third, statistical information in the target language appears to be crucial for shaping infants' and children's growing expertise in their target language. Statistics on the distribution of speech sounds (bimodal vs. unimodal) and the relative frequency of certain sound patterns (e.g., trochaic vs. iambic) play a role learners' behavior. We see in Chapters 4 and 5 that infants and children appear to be affected by other types of statistical patterns as well.

What do the studies presented in Chapter 3 have to say about the four theories of language development introduced in Chapter 1? The studies have at least three implications: First, early abilities with linguistic stimuli (e.g., /ba/ vs. /pa/ or the prosody of French vs. Russian) do not necessarily imply that the abilities rely on linguistic mechanisms. Rather, the specific examples of early abilities discussed in this chapter appear to rely on auditory processing mechanisms shared with other animals (e.g., chinchillas and rats). These studies are not consistent with any particular theory, but rather tell us that we must be cautious in interpreting early abilities as evidence for a learner with innate linguistic constraints. Second, several studies suggest that infants have excellent abilities to keep track of the statistics of their input. As noted elsewhere in the chapter, these abilities are a prerequisite for learning theories in which the learner is less strongly constrained by biology. Therefore, these studies indicate that such theories cannot be ruled out automatically. Finally, new studies are beginning to demonstrate that younger infants are able to learn phonological generalizations that do not occur in real languages and that older learners are unable to make. These results are not predicted by Triggering and Linguistic Hypothesis testing theories. They remind us that learners are not static entities and that development is characterized by both gains and losses of ability.

■ References

Aslin, R. N., & Pisoni, D. (1980). Some developmental processes in speech perception. In G. Yeni-Komshian, J. Kavanagh, & G. Ferguson (Eds.), *Child phonology Vol. 2: Perception*. New York: Academic Press.

Bosch, L., & Sebastián-Gallés, N. (2003). Simultaneous bilingualism and the perception of a language-specific vowel. *Language and Speech, 46*(2), 217-243.

Chambers, K. E., Onishi, K. H., & Fisher, C. L. (2003). Infants learn phonotactic regularities from brief auditory experience. *Cognition, 87*, B69-B77.

Cutler, A., & Carter, D. (1987). The predominance of strong initial syllables in the English vocabulary. *Computer Speech and Language, 2*, 133-142.

DeCasper, A. J., & Fifer, W. P. (1980). Of human bonding: Newborns prefer their mothers' voices. *Science, 208*, 1174-1176.

DeCasper, A. J., & Prescott, P. A. (1984). Human newborns' perception of male voices: Preference, discrimination and reinforcing value. *Developmental Psychobiology, 17*, 481-491.

DeCasper, A. J., & Spence, M. J. (1986). Prenatal maternal speech influences newborns' perception of speech sounds. *Infant Behavior and Development, 9*, 133-150.

Eimas, P., Siqueland, E., Jusczyk, P. W., & Vigorrito, K. (1971). Speech perception in infants. *Science, 171,* 303–306.

Fennell, C. T., Waxman, S. R., & Weisleder, A. (2007). With referential cues, infants successfully use phonetic detail in word learning. In *Proceedings of the 31st Boston University Conference on Language Development.* Somerville, MA: Cascadilla Press.

Fernald, A., Perfors, A., & Marchman, V. A. (2006). Picking up speed in understanding: Speech processing efficiency and vocabulary growth across the second year. *Developmental Psychology, 42,* 98–116.

Gerken, L. A. (2004). Nine-month-olds extract structural principles required for natural language. *Cognition, 93,* B89–B96.

Gerken, L. A., & Bollt, A. (2008). Three exemplars allow at least some linguistic generalizations: Implications for generalization mechanisms and constraints. *Language Learning and Development, 4*(3), 228–248.

Jusczyk, P. W. (1997). *The discovery of spoken language.* Cambridge, MA: MIT Press.

Jusczyk, P. W., Cutler, A., & Redanz, N. (1993). Infants sensitivity to predominant word stress patterns in English. *Child Development, 64,* 675–687.

Jusczyk, P. W., Friederici, A. D., Wessels, J. M., Svenkerud, V. Y., & Jusczyk, A. M. (1993). Infants' sensitivity to the sound patterns of native language words. *Journal of Memory and Language, 32*(3), 402–420.

Jusczyk, P. W., Luce, P. A., & Charles-Luce, J. (1994). Infants' sensitivity to phonotactic patterns in the native language. *Journal of Memory and Language, 33*(5), 630–645.

Kuhl, P. K., & Miller, J. D. (1975). Speech perception in the chinchilla: Voiced-voiceless distinction in alveolar plosive consonants. *Science, 190,* 69–72.

Lasky, R. E., Syrdal-Lasky, A., & Klein, R. E. (1975). VOT discrimination by four to six and a half month old. *Journal of Experimental Child Psychology, 20*(2), 215–225.

Maye, J., Werker, J. F., & Gerken, L. A. (2002). Infant sensitivity to distributional information can affect phonetic discrimination. *Cognition, 82*(3), B101–B111.

Mehler, J., Jusczyk, P., Lambertz, G., Halsted, N., Bertoncini, J., & Amiel-Tison, C. (1988). A precursor of language acquisition in young infants. *Cognition, 29*(2), 143–178.

Polka, L., & Werker, J. F. (1994). Developmental changes in perception of non-native vowel contrasts. *Journal of Experimental Psychology: Human Perception and Performance, 20,* 421–435.

Saffran, J. R., & Thiessen, E. D. (2003). Pattern induction by infant language learners. *Developmental Psychology, 39,* 484–494.

Shvachkin, N. (1948/1973). The development of phonemic perception in early childhood. In C. A. Ferguson & D. I. Slobin (Eds.), *Studies of child language development* (pp. 92–127). New York: Holt, Rinehart and Winston.

Seidl, A., & Buckley, E. (2005). On the learning of arbitrary phonological rules. *Language Learning and Development, 3-4,* 289–316.

Stager, C. L., & Werker, J. F. (1997). Infants listen for more phonetic detail in speech perception than in word-learning tasks. *Nature, 388*(6640), 381–382.

Streeter, L. (1976). Language perception in 2-month-old infants shows effects of both innate mechanisms and experience. *Nature, 259,* 39–41.

Swingley, D., & Aslin, R. N. (2002). Lexical neighborhoods and the word-form representations of 14-month-olds. *Psychological Science, 13,* 480–484.

Swingley, D., Pinto, J. P., & Fernald, A. (1999). Continuous processing in word recognition at 24 months. *Cognition, 71*(2), 73–108.

Toro, J. M., Trobalon, J. B., & Sebastián-Gallés, N. (2005). Effects of backward speech and speaker variability in language discrimination by rats. *Journal of Experimental Psychology: Animal Behavior Processes, 31*(1), 95–100.

Werker, J. F., Fennell, C., Corcoran, K., & Stager, C. L. (2002). Infants' ability to learn phonetically similar words: Effects of age and vocabulary size. *Infancy, 3,* 1–30.

Werker, J. F., Gilbert, J. H. V., Humphrey, K., & Tees, R. C. (1981). Developmental aspects of cross-language speech perception. *Child Development, 52,* 349–355.

Werker, J. F., & Tees, R. C. (1983). Developmental changes across childhood in the perception of non-native speech sounds. *Canadian Journal of Psychology, 37,* 278–286.

Werker, J. F., & Tees, R. C. (1984). Cross-language speech perception: Evidence for perceptual reorganization during the first year of life. *Infant Behavior and Development, 7,* 49–63.

4 Phonological Production

■ Precursors to Linguistic Production

Just as studies of infant speech perception reveal remarkable abilities at birth, studies of newborns suggest that they are able to associate the speech sounds that they hear with the vocal activity required to make those sounds. In one study, 25 newborns listened to /a/ and /m/ sounds while their mouth movements were recorded on video (Chen, Striano, & Rakoczy, 2004). Although none of the infants vocalized, they made more open mouth movements when they heard /a/ and more clutched mouth movements when they heard /m/ (Figure 4–1A and B). These findings suggest that newborns are highly prepared to produce speech sounds like the ones they will hear in their environment.

Oral Babble

In contrast to the study just described, the more frequent approach to studying infants' vocalizations involves collecting recorded audio

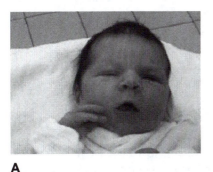   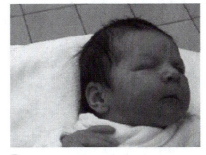

A   B

Figure 4–1. Infant mouth movements of an infant hearing /a/ (**A**) and /m/ (**B**). From Chen, X., Striano, T., & Rakoczy, H. (2004). Auditory-oral matching behavior in newborns. *Developmental Science, 15,* 217–221. Copyright 2004 by Wiley-Blackwell Publishing. Reprinted with permission.

samples of these vocalizations and coding them, either through careful listening or through acoustic measurements. Such studies suggest that during the first six months of life, infants may accidentally produce some sounds that resemble speech; however, researchers would not label these sounds as **babble** (Stark, 1980). That term is usually reserved for vocalizations in which particular sounds are obviously repeated and in which the timing properties (e.g., syllable duration) resemble those in speech. Babble is most frequent in infants from about 7 to 12 months of age, and it includes two subtypes: **reduplicated babble** and **nonreduplicated** or **variegated babble**. Reduplicated babble is characterized by repetitions of a single consonant-vowel (CV) syllable (e.g., [bababa]), and infants appear to concentrate on a single CV type (e.g., [ba]) for a period of time before concentrating on another. Variegated babble is characterized by strings of different syllables (e.g., [bamido]). In some forms of variegated babble, syllables are differentially stressed, with some syllables louder and/or higher in pitch, and pitch contours are given to syllable strings (e.g, rising across the whole set of syllables), giving productions a sentence-like quality. Research indicates that infants often produce both types of babble during the same developmental period (e.g., Mitchell & Kent, 1990).

There is some debate about nature of babble, and as you will see, the debate carries through nearly all work on children's phonological production. The nature of the debate concerns the degree to which the babble and word forms that infants and children produce are constrained by their ability to produce sounds (or hand gestures) or by other factors, including the specific language they are learning. In support of the first view that babble is a product of infants' developing vocal-motor system, there appear to be a number of properties shared by the babble of infants learning different languages. One pair of researchers (Davis & MacNeilage, 1990, 1995) suggests that both babble and early speech can be seen as rhythmic alternation between closed (consonant-like sound) and open (vowel-like sound) mouth positions, accompanied by phonation (vocal fold vibration). In support of their view, they note that some CV sequences are more frequent than others in babble, and these frequent sequences suggest that the basic syllable pattern is one of closing and opening the mouth, with tongue position held constant. For example, velar (back) consonants frequently pair with back vowels (e.g., /ka/, /gæ/). These researchers have further claimed that the preferred babble sequences can be related to a human "protolanguage" reconstructed from common form-meaning pairings across the world's languages (MacNeilage & Davis, 2000).

Although much of babble might be affected by articulatory forces common to all infants, language learners must ultimately come under the influence of their target language. The question is whether the influence of the target language can be seen in babble, or whether we must wait until children attempt to produce their first words. There are a number of reasons to believe that the target language shapes babble. First, despite an early claim that deaf and hearing infants show similar patterns of oral babble (Lenneberg, 1967), later research has demonstrated that deaf infants engage in different oral babble patterns than hearing infants (Oller, Eilers, Bull, & Carney, 1985). These findings suggest, at the very least, a role for hearing in oral babble. Second, despite early claims that babble and first word production were distinct stages with a "silent period" in between (Jakobson, 1968), it is now clear that late babble and first words overlap in time (e.g., Vihman, Macken, Miller, Simmons, & Miller, 1985).

Thought Question

Given how difficult it can be to understand young children's utterances, how might these researchers have gone about deciding whether what they were hearing was babble or a word?

More direct evidence of the role of the target language on babble is that infants from different linguistic environment demonstrate different babble characteristics. For example, 24 Mandarin-learning infants between the ages of 7 and 18 months produced a large number of labial consonants followed by back vowels, a pattern that is not predicted by accounts of babble that rely on universal articulatory patterns (Chen & Kent, 2005). However, these syllable productions are consistent with frequent syllables heard in Mandarin. Similarly, 18-month-old French infants produced babble with more rising pitch and longer final syllables than Japanese infants, patterns that are consistent with the target languages of the two groups (Hallé, de Boysson-Bardies, & Vihman, 1991).

How long is the developmental lag between when infants focus perceptually on the particular vowels and consonants in the target language and when this focus shapes their own productions? We currently have insufficient evidence to answer this question; however, one study provides at least a hint. Bénédicte de Boysson-Bardies and her colleagues examined the vowel productions of 10-month-old infants raised in homes where the ambient language was English, French, Cantonese, or Arabic (de Boysson-Bardies, Hallé, Sagart, & Durand, 1989). They found that the acoustic characteristics of the vowels were more similar among infants within a particular language community than among infants from different language communities. Furthermore, they found that infants' productions from a particular language community were more similar to adult productions from that community than to adult productions from another community. For example, adults and infants from English-speaking communities produced vowels with the highest pitch, whereas adults and infants from Cantonese-speaking communities produced vowels with the lowest. These results clearly indicate that infant babble is influenced by the infant's language environment. Recall from Chapter 3 that infants lose sensitivity to non-native vowel contrasts at about 6 months. Although we do not know if infants younger than 10 months would show an influence of the target language on their vowel production, we can hypothesize based on the current evidence that the lag between perceptual sensitivity and production is no more than four months.

In summary, the preceding discussion suggests that both universal articulatory (nonlinguistic) constraints and perceptual properties of the target language influence early vocalization. We will see a similar interplay between universal and language-specific properties in the section on children's early word production.

Manual Babble

Before leaving the topic of infant babble, we should acknowledge that not all babble is oral. Parallel to the debate about articulatory versus target language influences on oral babble, researchers studying the hand movements produced by infants exposed to signed languages are grappling with the source of these movements. Nearly all infants, regardless of whether they are exposed to sign language, produce some types of hand gestures. However, Laura Petitto and her colleagues have data suggesting that deaf and hearing infants exposed to a signed language produce other types of hand movements that (1) use the manual components seen in signed languages, (2) exhibit rhythmic properties like those found in oral babble, and (3) were not used to communicate (Petitto, Holowka, Sergio, Levy, & Ostry, 2004; Petitto & Marentette, 1991). Although infants not exposed to a signed language also produced some hand movements meeting these criteria, they did so approximately only one-tenth as frequently. From their observations, Petitto and colleagues have concluded that babble exhibits similar properties in both oral and manual domains and that the infant's linguistic input determines the form of babble that will ultimately be used as the precursor to language.

However, other researchers such as Meier and Willerman (1995) disagree with this view of manual babble and argue, just as Davis and MacNeilage have done in the domain of oral babble, that manual babble is more clearly a reflection of the infant's developing motor system than of her linguistic input. In support of this view, one group of researchers found that deaf and hearing infants engaged in the same amount of manual babble (Cormier, Mauk, & Repp, 1998). It is important to note that the criteria these researchers used to identify manual activity as babble were different from the characteristics used by Petitto and colleagues. Therefore, just as researchers in the early days of studying oral babble needed to develop definitions of different aspects of the phenomenon, researchers studying manual babble will need to determine what is and is not manual babble in order to make sense of conflicting research findings.

■ Protowords and Early Words

Near the end of the first year or beginning of the second year of life, most children produce their first meaningful utterances in the sense that the utterances appear to refer to some aspect of the child's environment. The observed timing of first meaningful utterances comes from diary studies of parents, and well as from audio- and video-taped recordings of learners' vocalizations. Two types of meaningful productions have been observed: protowords and words. A **protoword** is a sound sequence (often a syllable or two) that appears to be used consistently in a particular context. For example, children might consistently use the syllable [di] when their apparent goal is to draw an adult's attention to an object (Ferguson & Farwell, 1975). Early words differ from protowords in that the consistently produced sound sequence actually resembles an adult word that would be appropriate in the particular context in which it is used. For example, a child's use of the syllable [dæi] in the presence of her father is likely to be taken as an attempt to produce the adult form [dædi].

In keeping with the discussion above suggesting some overlap between babble and early words, children appear to choose their first words based partly on the production repertoire they developed in babble. Marlilyn Vihman and her colleagues recorded and coded the babble and speech of 9- to 16-month-old infants (Vihman et al., 1985). They found a good correspondence between sounds that infants favored in babble and sounds that appeared in their early words. For example, infants who produced an especially large number of velar sounds like [k] during babble are also likely to produce early words containing velar sounds. The origin of such "favorite sounds" is unclear. One possibility is that infants accidentally discover particular sounds during babble, and those sounds that they can produce consistently become favored in first words. Another possibility is that some infants hear a greater number of some sounds than others in their language environment. For example, an infant who hears an especially large number of words containing [l] in their environment might be likely to include [l] in both babble and early words.

Thought Question

Can you think of a reason that an infant might hear a particular sound more frequently?

Sound Properties of Early Words

Just as infants as a group are more likely to produce certain sounds in their babble, some consonants are likely to appear in early word productions. Perhaps not surprising, given the preceding discussion of the relation of babble to early words, many of the sounds that appear in babble are mastered first in word production. An examination of a parental checklist of first words (Fenson et al., 1993) reveals that /b/ is the most frequent first consonant of children's first words; /b/ is also mastered earliest, and it is a frequent target of babble (Stoel-Gammon, 1998). Why might there be such a bias in the sound structure of children's first words? There are at least two possibilities. By now you should guess that the possible answers focus on (1) articulatory constraints on what children are able to produce, and (2) the frequency of certain sounds in the target language.

Consistent with the articulatory constraints account, a number of researchers have suggested that labials might be relatively easier to produce than other sounds (Locke, 1983; Stoel-Gammon, 1998). Perhaps individual children choose to learn those words that they have the greatest likelihood of producing in a recognizable form. Evidence for this possibility can be found in two longitudinal studies in which young children (under age 2 years) were taught new words containing different types of sounds. In the first longitudinal study, the eight new words that contained sounds that children regularly produced before the study began were produced more often and in earlier sessions than the eight words that contained sounds that children never tried to produce (Schwartz & Leonard, 1982). Interestingly, the accuracy of children's productions of the two types of words did not differ. The second study contrasted new words of the two types in the first study, but added a third type of word—words containing sounds that children had tried in the past but never successfully produced (Schwartz, Leonard, Frome Loeb, & Swanson, 1987). Again, children attempted to say the new words containing sounds that they had accurately produced before the study began, although their comprehension of the three word types did not differ. These studies suggest that the words that children first produce are not a randomly selected subset of all the words they hear. Rather, they appear to select words that they are more likely to produce accurately.

Consistent with an influence of the target language, children learning different languages are more likely to produce those sounds that are frequent in their particular target language. For example, Greek children produce more /k/'s in their early words, probably because adult Greek has more words beginning with /k/ (Edwards & Beckman, 2008). Edwards and Beckman (2008) conclude that both universal articulatory constraints and the statistics of the target language play a role in children's early word productions.

Thought Question

Can you think of a way that languages might change over time to accommodate the articulatory constraints of young language learners? Hint, think of what we often called clothes that children wear to sleep in.

Early Words by Signing Children

Just as there are parallel lines of research on oral and manual babble of infants exposed to spoken and signed languages, respectively, there are parallel lines of research examining the first words of children exposed to these two linguistic modes. This is a domain of scientific research that has found a practical application. There is some evidence that children can produce recognizable hand gestures before they can accurately produce words. For example, researchers observed that a group of late talkers produced more communicative gestures than children whose productive vocabularies were within the normal range (Thal & Tobias, 1992). Indeed, some parents have taken to teaching a few manual gestures to young children with the goal of promoting communication before children produce any/many spoken words. In one study of this approach to early communication, Goodwyn and Acredelo (1993) taught parents of 11-month-olds eight gestures referring to meanings they might want to convey (e.g., arm-flapping for *bird*, hand-waving horizontally for *all gone*, etc.). The average age at which parents reported their child to use a manual gesture was 11.94 months vs. 12.64 months for vocal words. The age difference, although small, was statistically reliable, with 17 of the 22 children producing the first gesture before the first word.

There are at least two complications to evaluating the claim that children can produce recognizable manual gestures before spoken words. Both involve the fact that even children who have not been taught any gestures produce hand movements (Petitto & Marentette, 1991). One complication is that parents who have taught gestures to children may have a special investment in believing that their child is in fact using these gestures, so when they see a hand movement that resembles a taught gesture, they interpret the movement to be that gesture. The other related complication can be seen if you think of having to guess what a child might be saying when they produce something like a spoken word or something like a manual gesture. If you have taught your child a small set of manual gestures (e.g., 8), you could search through that set to guess what gesture your child might be producing. In contrast, if your child produces a spoken syllable, you might need to search through 50 or 100 similar sounding syllables to make a guess.

Even if the effects of a manual gesture advantage seen by Goodwyn and Acredolo is influenced by aspects of parental perception, can we therefore conclude that there is little point to teaching infants a small set of manual gestures? Probably not. If the parent can reduce the number of possible meanings that a child might be conveying, the guessing game that characterizes early communication with a young child may be simplified to some degree. Thus, the age of appearance of spoken words versus manual gestures represents a situation in which the "right" answer depends on what question you want answered.

■ The Relation of Children's Early Words Productions and Adult Forms

If you have ever heard a young child talk, you have almost certainly observed that child word forms typically differ from adult forms. Furthermore, children's early words deviate from adult forms in consistent ways. For example, a child might consistently produce the adult word *fish* as *fis* and *dish* and *dis*. This simple observation is the starting point for much of the research on phonological development. Child forms typically involve changes to or omissions of a phoneme

Table 4–1. Some Common Phonological Processes

Process	Example (adult form → child form)
Substitution Processes Fronting Stopping Gliding	*cow* → [tau], *fish* → [fɪs] *shoe* → [tu] *look* → [wʊk]
Assimilation Processes Place assimilation Voice initial and devoice final	*back* → [bæp], *mine* → [maim] *toes* → [dos], *bug* [bʌk]
Syllable and Word Shape Processes Final consonant deletion (CV) Consonant cluster reduction (CV or CVC) Reduplication ($\sigma_1\sigma_1$ or $\sigma_2\sigma_2$) Weak syllable deletion ($\sigma'(\sigma)$)	*boat* → [bo] *blue* → [bu], *mask* → [mæs] *water* → [wɔwɔ], *cookie* → [kiki] *giraffe* → [ræf], *banana* → [nænə]

C = consonant, V = vowel, σ = syllable.

or syllable of the adult form. These changes are generally said to reflect **phonological rules** or **phonological processes**. Phonological processes can be classified into three types: substitution, assimilation, and syllable or word shape processes. Each type comprises several subtypes, and examples are shown in Table 4-1.

Substitution Processes

In **substitution processes**, one class of sounds defined in terms of articulatory features (e.g., stops) is substituted for another class of sounds. Three substitution processes are shown in Table 4-1. In **fronting**, velar and palatal consonants (e.g., [k, ʃ] respectively) are replaced by alveolar (made more front in the mouth) consonants, generally with the same voicing ([t, s], respectively). In stopping, a fricative or affricate consonant like [ʃ] or [tʃ] is replaced by a stop with the same voicing and place of articulation. Thus, [t] replaces [ʃ], whereas [b] replaces [v]. In **gliding**, liquids ([r, l]) are replaced by glides ([j, w]).

Assimilation Processes

In **assimilation processes**, a change to one phoneme is based on the properties of another phoneme in the word. Two assimilation processes are shown in Table 4-1. In **place assimilation**, the place of articulation of the first and last consonants of a CVC sequence is made to be the same. Voicing and manner of articulation of the original consonant are retained. If voicing and manner of the two consonants is the same in the target word, the result after place assimilation is that two consonants are identical, as in *mine* produced as [maim], as situation referred to in some of the literature as **consonant harmony**. In the process labeled **voice initial and devoice final**, the vowel influences the surrounding consonants in a CVC sequence. Vowels are by definition voiced, and the first consonant is voiced in anticipation of the vowel. Voicing must stop at the end of a word, and the second consonant is made voiceless (devoiced) in anticipation.

Syllable and Word Shape Processes

In syllable and word shape processes, an adult form is changed in order to produce a syllable or word with a particular form. In **final consonant deletion**, an adult syllable that has a consonant-vowel-consonant (CVC) shape is produced with a CV shape. In **consonant cluster reduction**, a child produces an adult word form containing a consonant cluster, either at the beginning or end, with only one of the consonants in the cluster. This process can be conceptualized as the child attempting to produce a syllable with either a CV or CVC word shape. In **reduplication**, one of the syllables in the adult form, either the first or the second, is repeated in order to produce a word with a two-syllable form. In **weak syllable deletion**, the initial unstressed syllable of a word is omitted, revealing a preference for either a single stressed syllable or a two-syllable word with stress on the first syllable. Children can also adopt individual shape processes. For example, Macken (1979) noted that, for a period of development, her Spanish-learning subject assimilated new words into two-syllable word shapes in which the first syllable began with a labial consonant and the second with a dental. For example, the child produced *zapato* (shoe) as [pwato] and *Fernando* (a name) as [wano].

Other Important Relations Between Adult and Child Forms

In addition to changing adult forms in consistent ways, children often demonstrate a stage in which less mature forms alternate with more mature forms. Such **variability** is a hallmark of development, and as we see below, is difficult to explain under some theories of the relation between adult and child forms. An especially interesting relation between child and adult forms concerns the relation of child forms and data on frequently occurring forms in the languages of the world, or **cross-linguistic markedness**. Surveys of the world's language have revealed that some phonological forms occur much more frequently than others (e.g., Greenberg, 1978). Frequently occurring forms are called **unmarked forms** by linguists, whereas infrequently occurring forms are called **marked forms**. Among the unmarked forms that have been noted are CV syllables, voicing on syllable-initial consonants, and no voicing on syllable-final consonants. CVC syllables are also relatively unmarked, being much more frequent that other more complex syllable shapes such as CCVC. Researchers have noticed that such unmarked forms are they same forms produced by young children.

When considering the relation between adult and child word forms, it is important to note that children often appear to notice differences between their own forms and those of adults. That is, there is an asymmetric relation between discriminations that are made in perception versus production. Two phenomena are taken as evidence for this **perception/production asymmetry**. One of these is **avoidance**, which we have already discussed: Children appear to avoid words containing particular segments that they are presumably unable to accurately produce (Schwartz & Leonard, 1982; Schwartz et al., 1987). For example, a child who is unable to produce word-initial /d/ might avoid producing words like *dog* and *duck*, even though she can comprehend these words. Note that to selectively avoid a particular sound, a child must tacitly recognize that a word contains a sound that she is unable to produce. Another type of evidence for the existence of a perception/production asymmetry in early phonological development is the *fis* **phenomenon**. The reason for this name comes from an anecdote of a child who produced *fish* as *fis*, but who nevertheless became annoyed when an adult produced *fis*. Thus, at least some children can acknowledge that their word productions are not the same as those of adults.

Finally, there is evidence that children are able to produce most speech sounds, but not always when a particular sound is required. For example, some children engage in **regressions**, in which they achieve the adult form of a word the first few times they attempt to produce it, but thereafter produce a less mature form. Regressions indicate that the child can produce the form in question, but for some reason loses this ability once the word is firmly part of their productive vocabulary. A similar phenomenon can be seen in **chain shifts**. An example of a chain shift is a child who produces duck as [gʌk], but produces *truck* as [dʌk]. Thus, the child is able to produce the phonetic sequence associated with the word *duck* (i.e., [dʌk]), but does not do so when she intends to say that word.

■ Theories of the Relation Between Adult and Child Forms

Why do children's early words deviate from adult forms? Four broad classes of theories implicate perceptual factors, articulatory factors, innate grammar, or experience with the target language. In this section, we outline each type of theory and discuss how it fares in light of the available phonological production data. The highlights of the section are illustrated in Table 4–2. It might be helpful to note how

Table 4–2. Child Phonological Production Data and Four Theories Proposed to Explain Them

Data to explain	Perceptual Theories	Articulatory Theories	Innate Phonology Theories	Target Language Experience Theories
Substitution processes	Yes	Yes	Yes	Yes
Assimilation processes	No	Yes	Yes	Yes
Syllable and word shape processes	Yes	Yes	Yes	Yes
Variability within a child	No	Yes	No	No
Cross-linguistic markedness	Yes	Yes	Yes	Yes
Perception/production asymmetry	No	Yes	No	Yes
Regressions/chain shifts	No	No	Yes (chain shifts)	No

the theories in Table 4-2 relate to the four theories of language development that we have been discussing. The perceptual and articulatory theories are not theories of generalization at all and suggest that either the auditory system or the motor system is responsible for children's immature word forms. The innate grammar and experience with target language accounts are theories of generalization. As you might guess, the innate grammar view would fall to the left of the vertical line of Figure 1-4, and assumes innate linguistic constraints. The experience with the target language view would fall to the right of the vertical line and assumes that children's immature forms arise when a general purpose learning mechanism is applied to the child's input.

Perceptual Theories

One type of theory that accounts for some phonological processes is that perceptual biases make it difficult for the child to accurately perceive, and therefore produce, some adult word forms. Learning to produce all of the phonemes of the language requires the child to overcome these perceptual biases. On the perceptual view, a child who substitutes [d] for [g] misperceives [g] as [d] (Jakobson, 1968). Similarly, a child who omits the initial weak syllable of a word fails to fully perceive the omitted syllable (e.g., Echols & Newport, 1992). Thus, perceptual theories can easily account for substitution and word shape processes. Perceptual theories have more difficulty accounting for assimilation processes. For example, it is difficult to imagine a perceptual factor that would cause a child to misperceive the place of articulation of word initial consonants as the place of articulation of the final consonant, as in the process place assimilation.

Perceptual theories also have difficulty explaining variability in a child's production of a single word. If the child misperceives a word, she should not occasionally produce the adult form of the word. Conversely, if the child accurately perceives the adult form of a word, she should not occasionally produce an incorrect form. Perceptual theories can account for the relation between child forms and cross-linguistic markedness data by assuming that unmarked forms are the easiest to perceive and therefore the ones that are used by the largest number of languages. Perceptual theories have the greatest difficulty accounting for perception/production asymmetries. If child forms deviate from adult forms due to the child's misperception, it seems impossible to explain why some children appear to recognize that the adult form is not the same as their own. Finally, perceptual theories have difficulty accounting for regressions and chain shifts. In short, although some child forms might be due to misperception, perceptual failure cannot be a complete explanation of the relation between adult and child forms.

Articulatory Theories

Perhaps the most obvious answer to the question of why children produce different forms than adults do is that their developing articulatory systems make it difficult for them to produce some forms (e.g, Donegan & Stampe, 1979). This notion is consistent with observations that young children have considerably less neuromotor control over their articulation than do adults (e.g., Goffman & Smith, 1999). According to the articulatory theory, the phonological processes presented in Table 4-1 represent articulatory simplifications of adult forms. However, it is important to note that we have no independent articulatory theory of what makes one form simple and another complex. Therefore, saying that child forms are simpler than adult forms is not really an explanation of the nature of child forms. Perhaps, as speech researchers gather more information about the process of articulation in young children, they will develop a theory of what makes forms simple.

Assuming that we specify what is easy versus hard to say, articulatory theories are consistent with the variability observed in children's word forms, if we assume that speech articulation, like other neuromotor skills, is acquired slowly and punctuated by successes and failures. These theories are consistent with cross-linguistic markedness data, in the sense that frequently occurring forms across languages might be those forms that are easiest to articulate. However, such an account must then explain why some languages ever come to use phonetically more difficult forms. For example, if consonant clusters are more difficult than single consonants, why do any languages allow clusters? Articulatory theories can also account for perception/production asymmetries, because children might correctly perceive the adult form of a word but nevertheless not be able to produce that form with their own immature articulatory system.

With exception of the lack of an independently motivated theory of articulatory ease, the main difficulty for articulatory theories comes from regressions and chain shifts. Children who exhibit these behaviors provide evidence that they are able to produce the sound sequence in question. Therefore, articulatory constraints do not appear to be implicated in a straightforward way. It is these sorts of behaviors that led researchers studying child phonology thirty years ago to consider the possibility that children's immature forms might also involve generalization of the phonological system. The next two theories take this approach.

Innate Phonology Theories

The starting point for innate phonological theories is the cross-linguistic markedness data discussed earlier. That is, apparent constraints on child language forms often resemble preferred forms seen across the world's languages. Recall from Chapter 1 that, in the **Universal Grammar** (UG) view of human language originally proposed by Noam Chomsky, languages of the world differ from each other along relatively few dimensions or **parameters** (Chomsky, 1981). For example, languages differ in the types of syllable structures they allow, ranging from CV to CCCVCCC. In the UG approach, all children are born with the same default settings of their language parameters. Thus, children might be born with their phonology set to accept only CV syllables. They change this setting over time if they receive positive evidence of other types of syllables, such as CVC. On a recent version of innate phonology theory, called Optimality Theory, all languages share the same set of phonological constraints on word forms. Differences among adult languages are due to different orderings of these constraints. For example, English allows CCCVCCC syllables, because the constraint on syllables that do not conform to a CV form is relative low in rank. In contrast, this constraint is highly ranked in languages like Japanese that allow only CV syllables. Within this theory, children are born with a default constraint ranking and change their ranking over development to correspond to the adult ranking (Barlow & Gierut, 1999; Ohala, 1999).

On innate phonology accounts, phonological processes seen in child language reflect the default parameter values or constraint rankings of their innate grammar. Such theories have difficulty explaining variability, since all children should be born with the same grammar, and each child should apply this grammar to all word forms. Innate phonology theories generally are consistent with most cross-linguistic markedness data, since those data are central to this type of theory. Innate phonology theories do not naturally account for the perception/production asymmetry, as it seems reasonable that the same grammar would be used for both perception and production. For example, consider a child who is born thinking that her language will only contain CV syllables. What is to prevent that child from treating a word like *ask*, which has a VCC structure, as some kind of error? However, proposals do exist in which children maintain separate input and output grammars in order to account for perception/production asymmetries (e.g., Pater, 2004). Although innate phonology theories might have trouble dealing with regressions, there have been accounts within this framework of chain shifts, such as *duck* produced as [gʌk] and *truck* as [dʌk] (Dinnsen & Barlow, 1998).

Experience with the Target Language Theories

Experience theories (as we can call them for brevity) propose that children's word forms are influenced by the most frequent sounds and sound sequences in a language. They are highly similar to innate phonology theories in those aspects of children's productions they can explain, but with the driving force being what is frequent within a language, not what is frequent across languages. In this view, substituted sounds should be more frequent in the target language than the sounds they replace. Word forms resulting from assimilation and word shape processes should be more frequent in the target language than the forms they replace. The reason for the strong similarity between innate phonology and experience theories is that those forms that are most common across languages also tend to be most common within a particular language (e.g., Greenberg, 1978). However, sometimes a particular language makes frequent use of a phonological form that is atypical (marked) across languages. We already considered the case of Greek /k/, a sound that is frequent in Greek but not as frequent cross-linguistically (Edwards & Beckman, 2008). Recall that /k/ appeared earlier in the productions of Greek children than children learning other languages. Similarly, Zamuner and colleagues explored English-speaking children's final consonant deletion and found that children producing new CVC words were more accurate at producing the final consonant when CV and VC of the word were frequent in English than when these within-word sequences were less frequent (Zamuner, Gerken, & Hammond, 2004). Although few existing studies pit target language frequency against cross-linguistic frequency, those that have generally favor target language frequency as the critical factor in production.

Unlike innate phonology, experience with the target language can account for the perception/production asymmetry: Children might be able to accurately perceive most word forms but have difficulty producing those forms for which they have less practice, due to the infrequency of the form in their experience. Conversely, innate phonology theories can account for chain shifts, whereas it is difficult to see how experience theories could do so. Finally, neither innate phonology nor experience theories cope well with within-child variability.

Summary of Theories of the Relation Between Adult and Child Forms

Although children probably do misperceive some words they hear, the growing consensus among researchers studying children's early word forms is that these forms reflect more than misperception. Among the remaining three theories, articulatory theory appears to account for the most data; however, it fails to account for chains shifts. Both articulatory and innate phonology theories fail to account for recent observations that children learning different languages appear to be influenced by the frequency of a particular form in the target language (e.g., Greek /k/). One of the most promising explanations for children's early word forms is a hybrid approach that incorporates articulatory and experience theories (Edwards & Beckman, 2008). In this view, all children find some forms easier to produce than others; however, they are also influenced by their experience, such that they master more frequent forms sooner than less frequent ones. This hybrid theory accounts for a great deal of data, and it is appealing because it uses the same mixture of mechanisms that appear to account well for the development of babble. That is, articulatory proclivities are influenced by the statistics of the target language. One way that early researchers attempted to account for chain shifts is by suggesting that the two forms (e.g., *guck* for *duck* and *duck* for *truck*) entered the child's vocabulary at different times and therefore were subject to the phonological processes operating at the time (Ingram,

1974; Menn, 1978; Smith, 1973). Perhaps such a notion can be revived to account for chain shifts within the hybrid theory. Or perhaps what is needed is a three-way hybrid that includes some aspects of innate phonology. More research is needed for us to explain the whole set of child word production data.

■ Prosodic Properties of Early Productions

In Chapter 3, we demonstrated that infants and young children are perceptually sensitive to prosody, including the typical prosodic pattern of the mother's language and to word stress. Sensitivity to language prosody is also apparent in learners' early productions, beginning with babble and more clearly in early words and phrases. You already learned that French infants end strings of babble with rising pitch and lengthened syllables that are typical of French utterances, whereas Japanese infants exhibited falling pitch and no syllable lengthening that are typical of Japanese utterances (Hallé et al., 1991). In a classic study, Ann Peters (1983) noticed that, at a time when some children are beginning to produce their first words, other children produce longer utterances that retain the stress and pitch contour of the target utterance at the expense of consonants and vowels. For example, one child she studied produced an utterance that had the pitch contour of the phrase *open the door* and did so in appropriate situations. Snow (1994) also found that children, consistent with adult targets, lengthen utterance-final syllables at a time when they first begin to combine words.

Turning specifically to stress and rhythm, we noted in Chapter 2 that both of these aspects of prosody entail making some syllables in an utterance more prominent than others by making them louder, higher in pitch, or longer in duration. **Lexical stress** refers to the pattern of strong and weak syllables in a word, whereas **rhythm** refers to the pattern of stressed and unstressed syllables across a multiword utterance. For example, there are two stressed syllables in *octopus*, with primary stress on the first syllable and secondary stress on the third. The phrase *We could have been in Paris* has an alternating rhythm, with stress on *could, been,* and the first syllable of *Paris*. English-speakers tend to apply this kind of rhythm to their utterances, with every other syllable receiving more stress than the one next to it.

Although children's early words seem to most listeners to exhibit the same lexical stress as the adult targets, acoustic measurements reveal that young children do not produce stressed and unstressed syllables the way that adults do. For example, in adult English, unstressed syllables tend to be shorter in duration than stressed syllables. In contrast, young English-speakers tend to make both stressed and unstressed syllables of the same length, marking stress with pitch or amplitude instead (Goffman, 2004; Kent & Forner, 1980). Another way that researchers have examined lexical stress and rhythm in early language production has been to been to examine the effects of these factors on unstressed syllable deletion. Recall that the omission of unstressed word-initial syllables is a word-shape process (Table 4-1). Thus, both 1a and 1b in Table 4-3 are likely to be produced with the initial syllable omitted.

Research on children's sentence production suggests that 2-year-olds are also more likely to omit unstressed function words from the beginnings of utterances than from elsewhere in utterance. For example, children are more likely in a **Sentence Imitation** procedure to omit *the* from sentence 2a than sentence 2b. Similarly, they are more likely to omit *he* from 3a than *him* from 3b (Gerken, 1996). Several researchers have suggested that children learning English and other languages attempt to organize their utterances into strong-weak (trochaic) feet, shown in Table 4-3 (Allen & Hawkins, 1980; Demuth, 1996; Gerken, 1994; Wijnen, Krikhaar, & den Os, 1994). In this view, weak syllables that do not belong to a trochaic foot are more likely to be omitted than weak syllables that do belong to a foot. This proposal has the advantage of explaining observed differences in the omission of noninitial unstressed syllables. For example, when children were asked imitate sentences like 4, in which the verb inflection was itself a syllable (-es), they were more likely to omit *the* than they were in 2b. On the trochaic foot account, the verb inflection formed a trochaic foot with the verb, leaving *the* **unfooted** (not belonging to any foot). It is important to note that children's omissions of weak syllables, particularly those that are at the beginning of a word or sentence, probably reflect both articulatory constraints and properties of the target language. Although these omissions have been seen in a variety of languages, their prevalence and developmental course appear to be influenced by how frequent weak-strong sequences are in the target language (e.g, Demuth, 2006).

Table 4–3. Stress Patterns of Some Adult Forms of English Words and Phrases and Likely Child Forms

Adult Form and Stress Pattern	Likely Child Imitation
1a. giraffe w s	raffe
1b. banana w s w	nana
2a. The collie chased Robert w s w s s w	collie chased Robert
2b. Robert chased the collie s w s w s w	Robert chased the collie
3a. He chased Robert w s s w	chased Robert
3b. Robert chased him s w s w	Robert chased him
4. Robert chases the collie s w s w w s w	Robert chases collie

In summary, it appears that the forms of children's early utterances reveal a similar sensitivity to prosody as the one seen early perception.

■ Language Disorders Involving Phonology

Although we focus more fully on language disorders in Chapter 9, we briefly consider disorders of phonological production here, while accounts of normal development are still fresh in our minds. We can divide our discussion into disorders primarily affecting the production of consonants and vowels and those involving prosody.

Disorders Involving the Production of Consonants and Vowels

Probably the most frequent reason that preschool or young school-aged children are referred to speech-language pathologists is delay in mastering the phoneme inventory of the native language and maintenance of the phonological processes shown in Table 4–2. Indeed, speech-language pathologists have available a variety of tests for assessing a child's phoneme inventory and phonological processes. Typically, these tests compare a child's performance to that of a normative sample. Such tests may reveal, for example, that a four-year-old with a suspected phonological disorder produces word forms of the sort that we would more likely expect from a 30-month-old. This example is a case of an overall delay in phonological production ability.

However, there are other patterns that might be found in a child with a phonological disorder (Leonard, 1992). One is a chronologic mismatch, in which a child may exhibit some abilities that are usually later developing (e.g., accurate consonant clusters) along with processes that usually only occur in younger children (e.g., place assimilation). Another pattern is variable use of processes, in which the same word is produced in more than one way. A third pattern is systematic sound preference, in which a child substitutes a single sound for a variety of other sounds. For example, a child might substitute [t] for [f, s, ʃ, θ]. Note that such a substitution pattern would make it impossible for a listener to distinguish among the child's forms of words like *fox, socks* and *shocks*. Finally, a child with a phonological disorder might exhibit an unusual process, such as changing stops to fricatives. Recall that the more typical pattern is one in which fricatives are changed to stops.

Although a discussion of treatment for children with phonological disorders is beyond the scope of this book, let us describe one recent treatment approach that is especially interesting in light of the earlier discussion of cross-linguistic markedness. One group of researchers took as their starting point the view that more marked (rarer) sounds across the world's languages are more difficult to produce and less marked sounds are easier (Gierut, Morrisette, Hughes, & Rowland, 1996). From there, they made the counterintuitive prediction that helping children with phonological disorders to master the more marked sounds would allow them to master the less marked sounds "for free." Their approach turned out to be successful with a group of children, suggesting that studies of phonology and normal phonological development are valuable for treatment of language disorders.

Disorders Involving the Production of Prosody

The role of prosody in the production of children with specific language impairment (SLI) has been the focus of several investigations. Children with SLI, like children with normally developing language, frequently exhibit omissions of unstressed syllables from words and unstressed function morphemes, such as the word *the* and the *-es* verb inflection, from phrases (e.g, McGregor & Leonard, 1994). In fact, omission and incorrect use of function morphemes are often noted as a hallmark of SLI (Chapter 9). As we have already discussed with respect to children with normal phonology, weak stress alone does not fully predict the omission patterns observed in the utterances of children with SLI. Rather, position within the utterance is important. Thus, just as in the data from normally developing children illustrated in Table 4-3, children with SLI are more likely to omit grammatical morphemes from sentence-initial positions than from other sentence positions (McGregor & Leonard, 1994). These data have been taken to indicate the importance of trochaic feet in the productions of children with SLI. This apparent effect of trochaic feet appears to extend to children with SLI learning Italian (Leonard & Bortolini, 1998; and see Chapter 9).

■ Summary

At least four important themes are presented in this chapter. First, although it may take several years to fully master the phonology of adult targets, infants appear to be prepared to associate auditory input with the oral movements that are required to produce this input. Second, although it is controversial, there is some evidence that infants acquiring signed languages engage in the same sorts of babble, albeit manually, that hearing children do. Third, both babble and word production appear to be influenced by articulatory constraints coupled with sensitivity to the statistical properties of the target language. Finally, prosody appears to play an important role in the forms of utterances of children with both normally developing and disordered language.

■ References

Allen, G., & Hawkins, S. (1980). Phonological rhythm: Definition and development. In G. Yeni-Komshian, J. Kavanagh, & G. Ferguson (Eds.), *Child phonology, Vol. I: Production.* New York: Academic Press.

Barlow, J. A., & Gierut, J. A. (1999). Optimality theory in phonological acquisition. *Journal of Speech, Language, and Hearing Research, 42*(6), 1482-1498.

Chen, L. M., & Kent, R. D. (2005). Consonant-vowel co-occurrence patterns in Mandarin-learning infants. *Journal of Child Language, 32,* 507-534.

Chen, X., Striano, T., & Rakoczy, H. (2004). Auditory-oral matching behavior in newborns. *Developmental Science, 7*(1), 42-47.

Chomsky, N. (1981). *Lectures on government and binding.* Dordrecht: Foris.

Cormier, K., Mauk, C., & Repp, A. (1998). Manual babbling in deaf and hearing babies: A longitudinal study. In E. Clark (Ed.), *Proceedings of the child language research forum* (Vol. 29, pp. 55-61). Stanford, CA: CSLI.

Davis, B. L., & MacNeilage, P. F. (1990). Acquisition of correct vowel production: A quantitative case study. *Journal of Speech and Hearing Research, 33,* 16-27.

Davis, B. L., & MacNeilage, P. F. (1995). The articulatory basis of babbling. *Journal of Speech and Hearing Research, 38*(6), 1199-1211.

de Boysson-Bardies, B., Hallé, P., Sagart, L., & Durand, C. (1989). A crosslinguistic investigation of vowel formants in babbling. *Journal of Child Language, 16,* 1-17.

Demuth, K. (1996). The prosodic structure of early words. In J. L. Morgan & K. Demuth (Eds.), *Signal to syntax: Bootstrapping from speech to grammar in early acquisition* (pp. 171-184). Hillsdale, NJ: Lawrence Erlbaum Associates.

Demuth, K. (2006). Crosslinguistic perspectives on the development of prosodic words. *Language and Speech, 49*(2), 129-135.

Dinnsen, D. A., & Barlow, J. A. (1998). On the characterization of a chain shift in normal and delayed phonological acquisition. *Journal of Child Language, 25,* 61-94.

Donegan, P., & Stampe, D. (1979). The study of natural phonology. In D. A. Dinnesen (Ed.), *Current approaches to phonological theory.* Bloomington: Indiana University Press.

Echols, C. H., & Newport, E. L. (1992). The role of stress and position in determining first words. *Language Acquisition, 2,* 189–220.

Edwards, J., & Beckman, M. E. (2008). Some cross-linguistic evidence for modulation of implicational universals by language-specific frequency effects in phonological development. *Language Learning and Development, 4,* 122–156.

Fenson, L., Dale, P., Reznick, S., Thal, D., Bates, E., Hartung, J., et al. (1993). *MacArthur Communicative Development Inventories.* San Diego, CA: Singular.

Ferguson, C. A., & Farwell, C. B. (1975). Words and sounds in early acquisition. *Language, 51,* 419–439.

Gerken, L. A. (1994). Young children's representation of prosodic phonology: Evidence from English-speakers' weak syllable productions. *Journal of Memory and Language, 33*(1), 19–38.

Gerken, L. A. (1996). Prosodic structure in young children's language production. *Language, 72,* 683–712.

Gierut, J. A., Morrisette, M. L., Hughes, M. T., & Rowland, S. (1996). Phonological treatment efficacy and developmental norms. *Language, Speech, and Hearing Services in Schools, 27*(3), 215–230.

Goffman, L. (2004). Kinematic differentiation of prosodic categories in normal and disordered language development. *Journal of Speech, Language, and Hearing Research, 47*(5), 1088–1102.

Goffman, L., & Smith, A. (1999). Development and phonetic differentiation of speech movement patterns. *Journal of Experimental Psychology: Human Perception and Performance, 25,* 649–660.

Goodwyn, S. W., & Acredolo, L. P. (1993). Symbolic gesture versus word: Is there a modality advantage for onset of symbol use? *Child Development, 64*(3), 688–701.

Greenberg, J. H. (Ed.). (1978). *Universals of human language* (Vol. 2). Stanford, CA: Stanford University Press.

Hallé, P., De Boysson-Bardies, B., & Vihman, M. (1991). Beginnings of prosodic organization: Intonation and duration patterns of disyllables produced by Japanese and French infants. *Language and Speech, 34*(4), 299–318.

Ingram, D. (1974). Phonological rules in young children. *Journal of Child Language, 1,* 49–64.

Jakobson, R. (1968). *Child language, aphasia and phonological universals.* The Hague: Mouton.

Kent, R. D., & Forner, L. L. (1980). Speech segment duration in sentence recitations by children and adults. *Journal of Phonetics, 8,* 157–168.

Lenneberg, E. (1967). *Biological foundations of language.* New York: Wiley.

Leonard, L. (1992). Models of phonological development and children with phonological disorders. In C. Ferguson, L. Menn, & C. Stoel-Gammon (Eds.), *Phonological development.* Parkston, MD: York Press.

Leonard, L. B., & Bortolini, U. (1998). Grammatical morphology and the role of weak syllables in the speech of Italian-speaking children with specific language impairment. *Journal of Speech, Language, and Hearing Research, 41*(6), 1363-1374.

Locke, J. L. (1983). *Phonological acquisition and change.* New York: Academic Press.

Macken, M. (1979). Developmental reorganization in phonology. A hierarchy of basic units of acquisition. *Lingua, 49*, 11-49.

MacNeilage, P. F., & Davis, B. L. (2000). On the origin of internal structure of word forms. *Science, 288*, 527-531.

McGregor, K., & Leonard, L. B. (1994). Subject pronoun and article omissions in the speech of children with specific language impairment: A phonological interpretation. *Journal of Speech and Hearing Research, 37*, 171-181.

Meier, R. P., & Willerman, R. (1995). Prelinguistic gesture in deaf and hearing babies. In K. Emmorey & J. S. Reilly (Eds.), *Language, gesture and space* (pp. 391-409). Hillsdale, NJ: Lawrence Erlbaum.

Menn, L. (1978). Phonological units in beginning speech. In A. Bell & J. B. Hooper (Eds.), *Syllables and segments.* Amsterdam: North Holland.

Mitchell, P. R., & Kent, R. D. (1990). Phonetic variation in multisyllable babbling. *Journal of Child Language, 17*(2), 247-265.

Ohala, D. K. (1999). The influence of sonority on children's cluster reductions. *Journal of Communication Disorders, 32*, 397-422.

Oller, D. K., Eilers, R. E., Bull, D. H., & Carney, A. E. (1985). Prespeech vocalizations of a deaf infant: A comparison with normal metaphonological development. *Journal of Speech and Hearing Research, 28*, 47-63.

Pater, J. (2004). Bridging the gap between receptive and productive development with minimally violable constraints. In R. Kager, J. Pater, & W. Zonneveld (Eds.), *Constraints in phonological acquisition* (pp. 219-244). New York: Cambridge University Press.

Peters, A. (1983). *The units of language acquisition.* Cambridge: Cambridge University Press.

Petitto, L. A., Holowka, S., Sergio, L. E., Levy, B., & Ostry, D. (2004). Baby hands that move to the rhythm of language: Hearing babies acquiring sign languages babble silently on the hands. *Cognition, 93*, 43-73.

Petitto, L. A., & Marentette, P. F. (1991). Babbling in the manual mode: Evidence for the ontogeny of language. *Science, 251*, 1483-1496.

Schwartz, R. G., & Leonard, L. B. (1982). Do children pick and choose? An examination of phonological selection and avoidance in early lexical acquisition. *Journal of Child Language, 9*, 319-336.

Schwartz, R. G., Leonard, L. B., Frome Loeb, D. M., & Swanson, L. A. (1987). Attempted sounds are sometimes not: An expanded view of phonological selection and avoidance. *Journal of Child Language, 14*(3), 411-418.

Smith, N. (1973). *The acquisition of phonology.* Cambridge: Cambridge University Press.

Snow, D. P. (1994). Phrase-final lengthening and intonation in early child speech. *Journal of Speech and Hearing Research, 37*, 831–840.

Stark, R. (1980). Stages of speech development in the first year of life. In G. H. Yeni-Komshian, J. F. Kavanagh & G. A. Ferguson (Eds.), *Child phonology* (Vol. 1). New York: Academic Press.

Stoel-Gammon, C. (1998). Sounds and words in early language acquisition: The relationship between lexical and phonological development. In R. Paul (Ed.), *Exploring the speech/language connection* (pp. 25–52). Baltimore: Paul H. Brookes.

Thal, D. J., & Tobias, S. (1992). Communicative gestures in children with delayed onset of oral expressive vocabulary. *Journal of Speech and Hearing Research, 35*(6), 1281–1289.

Vihman, M., Macken, M., Miller, R., Simmons, H., & Miller, J. (1985). From babbling to speech: A reassessment of the continuity issue. *Language, 61*, 397–446.

Wijnen, F., Krikhaar, E., & den Os, E. (1994). The (non)realization of unstressed elements in children's utterances: A rhythmic constraint? *Journal of Child Language, 21*, 59–84.

Zamuner, T., Gerken, L. A., & Hammond, M. (2004). Phonotactic probabilities in young children's speech productions. *Journal of Child Language, 31*, 515–536.

5 The Lexicon

What Is the Lexicon?

The **lexicon** is the name given to people's mental list of words. Each word in the lexicon is called a **lexical entry**, and each entry is thought to include several types of information about the word. A schematic of the place of the lexicon in the linguistic system is shown in Figure 5–1. One type of information is the word's form, either in terms of sounds or signs. This component of a lexical entry is sometimes called a word's **lexeme**. A second type of information that must be part of a lexical entry is the word's meaning, sometimes called a word's **lemma**. Consider for a moment, the English word *cat*. In the lexicon, the lexeme of the word, perhaps encoded phonetically (e.g., /kæt/), must be linked to its meaning or lemma. We have reasons to believe that form and meaning are encoded separately. For example, in Tip-of-the-Tongue (TOT) states, we know that we know a word with a particular meaning (e.g., a device that measures air pressure), but we might not be able to think of its form at will (/bərɑmetə/, *barometer*). In addition to meaning, another type of information that might be part of the lemma tells how the word might combine with other words or morphemes, such as whether the word can be used as a noun, a verb, etc. and its gender in languages like French that make use of gender.

As you might guess from this description of the lexicon, a language learner's task in developing even a single lexical entry is a complex one. In order to learn about a word's form, the learner must first be able to find the word in a continuous stream of fluent speech. For example, when hearing someone say *What a lovely day*, the learner shouldn't store *alove* or *lyday* as possible word forms. This part of the learner's task is often called the **segmentation problem**. Once a learner has identified a particular word form, she must map that form onto the appropriate meaning, which is called the **mapping problem**. Finally,

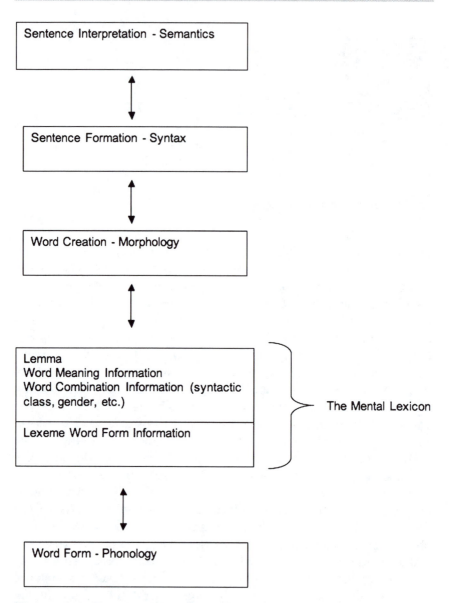

Figure 5-1. The place of the mental lexicon in human language.

the learner must determine the role that a particular word plays in sentences. For example, the word *brush* can be used as a noun, as in *Please hand me the brush*. But it can also be used as a verb, as in *Let me brush your hair*. Determining the sentence contexts in which a word can occur is often called the **syntactic labeling problem**. This chapter discusses the segmentation and mapping problems. Because the syntactic labeling problem is more concerned with the roles that words play in sentences, it is discussed in Chapter 7 on syntax.

■ The Segmentation Problem

It is difficult to understand the segmentation problem if you are listening to a language you know. It almost always feels as if each word is separate from each other word. However, if you think back to your childhood, you might remember making some mis-segmentations. For example, I can remember asking my mother what *elemeno* looked like. That is, I thought that the sequence of letters L-M-N-O was a single word. Other examples of childhood mis-segmentation include *dawnserly light* (for *dawn's early light*) in Beverly Cleary's (1968) "Ramona the Pest." Even adults occasionally make such errors, for example, the first time we hear the phrase *pay per view*, we might think we are hearing *paper view*.

Yet another way to understand the segmentation problem is to look at a visual representation of the acoustic properties of an utterance. One such representation is called a **waveform**, and is shown in Figure 5–2, below. The horizontal axis is time, and the vertical axis is amplitude (the acoustic dimension perceived as loudness). Places in the waveform that are very low in amplitude are potential breaks in the acoustic signal, and therefore possible word boundaries.

There are several things to note in Figure 5–2 that may help you understand the segmentation problem. First, note that there are no obvious breaks in the acoustic signal between the words *what* and *a* or *a* and *nice*. Thus, using the acoustic signal alone, it would be hard to guess where one word ended and the next began. Looking for areas of low amplitude is of no help either. If one takes that approach, the

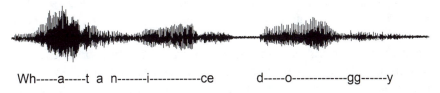

Wh-----a-----t a n-------i------------ce   d-----o-------------gg------y

Figure 5–2. Waveform of a person saying, *What a nice doggy.*

wha appears separate from the *ta* in *what a*, which blends into the *n* of *nice*. There is a break in the signal between *nice* and *doggy*, which might help a listener to treat *doggy* as a new word. However, there is also a break between the first and second syllable of *doggy*, which might cause the listener to mistakenly segment the speech signal into two words *dog* and *gy*.

Thinking about children's mis-segmentation errors, listening to speech of an unknown language, and looking at a waveform of a language you know, each demonstrate that the child cannot depend on the acoustic signal alone to determine where words begin and end. Rather, she must use some additional **segmentation cues** to begin storing word forms in her lexicon. These cues include: (1) encountering single-word utterances, (2) encountering words at the ends of utterances, (3) statistical information about what syllables predictably occur next to other syllables, (4) encountering words adjacent to frequent function morphemes such as *the*, (5) language-specific typical stress patterns, and (6) language-specific typical sound sequences. The first three cues are useable without knowing anything about the target language, whereas the 4th, 5th, and 6th cues require the learner to have already learned something about words in her language. Each cue is discussed below.

Single-Word Utterances

Perhaps the most obvious way to solve the segmentation problem is not to encounter it to begin with. The segmentation problem arises because, as efficient language producers, we are able to plan farther ahead than a single word when we speak (e.g., Garrett, 1975), and therefore we do not pause between the words of an utterance. However, if the first utterances that a child encountered contained only single words, the beginning and end of an utterance would be the beginning and end of a word form that could then be stored in the child's mental lexicon. Luckily for children, caregivers do produce some single-word utterances; however, one estimate for middle-class American parents places the percentage of single-word utterances at only about 9% (Brent & Siskind, 2001). Importantly, the words that parents produce in isolation are among the first that children produce, suggesting that these words might be particularly salient or important to children. Nevertheless, the small number of single-word utterances that children encounter suggests that they must quickly move beyond this cue to a more sophisticated approach to lexical segmentation.

Words at Ends of Utterances

Even if a single utterance does not always correspond to a single word, it still might helpful to have a word align with either the beginning or end of an utterance, thereby reducing the segmentation problem in half. Although logically speaking, utterance beginnings and endings might provide equally helpful information about word forms, recall from Chapter 2 that words at the ends of utterances are typically lengthened. Thus, words in this position might be acoustically more salient and also less likely to be produced in ways that make it difficult to determine which segments they contain. For example, consider the utterances *That tart is so sweet* and *That sweet tart is delicious.* You may notice that you are more likely to hear the /t/ at the end of *sweet* in the first sentence than the second. If this were your first encounter with the word *sweet*, you might extract and store a more accurate lexeme after hearing the first sentence.

Children are also better at recognizing words in utterance-final position. In one study, Shady and Gerken (1999) found that 24- to 26-month-olds were more likely to point to a picture of a named referent if the referring word was in sentence-final position (e.g., *Find the dog*) than when it was sentence-internal (e.g., *Find the dog for me*). Other researchers using the Looking-While-Listening procedure showed that 15–month-olds also benefit from hearing the name of an object in utterance-final position (Fernald, McRoberts, & Swingley, 2001). In keeping with children's abilities, many parents place words that they want their children to learn in utterance-final positions (Fernald & Mazzie, 1991, e.g., *Look! That's an aardvark!*).

Thought Question

How might you test whether utterance-final lengthening or some other factor (such as memory) is playing a role in children's increased ability to identify the referent of a word in utterance-final position?

Statistical Cues

Another cue for lexical segmentation that requires no prior knowledge of words in the target language is the probability with which one syllable is followed by another. For example, an infant might hear the word *baby* in the phrases *pretty baby, silly baby, darling baby*, and so forth. In each phrase, the syllable *ba* is always followed by the syllable *by*, because *baby* is a word. In contrast, *ba* only follows *ty, ly,* and *ling* (from *pretty, silly, darling)* some of the time. Could the probability of one syllable following another be used for finding words in the speech stream? To find out, Saffran, Aslin, and Newport (1996) used the HPP to familiarize 8-month-olds for about two minutes with four trisyllabic nonsense words (e.g., *bidaku, padoti, golabu, tupiro*), which were strung together in random order (the same word could not occur twice in sequence) and with no breaks between words (e.g., *bidakupadotigolabubidakutupiro* . . .). Infants were then tested to see whether they would discriminate two of the familiarized words (e.g., *bidaku*) from two "part words" made up of one syllable of one familiarized word and two syllables from another (e.g., *kupado*). They listened longer to part word stimuli than to familiarized words (a novelty preference), indicating that they could discriminate the two word types. The researchers proposed that infants were able to use the statistical likelihood of one syllable following another to extract the actual trisyllabic words from the familiarization stimuli. For example, in the familiarization word *bidaku* the syllable *bi* is followed by *da* and *da* is followed by *ku* with a probability of 100%. The syllable *pa* follows *ku* only 33% of the time (because each three-syllable word can be followed by three other words). One alternative explanation is that infants were sensitive to trisyllabic sequences that occurred more frequently in the familiarization stimuli, rather than **transitional probabilities** (the statistical likelihood of one syllable following another) between adjacent syllables. For example, the syllable sequence *bidaku*, which was a word, occurred about three times more often than the syllable sequence *kupado*. It would be impressive even if infants were sensitive to such frequency differences. However, a subsequent study ruled out the possibility that frequency alone was responsible for infants' responding, suggesting that infants possess the even more impressive sensitivity to transitional probabilities (Aslin, Saffran, & Newport, 1998).

Following the studies on infants' ability to extract stable sequences from syllable strings, similar studies using either tone or visual sequences revealed that infants' ability to track transitional probabilities is not limited to linguistic stimuli (Aslin, Slemmer, Kirkham, & Johnson, 2001; Saffran, Johnson, Aslin, & Newport, 1999). Therefore, whatever the mechanism underlying infants' abilities in this domain, it appears to be a general one, and not specific to language.

Occurrence of Words Adjacent to Frequent Function Morphemes

Most readers will have encountered the following lines from Lewis Carroll at some point in their lives *Twas brillig and the slithy toves, and gire and gimble in the wabe* (Carroll, 1872). Just like any connected speech, the words "slide" together, such that there are no silences between words and sections of low amplitude are as likely to occur within as between words. The segmentation problem for the line from Lewis Carroll is illustrated in Figure 5–3. The first time you heard this line, you did not know any of the **content words**, that is,

Twas b-ril-lig and the s-li-thy t-ove---s did gire and gim-ble in the wa-be

Figure 5–3. The segmentation problem illustrated with a line from Lewis Carroll's "Jabberwocky."

the nouns, verbs, adverbs, and adjectives that carry most of the meaning or content of an utterance. This situation is similar to the one that the child is in, before she has a substantial lexicon. How did you determine where the words began and ended? One possibility is that you recognized a few very frequent **function morphemes** (also called **grammatical morphemes**), such as *and*, *the*, *did*, and so forth, which gave you a way of segmenting the intervening material into likely word candidates.

Are infants and children able to make use of function morphemes, which are specific to each language, in this way? There is some reason to believe that, even if infants do not know specific function morphemes, the phonological properties of function morphemes as a set might help them with lexical segmentation. In English, function morphemes share a set of phonological properties. For example, many function morphemes contain the vowel schwa (/ə/) and fricative consonants such /ð/ (*the*), /s/, and /z/ (Gerken, Landau, & Remez, 1990; Shi, Werker, & Morgan, 1999). Although not all function morphemes exhibit each phonological property, the set of properties may help to identify function morphemes as a set largely distinct from content words. There is evidence that even newborn infants are able to distinguish content words from function morphemes based on their phonological properties (Shi et al., 1999). These data suggest that infants might be able to use even a fuzzy representation of a function morpheme to help them segment the speech stream into possible word candidates.

What is the evidence that learners are able to use function morphemes in this way? In a study by Gerken and Macintosh (1993), 24- to 26-month-olds were better able to select a named referent when they heard sentences containing a correctly used function morpheme preceding the target word (e.g., *Find the dog for me*) than no function morpheme (e.g., *Find dog for me*). Other researchers (Kedar, Casasola, & Lust, 2006; Zangl & Fernald, 2007) found that even 18-month-olds were faster and more accurate in looking at the referent of a target noun when the noun was preceded by a determiner. Because a singular count noun (such as *dog*) must be preceded by a determiner for the sentence to be grammatical (i.e., *Find dog for me* is not a grammatical sentence), we cannot be sure from these studies whether children's better performance for utterances with than without function morphemes is due to their better ability to segment the utterance or to a rudimentary expectation about sentence structure.

At least one study does suggest that infants can use function morphemes for lexical segmentation. Researchers studying French-learning 8-month-olds used the HPP and familiarized infants with a phrase containing a French function morpheme (e.g., *des*, /de/ = *some*) plus a noun, or with a nonsense syllable (e.g., *kes*, /ke/) plus a different noun (Shi & Lepage, 2007). Both nouns were infrequent words in French. During test, infants heard the two nouns in isolation. They listened significantly longer to the noun that previously co-occurred with a function morpheme than that with a nonsense syllable. This finding suggests that infants hearing *kes* + *noun* treated the sequence as a single word and therefore failed to recognize just the second syllable of that word during test. Furthermore, as the nonsense function morpheme differed from the real one only in the first consonant, the results suggests that 8-month-olds already have a relatively accurate representation of at least some function morphemes, which they can use in lexical segmentation.

Language-Specific Stress Patterns

Another type of language-specific segmentation cue is frequent lexical stress patterns. We have noted elsewhere that a majority of English content words begin with a stressed syllable; therefore, a good strategy for finding English words in the speech stream is to guess that a new word is starting when you hear a stressed syllable. Returning to the "Jabberwocky" example, *brillig, slithy, toves, gire*, and *gimble* all begin with a stressed syllable. There is good evidence that, by age 9 months, American infants use stress to locate possible word candidates. We already discussed in Chapter 3 that 9-month-old American infants prefer to listen to lists of words with a strong-weak pattern over words with a weak-strong pattern (Jusczyk, Cutler, & Redanz, 1993). Other research indicates that infants are more likely to extract words with a strong-weak pattern from running speech. For example, one group of researchers used the HPP to familiarize 7.5 months with passages containing words that either had a strong-weak (*kingdom, hamlet*) or a weak-strong (*guitar, device*) stress pattern (Jusczyk, Houston, & Newsome, 1999). After familiarization, infants were tested on lists of words that either did or did not occur in the familiarization passages. Infants who had been familiarized with strong-weak words were able to recognize them in the word lists. They demonstrated this by listening longer to lists containing familiar words. However, infants familiarized with passages containing weak-strong words showed no evidence of recognizing the familiarization words. However, by 10.5 months of age, infants were able to recognize both strong-weak and weak-strong words, perhaps because they were using combinations of cues to make word segmentation more efficient and adultlike.

Language-Specific Typical Sound Sequences

The final lexical segmentation cue to be discussed in this chapter concerns the fact that the words of a language exhibit some very frequent sequences of sounds or frequent **phonotactics**. Within-word phonotactics tend to be quite different from between-word phonotactics, that is, sound sequences created when the right edge of one word is next to the left edge of the following word. If within-word and between-word phonotactics are different enough from each other, language learners might use phonotactic information to guess where the edges of words are. For example, the sequence /sp/ is quite frequent in English words (e.g., *spinach*). In contrast, the sequence /sð/ never occurs within English words but occurs often between words in phrases like *pats the*, *likes the*, and so forth. Computer counts of the phonotactics of English **corpora** (large samples of the language) indicate that there are sufficient differences between within-word and between-word phonotactics to allow accurate segmentation of a large number of words (Hockema, 2006). Researchers have found that infants as young as 9 months of age are able to use phonotactics to segment words from running speech (Mattys & Jusczyk, 2001b). Infants were familiarized with passages containing the nonsense words *gaffe* and *tove*. The words either occurred in contexts in which phonotactic information should make them easy or hard to find. For example, in the sequence *bean-gaffe-hold*, the /ng/ cluster created between *bean* and *gaffe* and the /fh/ created between *gaffe* and *hold* are rare within English words, which should suggest that *gaffe* is a separate word. In contrast, in the sequence *fang-gaffe-tine*, the /ŋg/ and /ft/ clusters created on either side of *gaffe* are very frequent in English words (e.g., *angle, sifter*), making it difficult to separate *gaffe* from the surrounding words. At test, infants heard lists of words from the familiarization phase as well as lists of new words. Only infants who had heard the words in the phonotactic contexts that should have promoted segmentation distinguished the familiarization words from new words, suggesting that only they had succeeded in segmentation.

A segmentation cue that is related to phonotactics is differences in within-words versus between-word allophones, or pronunciation variants of a phoneme (recall Chapter 2). For example, different allophones of the phonemes /t/ and /ɾ/ appear in the word *nitrate* than in the phrase *night rate*. One team of researchers found that 2-month-old infants easily distinguish these allophones (Hohne & Jusczyk, 1994). Other researchers have shown that 7.5- to 8-month-olds are able to use allophonic cues in segmentation (Mattys & Jusczyk, 2001a). In this study, infants were familiarized with passages containing words like *dice* and *cash*. For half of the infants, these words were not really words, but were spliced out of phrases like *cold ice* and *hard ice*, whereas for the other half, the words *ice* and *cash* were pronounced as single words. Note that the words formed accidentally from phrases have different allophones than the ones produced as single words. At test, infants heard word lists containing familiarized versus novel words, and only the infants who had been familiarized with the words pronounced as single words distinguished the two word lists. Like the study on phonotactic cues, this study suggests that infants were able to use their knowledge of language-specific allophones to segment words from running speech.

■ The Mapping Problem

Once learners have found words in the speech stream, the next major step to creating a mental lexicon is to associate segmented word forms with meanings. For example, a child might hear the word *mommy* very frequently and store this sound string in her memory. However, at some point, she must realize that the sound string *mommy* has a particular meaning.

What do we mean by "word meaning"? When just about anyone is asked this question, they respond that the meaning of a word has something to do with what the word refers to in the world. Although there is probably at least a grain of truth in this idea, **reference** is not a complete account of meaning. If you think for a moment about the words you know, you will understand why. On the "meaning is reference" view, what do words like *truth* or *want* or *very* mean? That is, once we leave the domain of picturable objects, properties, and actions, it is difficult to equate meaning with reference. So what is meaning? One way to think about word meaning is that words refer to the contents of the minds of our fellow humans. The particular mental contents that are important for meaning are called **concepts**. Many concepts concern the objects and events we humans encounter in the world, and a good way of conveying those concepts to a novice is to simply indicate which aspect of the world is involved in the concept. That is, if I want to get a child to learn about the concept *cat*, pointing to a cat in the world is probably a good start. Most of the research on early word learning involves concepts that have some origin in the world, and much of the discussion of mapping will focus on word-world mapping. But other human concepts, like *truth*, arise in other ways, and we must also consider how children map words to these. Therefore, we consider some examples of how children might map more directly from words to concepts, without using world reference as an intermediary.

When do learners first begin to map words to sound sequences? Looking at language production, many children produce their first words by their first birthday, and by the middle of the second year, children are thought to have vocabularies of about 50 words, on average. However, looking at comprehension, we can see that infants understand common words like *mommy* and *daddy* as early as about 6 months of age (Tincoff & Jusczyk, 1999). Using the **Intermodal Preferential Looking** procedure (**IPLP**), infants were shown side-by-side videos of their parents while listening to the words *mommy* and *daddy*. Infants looked significantly more at the video of the named parent. A second experiment revealed that infants do not associate these words with men and women in general, indicating that they treated the names as referring to specific individuals. This observation brings us to our next question:

How do children begin to map word meanings to sound sequences? Even if we assume that children begin learning word meanings by mapping word forms to referents in the world, we already face a considerable problem, which was made famous by the philosopher Quine (1960). Quine considered the problem of an adult who is trying to learn what the words in a new language mean from a native speaker of the language. The native speaker points to a furry creature hopping into the bushes and says *Gavagai!* What are you to think that *gavagai* means? Logically speaking, it could mean the creature itself (e.g., the equivalent of *rabbit*), the creature's name (e.g., *Harvey*), the creature's tail, leg, ears, and so forth, the creature's lair (under the bush), the statement that the creature is really good to eat, or any one of a number of other possibilities. You should recognize this situation as an instance of the induction problem. How do you determine what the native speaker is referring to? That is, how do you constrain your guess about the word-world mapping? The literature on child word learning offers several possible constraints on word-world mapping, six of which are discussed below. This is followed by discussion of two types of mapping errors and what they might tell us about the mapping process, and exploration of the mapping problem across languages.

The Whole Object Assumption

The **whole object assumption** states that, unless they have evidence to the contrary, children will assume that words refer to whole objects rather than object parts (Markman, Gelman, & Byrnes, 1991). In the example above, the whole object assumption would prevent a learner from thinking that *gavagai* refers to the animal's tail, ears, and so forth. American parents appear to act as though their children operate with the whole object assumption, providing whole object labels 95% of the time (Ninio, 1980). On the rare occasions that parents label object parts, they use particular sentence forms, such as *That's a dog, and that's his tail*, which may help children to know that the labeling is unusual.

The Taxonomic Assumption

The **taxonomic assumption** states that children assume that words refer to classes, not individuals (Markman et al., 1991). In the example above, the taxonomic assumption would prevent the word learner from thinking that *gavagai* means the creature's proper name (e.g., *Harvey*). What is the evidence the children obey the taxonomic constraint? The typical method for testing for this constraint is to present children with a new object that is either labeled with a word (e.g., *this is a blicket*) or simply commented on (*look at this one*). The child is then shown other instances of the category along with non-category members and asked to *find another blicket* or *find another* *one.* The typical finding is that children in the word condition, but not the no-word condition, select another member of the original category. Children by about age 2 years show this effect (Woodward & Markman, 1998).

Thought Question

Are the data on 6-month-olds association of *mommy* and *daddy* with their parents but not with other women and men consistent or inconsistent with the taxonomic assumption?

The Mutual Exclusivity Assumption

The mutual exclusivity assumption states that children think that every object can have only one name (Markman et al., 1991). Imagine that I showed you two objects, one that is familiar to you (e.g., a cup) and one that you had never seen. Then I said, *Hey, can you hand me the ziffle?* Which object would you hand me, the cup or the unfamiliar object? Many studies similar to the thought experiment just described have been done, and the typical finding is that both adults and children would select the unfamiliar object. For example, in one study, 3-year-olds chose the unfamiliar object when presented with the novel label about 80% of the time (Markman & Wachtel, 1988). The mutual exclusivity assumption says that they do so because the cup already has a label. There is even evidence that infants as young as 12 months of age have some expectation that, all other things equal, there is a one-to-one correspondence between labels and objects (Xu, Cote, & Baker, 2005). In one experiment, a researcher looked into a box while the infant was watching and provided two labels (e.g., *Look, a fep!* and *Look, a wug!*) or just repeated the same label (e.g., *Look, a fep! Look, a fep!*). Infants were then allowed to reach into the box. After each infant retrieved one object from the box, their subsequent search behavior was recorded, and the data showed that infants searched for a longer duration after hearing two labels than one. These data suggest that hearing two labels led the infants to expect two objects inside the box.

Although there is evidence that word learners make use of the whole object, taxonomic, and mutual exclusivity assumptions, we must still ask whether these constraints are specific to language (to the left of the vertical line in Figure 1–4), or whether they reflect general purpose cognitive constraints that are employed in service of learning the words of a language. For example, whole objects might be visually salient to infants or interesting because they can be picked up. Therefore, when an adult provides a label, infants might consider the whole object as a likely referent simply because their attention is already focused on the whole object. Similarly, with respect to the mutual exclusivity assumption, we can ask whether learners choose the unlabeled object because they are assuming that each object has only one label, or because they think that, if the requester had wanted the previously named object, he or she should have used the recently provided label. The latter type of information is called **pragmatics**.

To address the question of whether mutual exclusivity is an assumption about language learning or an expectation about pragmatics, Gil Diesendruck and Lori Markson (2001) showed 3-year-olds two novel objects and provided information about one of them, either in the form of a label (*This is a zev*) or in the form of a fact (*My sister gave this to me*). They then asked children to retrieve one of the objects. In the label condition, the child was given a new label in the retrieval request (*Hand me the bip*), and in the fact condition, the child was given a fact (*Hand me the one my dog likes to play with*). In the label condition, children retrieved the second, previously unlabeled object about 82% of the time, similar to previous results using this technique. In the fact condition, children retrieved the second object about 73% of the time, somewhat less than in the label condition, but still significantly above chance. These results suggest that children's expectations about human interaction at least partly may be responsible for the results from previous studies on mutual exclusivity. Therefore, word learning may rely on general purpose mechanisms for problem-solving and interacting with our fellow humans, and not on mechanisms specific to the task of learning words. We consider another such example in the next section.

The Shape Bias

The **shape bias** states that when learning a new word for an object, that word should apply to objects with similar shapes. In one of the earliest studies exploring the shape bias, researchers taught new object labels to 2- and 3-year-olds, as well as adults (Landau, Smith, &

Jones, 1988). Depictions of similar 3-dimensional training objects are shown in Figure 5–4. At test, participants were shown pairs of items and asked, *Which one is the dax* or *Which one is the riff?* The test items differed from the original labeled items in terms of shape (e.g., one arm of the dax was at more than a 90° angle from the bottom), size (e.g., a larger dax), or texture (e.g., a dax made out of cloth instead of wood). Both children and adults selected items of the same shape much more often than items with the same size or texture. Nevertheless, adults demonstrated a much greater shape bias than did the children. Fourteen years after the 1988 study, the same group of researchers and their colleagues explored the reason for the increase in shape bias over development (Smith, Jones, Landau, Gershkoff-Stowe, & Samuelson, 2002). They asked whether the particular words that children learn earliest are ones referring to objects that are categorized based on shape and whether this early word learning created a shape bias where there was not one originally. In a longitudinal study,

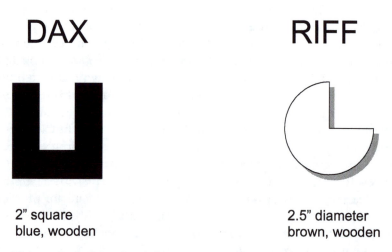

DAX

RIFF

2" square
blue, wooden

2.5" diameter
brown, wooden

Figure 5–4. Stimuli used in an experiment by Landau, Smith, and Jones (1988) to explore the shape bias in word learning. Adapted from *Cognitive Development, 3*(3), Landau, B., Smith, L. B., and Jones, S.S. The importance of shape in early lexical learning, pp. 299–321, Copyright (1988), with permission from Elsevier. Reprinted from *The Lancet, 3*, Landau, B., Smith, L. B., and Jones, S.S. The importance of shape in early lexical learning, pp. 299–321, Copyright (1988), with permission from Elsevier.

they taught 17-month-olds new words for object categories that were organized by shape (e.g., only objects with similar shapes have the same name). These children, compared with a control group, showed a dramatic increase in learning of new object names outside of the laboratory during the course of the study. The results suggest that children learn the basis by which different types of word categories are formed, resulting in biases like the shape bias.

Thought Question

Can you think of a parallel experiment to the one by Smith et al. (2002) in which you test whether the whole object assumption, taxonomic assumption, or mutual exclusivity assumption could result from learning a few words?

Statistical Constraints

Up until now, we have been discussing how a child who hears a word for the first time maps that word form onto possible word meanings. **Statistical constraints** on word learning are different, because they focus on how children use multiple encounters with a word to home in on the word's meaning. Two main types of statistical constraints have been proposed. In the first approach, the learner uses multiple encounters with the word to determine which part of the environment the word might refer to (Yu, 2008). To get the flavor of this approach to statistical constraints, consider the *gavagai* problem spread over multiple encounters. Your native informant uses the word *gavagai* in five different circumstances, represented in Table 5-1. The table shows a variety of entities that are present when the word *gavagai* is uttered. In the first encounter, six different possible referents are listed. However, in subsequent encounters, two of those referents are not listed: the spear is missing from encounters 3 and 5, and the bush from encounters 4 and 5. Therefore, over multiple encounters, you might conclude that the spear and the bush are less likely possible referents for *gavagai* than are rabbits, rabbit ears, animals, and the sky, all of which are present on every occurrence of *gavagai*. But how might you rule out rabbit ears, animals, and sky as referents, if the

Table 5–1. Schematic of How Statistical Constraints Might Help a Word Learner to Home in on the Appropriate Reference for the Word *Gavagai*

Encounter with word	Possible Meaning					
	rabbit	rabbit ears	animal	sky	spear	bush
1	X	X	X	X	X	X
2	X	X	X	X	X	X
3	X	X	X	X		X
4	X	X	X	X	X	
5	X	X	X	X		

correct referent of the word is actually *rabbits?* Ruling out the sky is relatively easy under the statistical constraints, if we consider that you are not only hearing the word *gavagai*, but many other words as well. The sky might be present during many of those word encounters. That is, the sky referent is not strongly correlated with any particular word, suggesting that it is an unlikely referent for any of the words. With respect to rabbit ears, these are present whenever the word *gavagai* is uttered. A learner who could supplement statistical constraints with other constraints, such as the whole object assumption, would be more likely to think that *gavagai* referred to the whole rabbit.

A somewhat different problem arises when determining whether *gavagai* refers to rabbits or animals more generally, and this problem brings us to the second way in which statistics might be used to solve the mapping problem. Imagine that there is a word *vigado* which means *animal* in the language, as well as the word *gavagai*, which means *rabbit*. The particular creature that has been indicated for you is both a *vigagdo* and a *gavagai*, because the two words refer to different levels of meaning. In English, *rabbit* is said to be a **basic level** category label, whereas *animal* is a **superordinate** category label (and the term for a specific kind of rabbit is called a **subordinate** category label). The first time you encounter the rabbit and hear the word *gavagai*, you have no evidence at all as to whether the term refers to rabbits or animals. However, if you hear *gavagai* in three different encounters with the rabbit, and in no encounters with other animals, you will have stronger evidence that *gavagai* refers to rabbits. That is, if *gavagai* really refers to animals, it is quite an unlikely coincidence that you have only heard it used to refer to rabbits. Once the coincidence becomes sufficiently unlikely, you have good evidence that *gavagai* indeed refers to rabbits. In contrast, if you hear *gavagai* in encounters with other animals, you will have good evidence that *gavagai* refers to animals in general and not just rabbits. To ask whether children are able to build on statistical evidence to determine the meaning level to which a word refers, researchers showed 3- to 4-year-olds either one Dalmation or three different Dalmations and labeled each one a *fep* (Xu & Tenenbaum, 2007). Children who heard *fep* refer to three Dalmations were less likely to think that *fep* referred to dogs in general than children who heard *fep* refer to a single Dalmation. These data suggest that children can use the pattern of word-referent pairings in their input to form increasingly accurate ideas of what words mean over experience.

Syntactic Constraints

Up until now, we have been considering the problem of how children map words onto objects in the world. However, many words that children know do not refer to objects, but refer instead to substances (e.g., *water, sand*), properties (e.g., *blue, bumpy, big*), actions (e.g., *run, kiss*), and relations (e.g., *in, on, under*). One of the most powerful cues that children can use to determine a word's referent is the sentence structure in which the word is used. In this section, we explore these **syntactic constraints** or cues. Syntactic cues not only provide information about how to map word forms onto the world, but also have the potential to help map word forms onto more abstract concepts.

In one experiment that examined syntactic cues to properties (adjectives), 2-year-olds were introduced to a new word that was used either as a noun or an adjective: *This is a biv* versus *This is a biv one* (Taylor & Gelman, 1988). The referent for the word was a whalelike creature with a long green tail, round ears, and large eyes, and it was made of pale green fake fur. During test, four toys were present: the original toy, a similar toy with a plaid body covering, another creature covered with pale green fur, and another creature with a plaid body covering. Children were asked to perform some simple actions (e.g., *Can you put a biv in the box?*, *Can you put a biv one in the box?*, *Can you put this in the box?*), and the animal they chose was noted. More children who heard the new word used as a noun chose toys from the same object category and ignored body covering, while more children who heard the word used as an adjective chose based on body covering (green fur versus plaid). Therefore, children appeared to detect the subtle differences in sentence structure and use it to help determine what the words referred to.

Turning to the use syntax to learn about verb meaning, researchers working with adult participants have demonstrated clearly that they are unable to guess the meaning of a verb that is used to refer to a video-taped event unless that verb is used in a sentence context (Gillette, Gleitman, Gleitman, & Lederer, 1999). That is, even when you know the language and know that you are trying to guess a particular word that you already know (e.g., the verb *call*), you cannot guess it without syntactic evidence. To ask whether young children can use syntax to learn new verbs, Fisher (2002) taught 2.5-year-olds new verbs and tested them on what they thought the verbs meant. Table 5-2 shows the events and sentences to which children were exposed.

Notice that each sentence in Table 5-2 has the direct object *her* in parentheses, which is meant to indicate that some children learned

Table 5–2. Verb-Learning Events and Sentences Reported in Fisher (2002)

Event	Sentence
Participant A pulls B backward along a slippery surface by pulling on B's backpack.	She stipes (her) over there!
A rolls B toward her on a wheeled dolly by pulling on a feather boa tied around B's feet.	She braffs (her) over there!
A wheels B forward and back in a red wagon.	She pilks (her) back and forth!
A rotates B on a swivel stool by pulling on the ends of a scarf around B's waist.	She gishes (her) around!

the word in a sentence naming two actors (i.e., the subject *she* and the direct object *her*), whereas others learned the word in a sentence naming only one actor. The sentences with two actors are called **transitive**, and in English syntax, they should indicate that the subject of the sentence did something to someone or something (i.e., to the direct object). Therefore, if you hear *She gishes her around*, and are then asked *Who gished?*, you should have a very good idea about the correct answer. In contrast, if you hear *She gishes around* referring to a scene with two participants, either participant might be the one *gishing*. Both adults and 2.5-year-olds showed this pattern of responding, pointing to character A significantly more often than character B after hearing the new verb in a transitive sentence. These data suggest that young children are able to make use of sentence syntax when learning new verb meanings. However, other research suggests that children are very conservative about generalizing newly learned verbs to sentence contexts that are different from the one in which they learned the verb, an observation that seems to contrast with children's willingness to generalize new nouns (Tomasello, 2000). We discuss the issue of syntactic generalization in more detail in Chapter 8.

Children's Mapping Errors

Children have been observed to make two main types of mapping errors, each of which might inform us about how they approach the mapping task. One type of error is called **underextension**. These errors occur when a child uses a word to refer to a smaller range of referents than expected based on the adult meaning. Underextensions are more likely to occur in children younger than 18 months of age. In one study, 12-, 15-, and 18-month-olds were taught the name for a live rabbit or hamster and subsequently asked on separate trials to choose a hamster or rabbit from drawings, photos, and stuffed animals from these two categories (Oviatt, 1982). Only five of the 14 12- and 15-month-olds chose a new object from the category on which they had been trained, whereas all seven of the 18-month-olds were able to generalize appropriately. This study suggests that young children are not particularly adept at extending words to new members of a category. Such a finding implies either that the taxonomic constraint is learned through exposure to naming conventions in the language, or that very young children have difficulty determining the bases on which to extend new labels.

A more common mapping error seen in many young children is **overextension**, in which the child uses a word for a broader range of referents than the adult meaning. Children calling horses and cows *dogs* or calling all men *daddy* are examples of overextension. Overextensions might reveal something about the hypotheses that children have about how a word should generalize to new referents. For example, recall the previous discussion of deciding whether a word refers to Dalmations or the broader class of dogs. Overextensions appear to reflect three types of hypotheses, or ways in which children see the referents of a word as being like each other. One basis of overextension is **perceptual features.** A child who calls horses and cows *dogs* might notice that the three animals share fur, four legs, and domestication, but fail to treat as relevant size or other features that differentiate the animals. Another observed basis of overextension is **functional features**. An example of an overextension based on functional features is a child calling a thrown disk *a ball*. Thus, the function of being "throwable," and not shape, is taken to be the basis of generalizing *ball* to other referents. Finally, children sometimes appear to overextend based on a **family resemblance** structure. An example of such an overextension is a child who used the word *baby* to refer to herself reflected in a mirror, a framed picture of a baby, and a picture frame (Bowerman, 1978). Here, the child seems to treat something like a framed picture of a baby as a category **prototype** for *baby* and treats items have some overlap of features as possible babies as well, hence using *baby* to refer to the picture frame with no baby picture.

One question we can ask about overextension is whether the learner really believes that horses are the same as dogs or throwing disks are the same as balls, or whether she knows what the correct mappings are but fails to use to correct word for some reason. Three accounts of overextension errors have been offered, and there is good evidence that some children do each, suggesting that overextensions have multiple causes. The three causes for overextensions are illustrated in Figure 5-5. One possibility is that children truly have the wrong hypothesis about the basis of the category, which is indicated in the "category error" column of Figure 5-5. In this situation, children who are asked to look at or point to *the dog* when shown a picture of a dog and a horse would be equally likely to select either picture. The second possibility, "pragmatic errors," is that children know that a horse is really not a member of the dog category but do not have a word for *horse*. An interesting twist on this type of overex-

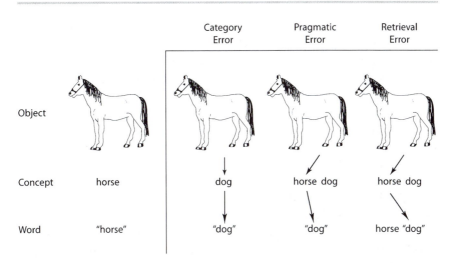

Figure 5–5. Possible reasons for children's overextension errors. From: The course of children's naming errors in early word learning. Gershkoff-Stowe, L., *Journal of Cognition and Development, 2*, pp. 131-155, 2001, Taylor & Francis, Ltd. Adapted by permission of Taylor & Francis, Ltd.

tension was found by Elsen (1994), who found using a diary study that one German-speaking child's overextensions were cases in which the child substituted a more easily pronounced, semantically related word, for one that the child had difficulty producing. An English parallel might be a child who calls giraffes *horses*, not because the child thinks that *horse* is the appropriate label, but because she cannot accurately produce *giraffe*. Finally, the third possibility, "retrieval errors," is that children's overextensions are akin to adult speech errors. For example, an adult might say, *Can you hand me the knife, no, I mean the fork*. Thus, the adult had a temporary lapse in retrieving the intended word. Gershkoff-Stowe (2001) has demonstrated that such retrieval errors are particularly likely during a narrow window of time when children have between 50 and 150 words in their productive vocabularies. She proposes that children during this time are still mastering how to access their growing lexicons in a fast an efficient way. Note that in both pragmatic and retrieval errors, children should be more likely to select the correct picture in comprehension for a word that they overextend in production. That is, when shown a horse and a dog picture and asked to look at or point to *the dog*, children who overextend *dog* to horses in production nevertheless should choose the dog. Such a result has been shown in a number of studies (e.g., Naigles & Gelman, 1995; Rescorla, 1980). Here we have another case of a perception/production asymmetry like the one we discussed in Chapter 4. We will see other such cases in Chapters 7 and 8.

The Mapping Problem Across Languages

The majority of the experiments on children's word mapping that have been reported in this chapter so far have focused on American children learning English. We end the chapter by considering three examples of cross-linguistic research on children's word learning and what this research might tell us beyond what we have already discussed. The three examples include noun learning by Japanese children, preposition learning by American versus Korean children, and word learning by English-Hebrew bilingual children. Beginning with proper nouns versus common nouns, research with American 17-month-olds showed that girls were able to use the presence or absence of a determiner to infer whether a new word was a proper noun that referred only to an individual (*This is Dax*) versus a common noun that referred to a category of objects (*This is a dax*). Children who were introduced to the word as a proper noun did not use the word to refer to any other objects than the one that had been labeled for them, whereas children introduced to the word preceded by *the* used the word to refer to other similar objects (Katz, Baker, & MacNamara, 1974). Thus, in English, the presence of a preceding determiner is an excellent (syntactic) cue about the taxonomic status of a noun, and children are sensitive to this cue quite early. But what about languages like Japanese that do not use determiners? In one study, 2-year-old Japanese children were taught novel words referring to animate and inanimate objects (Imai & Haryu, 2001). When the objects were unfamiliar to children, they automatically interpreted the noun as though it referred to an object category. Children indicated this interpretation by agreeing that the new word could be applied to new objects that were similar to the one that was originally named. However, when new words were taught for already familiar objects, children seemed to think that the new word was a proper name if the object was animate and a subordinate category name if the object was inanimate. That is, in the absence of syntactic cues to the taxonomic status of a noun, Japanese children appear to use the taxonomic assumption when a new word refers to an unfamiliar object and mutual exclusivity plus knowledge about what objects are likely to have proper names when a new word refers to a familiar object.

Turning to children's learning of prepositions, languages differentially divide up what aspects of space are categorized together to be labeled by a single preposition. As shown in Figure 5-6, English uses the preposition *on* to refer to situations where object A contacts the surface of object B, but object A is not contained within object B. The latter situation is described by the English preposition *in*. In contrast, Korean has a preposition *kkita* that partially aligns with English *in* and partially with English *on*. Korean *kkita* is used when there is

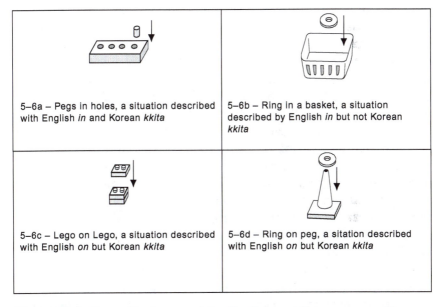

5–6a – Pegs in holes, a situation described with English *in* and Korean *kkita*

5–6b – Ring in a basket, a situation described by English *in* but not Korean *kkita*

5–6c – Lego on Lego, a situation described with English *on* but Korean *kkita*

5–6d – Ring on peg, a sitation described with English *on* but Korean *kkita*

Figure 5–6. Four situations and the English and Korean prepositions used to describe them. Reprinted from *Cognitive Development*, 14(2), Choi, S., McDonoug, L., Bowerman, M., and Mandler, J. M. Early sensitivity to language-specific spatial categories in English and Korean, pp. 241–268, Copyright (1999), with permission from Elsevier. Reprinted from *The Lancet*, 14, Choi, S., McDonoug, L., Bowerman, M., and Mandler, J. M., Early sensitivity to language-specific spatial categories in English and Korean, pp. 241–268, Copyright (1999), with permission from Elsevier.

a tight-fit relation between object A and object B. Thus, Figure 5–6A is described with English *in* and Korean *kkita*, whereas 5.6B is still described with English *in* but not *kkita*. Figures 5–6C and 5–6D are both described with Korean *kkita*, but described with English *on*. Interestingly, all four situations shown in Figure 5–6 would be described by the Spanish preposition *en*.

One question that arises, given the different mappings of prepositions to situations show in Figure 5–6, is whether one way of categorizing spatial relations is easier for children to learn than another. For example, is containment in general easier to think about and therefore easier for preposition mapping than tight fit? For an adult English-speaker, the answer might seem to be *yes*. But what about for children learning English versus Korean? One group of researchers showed English- and Korean-learning 18- and 23-month-olds pairs of pictures like Figures 5–6B and 5–6D on a video screen. Children would hear sentences like *Where is she putting it in?* or the Korean equivalent using *kkita* (Choi, McDonough, Bowerman, & Mandler, 1999). Children of both language groups and both age groups looked significantly longer at the picture that matched the sentence, suggesting that by 18 months, they had mastered the way in which their particular language had divided up and labeled the world. Therefore, it seems that both the Korean and English spatial concepts were equally easy for children to learn.

The last study in this section focuses on bilingual children, who often hear two labels for the same object, one in each language. If bilingual children applied the mutual exclusivity assumption, they should fail to treat the second label as referring to the intended object. For example, if a Spanish-English bilingual knows the word *gato* (*cat*) in reference to cats, she should not think that *cat* also refers to cats if she rigidly applies mutual exclusivity. In contrast, if children use their knowledge of pragmatics to determine when a new word refers to an old or new object, they will probably be influenced what language(s) the person providing the new label speaks. To ask whether bilingual children use pragmatics in word learning, Diesendruck (2005) taught 3-year-olds a new English word for novel object A, and children were subsequently asked to retrieve an object by a puppet who asked them in Hebrew. The question was whether they would give the puppet object A, thereby violating mutual exclusivity or object B, consistent with mutual exclusivity. For half of the children, it was made clear that the puppet was a Hebrew-English bilingual and for other half that the puppet was a monolingual Hebrew speaker. When children thought the puppet was bilingual, they chose object B more often, but when they thought he was monolingual, they chose A more often. One explanation for this effect is that, if children thought that the puppet knew the English word that the experimenter used to label object A, the pragmatics of the situation should have caused the puppet to ask for object A using the same label that the experimenter did. Therefore, when the puppet used a different label, children inferred that he wanted the other object. In contrast, if children thought that the puppet did not know the English word that the experimenter used to label object A, the pragmatics of the situation focused everyone's attention on the labeled object. Therefore, children thought that the puppet was referring to the previously labeled object, but in his own language.

■ Summary

At least four important themes are seen in Chapter 5. First, developing a lexicon entails finding word forms in the speech stream (the segmentation problem) and attaching these forms to meaning (the mapping problem). Second, there are a number of cues to the segmentation problem, some of which require no prior knowledge of language, and some of which make use of typical properties of particular languages. Third, although solving the mapping problem might begin with children mapping word forms onto the world, children must ultimately map word forms onto concepts shared by their linguistic community. Finally, because any word can refer to a number of possible referents, children rely on certain assumptions or constraints to successfully solve the mapping problem. Whether or not the constraints on word learning must be specific to language, or whether they reflect general purposed learning mechanisms is not clear. However, a number of studies suggest that children change over development in how they apply these constraints (e.g., the shape bias, early underextension). These studies, like the ones reported in Chapter 3, might be taken to indicate that children begin learning at least some aspects of language using general purpose learning mechanisms that become more language-specific through experience.

■ References

Aslin, R. N., Saffran, J. R., & Newport, E. L. (1998). Computation of conditional probability statistics by 8-month-old infants. *Psychological Science, 9*(4), 321-324.

Aslin, R. N., Slemmer, J. A., Kirkham, N. Z., & Johnson, S. P. (2001). *Statistical learning of visual shape sequences.* Paper presented at the meeting of the Society for Research in Child Development, Minneapolis, MN.

Bowerman, M. (1978). The acquisition of word meaning: An investigation into some current conflicts. In N. Waterson & C. Snow (Eds.), *The development of communication* (pp. 263-287). New York: Wiley.

Brent, M. R., & Siskind, J. M. (2001). The role of exposure to isolated words in early vocabulary development. *Cognition, 81*(2), B33-B44.

Carroll, L. (1872). *Through the looking-glass and what Alice found there.* London: MacMillan.

Choi, S., McDonough, L., Bowerman, M., & Mandler, J. M. (1999). Early sensitivity to language-specific spatial categories in english and korean. *Cognitive Development, 14*(2), 241-268.

Cleary, B. (1968). *Ramona the pest.* New York: Harper Collins.

Diesendruck, G. (2005). The principles of conventionality and contrast in word learning: An empirical examination. *Developmental Psychology, 41*(3), 451-463.

Diesendruck, G., & Markson, L. (2001). Children's avoidance of lexical overlap: A pragmatic account. *Developmental Psychology, 37*(5), 630-641.

Elsen, H. (1994). Phonological constraints and overextensions. *First Language, 14*, 305-315.

Fernald, A., & Mazzie, C. (1991). Prosody and focus in speech to infants and adults. *Developmental Psychology, 27*, 209-221.

Fernald, A., McRoberts, G. W., & Swingley, D. (2001). Infants' developing competence in understanding & recognizing words in fluent speech. In J. Weissenborn & B. Höhle (Eds.), *Approaches to bootstrapping. Phonological, lexical, syntactic and neurophysiological aspects of early language acquisition* (Vol. 1, pp. 97-123). Amsterdam: John Benjamin.

Fisher, C. (2002). Structural limits on verb mapping: The role of abstract structure in 2.5-year-olds' interpretations of novel verbs. *Developmental Science, 5*(1), 55-64.

Garrett, M. F. (1975). The analysis of sentence production. In G. Bower (Ed.), *Psychology of learning and motivation* (Vol. 9, pp. 133-177). New York: Academic Press.

Gerken, L. A., Landau, B., & Remez, R. E. (1990). Function morphemes in young children's speech perception and production. *Developmental Psychology, 26*(2), 204-216.

Gerken, L. A., & McIntosh, B. J. (1993). The interplay of function morphemes and prosody in early language. *Developmental Psychology, 29*, 448–457.

Gershkoff-Stowe, L. (2001). The course of children's naming errors in early word learning. *Journal of Cognition and Development, 2*, 131–155.

Gillette, J., Gleitman, H., Gleitman, L., & Lederer, A. (1999). Human simulations of vocabulary learning. *Cognition, 73*(2), 135–176.

Hockema, S. A. (2006). Finding words in speech: An investigation of American English. *Language Learning and Development, 2*(2), 119–146.

Hohne, E. A., & Jusczyk, P. W. (1994). Two-month-old infants' sensitivity to allophonic differences. *Perception and Psychophysics, 56*, 613–623.

Imai, M., & Haryu, E. (2001). Learning proper nouns and common nouns without clues from syntax. *Child Development, 72*(3), 787–802.

Jusczyk, P. W., Cutler, A., & Redanz, N. (1993). Infants' sensitivity to predominant word stress patterns in English. *Child Development, 64*, 675–687.

Jusczyk, P. W., Houston, D., & Newsome, M. (1999). The beginnings of word segmentation in English-learning infants. *Cognitive Psychology, 39*, 159–207.

Katz, B., Baker, G., & MacNamara, J. (1974). What's in a name? On the child's acquisition of proper and common nouns. *Child Development, 45*, 269–273.

Kedar, Y., Casasola, M., & Lust, B. (2006). Getting there faster: 18- and 24-month-old infants' use of function words to determine reference. *Child Development, 77*(2), 325–338.

Landau, B., Smith, L. B., & Jones, S. S. (1988). The importance of shape in early lexical learning. *Cognitive Development, 3*(3), 299–321.

Markman, E. M., Gelman, S. A., & Byrnes, J. P. (1991). *The whole-object, taxonomic, and mutual exclusivity assumptions as initial constraints on word meanings.* New York: Cambridge University Press.

Markman, E. M., & Wachtel, G. F. (1988). Children's use of mutual exclusivity to constrain the meaning of words. *Cognitive Psychology, 20*(2), 121–157.

Mattys, S. L., & Jusczyk, P. W. (2001a). Do infants segment words or recurring contiguous patterns? *Journal of Experimental Psychology: Human Perception and Performance, 27*(3), 644–655.

Mattys, S. L., & Jusczyk, P. W. (2001b). Phonotactic cues for segmentation of fluent speech by infants. *Cognition, 78*(2), 91–121.

Naigles, L., & Gelman, S. A. (1995). Overextensions in comprehension and production revisited: Preferential-looking in a study of dog, cat, and cow. *Journal of Child Language, 22*, 19–46.

Ninio, A. (1980). Ostensive definition in vocabulary teaching. *Journal of Child Language, 7*(3), 565–573.

Oviatt, S. L. (1982). Inferring what words mean: Early development in infants' comprehension of common object names. *Child Development, 53*(1), 274–277.

Quine, W. V. O. (1960). *Word and object.* Cambridge: Cambridge University Press.

Rescorla, L. A. (1980). Overextension in early language development. *Journal of Child Language*, 7, 321–335.

Saffran, J. R., Aslin, R. N., & Newport, E. (1996). Statistical learning by 8-month-old infants. *Science*, 274, 1926–1928.

Saffran, J. R., Johnson, E. K., Aslin, R. N., & Newport, E. L. (1999). Statistical learning of tone sequences by human infants and adults. *Cognition*, 70(1), 27–52.

Shady, M. E., & Gerken, L. A. (1999). Grammatical and caregiver cues in early sentence comprehension. *Journal of Child Language*, 26(1), 163–175.

Shi, R., & Lepage, M. (2007). The effect of functional morphemes on word segmentation in preverbal infants. *Developmental Science*, 11(3), 407–413.

Shi, R., Werker, J., F., & Morgan, J. (1999). Newborn infants' sensitivity to perceptual cues to lexical and grammatical words. *Cognition*, 72, B11–B21.

Smith, L. B., Jones, S. S., Landau, B., Gershkoff-Stowe, L., & Samuelson, L. (2002). Object name learning provides on-the-job training for attention. *Psychological Science*, 13(1), 13–19.

Taylor, M., & Gelman, S. A. (1988). Adjectives and nouns: Children's strategies for learning new words. *Child Development*, 59(2), 411–419.

Tincoff, R., & Jusczyk, P. W. (1999). Some beginnings of word comprehension in 6-month-olds. *Psychological Science*, 10(2), 172–175.

Tomasello, M. (2000). Do young children have adult syntactic competence? *Cognition*, 74(3), 209–253.

Woodward, A., & Markman, E. M. (1998). Early word learning. In D. Kuhn & R. S. Siegler (Eds.), *Handbook of child psychology: Vol. 2, Cognition, perception and language* (5th ed.). New York: Wiley.

Xu, F., Cote, M., & Baker, A. (2005). Labeling guides object individuation in 12-month-old infants. *Psychological Science*, 16(5), 372–377.

Xu, F., & Tenenbaum, J. B. (2007). Word learning as Bayesian inference. *Psychological Review*, 114(2), 245–272.

Yu, C. (2008). A statistical associative account of vocabulary growth in early word learning. *Language Learning and Development*, 4(1), 32–62.

Zangl, R., & Fernald, A. (2007). Increasing flexibility in children's online processing of grammatical and nonce determiners in fluent speech. *Language Learning and Development*, 3, 199–231.

6 Overview of Syntax and Morphology

■ What Is Morphosyntax?

Recall from Chapter 1 that the meaningful units of language can be combined in two ways. One type of combination is **morphology**, which entails forming new words by combining meaningful units called **morphemes**. Linguists have further divided morphology into two types. **Derivational morphology** is used to change the syntactic category of words. For example, the adjective *false* can be turned into the verb *falsify*, which can be turned into the noun *falsification*. We will not discuss derivational morphology further. **Inflectional morphemes** do not change the syntactic category of a word, but either modify its meaning (e.g., *dog* → *dogs*, *walk* → *walked*) or are required as part of the form of a sentence (e.g., *I walk*, *He walks*).

The second way that meaningful units can be combined is **syntax**, which entails putting words together to make **phrases** and **clauses**. Morphology and syntax work in tandem to allow us to use the limited number of meaningful units in our mental lexicons to create and understand an infinite number of utterances. We refer to the joint role of morphology and syntax in the comprehension and production of meaningful and grammatical sentences as **morphosyntax**, which is the focus of Chapters 6 through 8.

You have probably never read or heard the particular sentences in this paragraph before, but you are able to understand them. Furthermore, understanding the sentences in this paragraph, as well as those you encounter every day, probably involves more than simply understanding the words and morphemes and trying to piece together the writer's or speaker's likely intended meaning. Rather, using morphosyntax to understand and produce sentences requires sensitivity to several aspects of language: (1) **syntactic constituents**, (2) **syntactic categories**, (3) **structural positions**, and (4) **thematic**

roles. Most theories of language development include some version of these four aspects of language in some way, and the next section provides a brief overview of each of them. Morphosyntactic development has perhaps been the arena in which the theoretical approaches to language development outlined in Chapter 1 have been most debated. The discussion of the components of morphosyntax is followed by an outline of four of these debates. Following this overview chapter, Chapter 7 presents data on infants' and children's sensitivity to morphosyntax as it pertains to the form of sentences, without regard to the sentences' meaning. This way of viewing syntax is very similar to the idea of "word forms" (grammatical sound sequences) discussed in Chapters 4 and 5. Chapter 7 focuses on syntactic constituents, syntactic categories, and structural positions insofar as the latter are reflected in word order. Chapter 8 presents data on how infants and children learning English and other languages use a variety of cues to extract meaning from sentences. Chapter 8 also provides sample studies illustrating the four debates outlined below.

■ Four Components of Morphosyntax

This section provides an overview of four components of morphosyntax that are assumed in some form by many approaches to morphosyntactic development.

Syntactic Constituents

One aspect of morphosyntax concerns how the words in a sentences form smaller groups of words, or **syntactic constituents**. For example, in sentence 6a, you need to determine that the **phrase** *the old yellow cat* forms an important unit, as do the words *doesn't drink*. Similarly, in sentence 6b, the **clause** *after he chased the old yellow cat* is a minisentence (containing a subject and a verb) inside the whole sentence. Determining where the sentence constituents are is an important first step in sentence comprehension.

6a. The old yellow cat doesn't drink milk.
6b. After he chased the old yellow cat, my dog took a nap.

Recall that in Chapter 5, we discussed the **segmentation problem** for finding words in the speech stream. The same problem and many of the same solutions apply to finding syntactic constituents. One of the solutions is **prosody**. For example, an infant or child hearing sentence 6b might be able to use pausing, pitch changes, and syllable lengthening to determine that a new clause begins after the word *cat* (see Table 2-3 and Figure 2-4). However, not all syntactic constituents are marked prosodically. For example, *the old yellow cat* and *a nap* are both syntactic constituents of 6b, but they might not exhibit noticeable prosodic properties to set them off from the preceding verbs *chased* and *took*.

Another cue that might be used to solve the segmentation problem for both words and syntactic constituents is **function morphemes** (see Chapter 5). For example, although the phrase *the old yellow cat* in 6b is probably not marked by prosody as a separate constituent, the determiner *the* occurs at the beginning of many sentences (e.g., 6a), which is a clue that it can begin a syntactic constituent. When *the* occurs within a sentence, as in 6b, it can cue the beginning of a phrase even though the phrase is not marked as a constituent by prosody. Evidence that children use function morphemes in aid of word segmentation was presented in Chapter 5.

A third type of cue to syntactic constituents is comparisons across sentences. For example, even though the phrase *some milk* may not be prosodically marked as a constituent in 6c, hearing 6c in the close temporal proximity to 6d might allow a language learner to determine that *some milk* is a constituent, because it is replaced by a single word (*it*). Similarly, the fact that *some milk* moves as a unit between 6c and 6e might also provides a cue that it is a constituent.

6c. The cat spilled some milk.
6d. The cat spilled it.
6e. Some milk was spilled.

Syntactic Categories

Related to locating the sentence constituents is determining how particular words and phrases are being used in the sentence, that is, determining the words' and phrases' **syntactic categories**. The syntactic categories that apply to words are often called **lexical categories** and include **noun, verb, adjective, preposition, determiner**, and **auxiliary**, to name a few. The syntactic categories that apply to phrases are often called **phrasal categories**, and include **noun phrases** or **NP's** and **verb phrases** or **VP's**, as well as others. We can describe the sentences of a language in terms of **phrase structure rules**, which specify the order of phrasal constituents, which are in turn made up of lexical constituents. One simple version of phrase structure rules is shown in Table 6–1. The way that these rules can be used to describe a sentence is shown in 6f. The parentheses show the constituents, with some constituents (*the milk*) embedded within larger constituents (the VP). This embedding is part of the hierarchical structure of language, which we discuss further in Chapter 8.

6f.   (The$_{det}$ cat$_{noun}$)$_{NP}$ ([drank$_{verb}$] [the milk]$_{NP}$)$_{VP}$

How does a language learner determine the syntactic categories of sentence constituents? You can get a sense of the problem by noting that *brush* is being used as a verb in sentence 6g, but as a noun in sentence 6h. You may have learned in grade school that "a noun is a person, place, or thing." Although the meaning of the word may provide you with some clue about its syntactic category, the examples in 6g and 6h suggest that there is some circularity in this approach. That is, in 6g, *brush* is a verb, because it refers to an action, but in 6h, *brush* is a noun, because it refers to a thing. But how do you know

Table 6–1. Some Phrase Structure Rules and Sample Phrases That They Generate ("det" stands for "determiner")

Phrase Structure Rule	Sample Phrases
S → NP VP	This rule can generate any sentence.
NP → (det) (Adj) N	*the dog, the big dog, big dogs*
VP → V (NP) (NP) (PP)	*sleep, chase small dogs, chase small dogs around the park, brought him the newspaper*
PP → P (NP)	*around the park, inside*

that *brush* refers to an action in 6g and a thing in 6h? Because the word is used as a verb in the first sentence and as a noun in the second sentence. This chain of logic is clearly circular.

6g. Jenny can brush her hair.
6h. Max found a brush in the drawer.

If using meaning to determine a word's syntactic category introduces such circularity, what other information can be used? In 6g, the auxiliary verb *can* (a type of function morpheme) preceding *brush* tells you that it belongs in the same category as other words that can be preceded by *can*, such as *jump, eat*, and so forth. As linguistically aware adults, we would call words in this group "verbs." Similarly, the determiner *a* (another type of function morpheme) preceding *brush* in 6h tells you that it can be grouped with other words preceded by *a*, such as *dog, house*, etc. We would call the words in this group "nouns." In addition to function morphemes, the location of a word in relation with other words in a sentence can help you determine its syntactic category. For example, if you know that *her hair* is a noun phrase and you know that verbs often precede noun phrases, you can use that information to tell you that *brush* is a verb in 6g. The main point to remember is that different syntactic categories (nouns, verbs, adjectives, etc.) are distributed differently from each other in sentences. That is, they occur in different sentence contexts. Function morphemes and location with respect to other constituents in the sentence are called **distributional cues** to syntactic categories. Mintz (2003) has identified a particular type of distributional cue that he calls "frequent frames," which he has shown using computer models to reliably group words into syntactic categories, at least in English. Examples of frequent frames that have been identified in parental input to young children are *I ___ it* and *the ___ and*. Words that we would call "verbs" can often appear in the first frame, and words that we would call "nouns" would often appear in the second frame.

You might have noted some puzzling wording in several places in the previous paragraph; for example "As linguistically aware adults, we would call words in this group. . ." This wording points to a potential complication of distributional cues to syntactic categories. Distributional cues allow us to collect words into groups, but although we as adults can say, *The words in that group are all nouns*, the infant or child might only treat the words as unlabeled groups. Why do we care if the groups can be assigned labels like "noun" or "verb"? Because within Triggering theories of language acquisition, humans are born with parameters like those shown in Table 6-2. Note that these proposed parameters assume that children know what words in their language are nouns, verbs, adjectives, and so forth. Many versions of Linguistic Hypothesis Testing also make this assumption. Therefore, these theories need to propose how language learners might determine which groups of words belong to which innately specified categories. We discuss one proposal and the evidence for it in Chapter 7.

Structural Positions

Much of the job of understanding sentences entails determining the relation of the noun phrase(s) to the verb—that is, determining the **structural position(s)** of the NP(s). All sentences have a **subject** NP, and sentences like 6i that have only a subject and no other NP's are called **intransitive** sentences. In English sentences containing

Table 6–2. Sample Parameters Proposed by Baker (2001) and the Syntactic Categories Referred to by the Parameter

Parameter	Syntactic Category Referred to
Only one verb can be contained within each verb phrase or more than one verb can be contained in a single verb phrase	verb
The subject of a clause is merged with the verb phrase or it is merged with the auxiliary phrase	verb phrase
Adjectives are treated as a kind of verb or adjectives are treated as a kind of noun	adjective, verb, noun
If agreement with a noun phrase X is not required, use the agreement to show that the noun phrase X is animate and/or definite in its reference	noun phrase

a single clause, the first noun is almost always the subject. In other languages, the subject occupies other positions in the sentence. In languages like Spanish, the subject is sometimes only understood from context, as in the sentence *Quiero helado* (*I want ice cream*). The *-o* inflection on *quiero* (*want*) tells you that the subject of the sentence is *I*, even though it is not overtly present. Not only does each sentence have a subject, but each clause within the sentence does as well. Thus, in 6j, *the cat* is the subject of the subordinate clause, and *she* is the subject of the main clause, and therefore of the entire sentence. Some sentences also have a **direct object**, as exemplified by *some milk* in 6k. Sentences with a subject and direct object are called **transitive** sentences. Other sentences like 6l have both a direct object and **indirect object**. In 6l, *the cat* is the indirect object, and *some milk* is the direct object. Sentences with both a direct and indirect object are called **dative** sentences. The phrase that is the indirect object in a dative can also be expressed as the **object of a preposition** as illustrated in 6m (*to the cat*). Sentences that have this structure are often referred to as **prepositional datives**.

6i. The cat is sleeping.
6j. When the cats drinks milk, she purrs.
6k. The cat is drinking some milk.
6l. Max gave the cat some milk.
6m. Max gave some milk to the cat.

One reason that we need to consider the structural positions of sentence constituents, and particularly of NP's, is the role of these positions in determining sentence meaning. We discuss how structural positions are related to meaning below. Before we can do that, we need to consider how to determine which nouns are in which structural positions in a sentence. In languages like English that rely heavily on word order, determining which NP constituent is the subject of the sentence is accomplished based on word order. As noted above, the first NP in English sentences is almost always the subject. In sentences containing pronouns, the subject is further indicated by pronoun **case marking**. For example, the pronouns *I*, *he*, *she*, and *they* are said to mark the **nominative case** and can only be subjects. The pronouns *me*, *him*, *her*, and *them* mark the **accusative** or **dative case** and can be either direct objects (e.g., *Chris chased me*) or indirect objects (e.g., *Chris gave me a book*). Thus, syntactic cases, such as nominative, accusative, and dative, correspond to the structural positions subject, direct object, and indirect object, respectively.

The fact that English only marks syntactic case on pronouns stands in contrast with the morphosyntactic systems found in many other languages of the world. Languages such as Latin and Russian, which have freer word orders than English, employ case markers on most or all nouns to indicate which NP is the subject, object, etc. For example, the Latin word that means *master* has the root *domin* (as in *dominate*) to which case endings are added, as shown in Table 6-3. Thus, the noun *dominus* in the nominative case would be the subject of a sentence in which it appeared.

An example of how case markings and not word order are used to assign structural positions can be seen in the Russian sentences 6n and 6o. In 6n, the first noun is in nominative case and is therefore interpreted as the one doing the action. In 6o, the first noun is in accusative case and is therefore interpreted as the one who is acted upon. Comparing how you determine structural positions in 6i–m versus 6n–o illustrates that children learning different languages need to attend to different cues to understand, and ultimately produce, sentence of their language. We discuss how children learning languages like Russian achieve this ability in Chapter 8.

6n. Devushka razbudila mal'chika
    girl+nominative woke up boy+accusative
    The girl woke up the boy.
6o. Damu udaril mal'chik
    lady+accusative hit boy+nominative
    The boy hit the lady.

Table 6–3. Examples of the Latin Case Marking System

Word Form	Syntactic Case
domin<u>us</u>	nominative
domin<u>um</u>	accusative
domin<u>o</u>	dative

Thematic Roles

Thematic roles are a way of keeping track of who did what to whom in a sentence. Some thematic roles and their descriptions are shown in Table 6-4. It is the linking of thematic roles to structural positions that determines much of sentence interpretation.

How are thematic roles linked to structural positions? The answer to this question is complex and largely governed by the particular syntactic theory to which one subscribes. However, for the present purposes, we can say that the way in which this linking is achieved depends on two factors: the particular verb that is used and the type of sentence.

With respect to particular verbs, consider the difference between the verbs *wept, liked, kissed, gave,* and *put* in Table 6-5. These verbs obviously differ in meaning, and their meaning differences are partially reflected in the thematic roles that they require be present. For example, the act of weeping requires only the weeper be specified. Liking and kissing requires both the one doing the liking or kissing and the one who is liked or kissed be specified. The act of giving requires the one giving, what is given, and to whom it is given be specified. Finally, the act of putting requires specification of the one putting, what is put, and where it is put.

Although knowing specific verbs is very helpful in determining the thematic roles used in a sentence, this knowledge isn't necessary

Table 6–4. Some Thematic Roles and Their Descriptions

Thematic Role	*Brief Description*
Agent	someone or something that performs an action
Theme	someone or something to which an action is done
Experiencer	someone who experiences a sensation or emotion
Recipient	someone or something who receives something
Location	a place where something ends up at the end of an action

Table 6–5. Some Sentence Types and the Thematic Roles of Their NP Constituents

Sentence	Type	NP 1 (Subj)	NP2	NP3
Oscar wept.	Active intransitive	Agent		
Oscar liked Lucinda	Active transitive	Experiencer	Theme	
Oscar kissed Lucinda	Active transitive	Agent	Theme	
Lucinda was kissed by Oscar	Passive	Theme	Agent	
Lucinda was kissed	Reduced passive	Theme		
Oscar gave Lucinda a book	Dative	Agent	Recipient	Theme
Oscar gave a book to Lucinda	To-Dative	Agent	Theme	Recipient
Oscar put a book on the table	Locative	Agent	Theme	Location

to make a good guess about the meaning of a sentence that contains an unfamiliar verb. For example, if you hear sentence 6p, you would probably be able to produce 6q and also know that 6r is ungrammatical. You further could guess that the verb *mip* entails transferring something between two entities. Recall from Chapter 5 that young children appear to have some rudimentary ability to determine verb meaning from sentence structure.

6p. She mipped him the snerg
6q. The snerg was mipped by her
6r. *He was mipped.

With respect to how the type of sentence influences thematic role assignment, several sentence types are listed in Table 6–5. Consider the three sentences containing the verb *kissed* in Table 6-5. In the first sentence containing *kissed*, the subject is the agent, whereas in the other two sentences, the subject is the theme. What is the basis of the difference? The first sentence is **active**, whereas the other two are **passive**. Passive sentences place the theme in the subject position to acknowledge that it is the topic of the conversation. For example, you might be discussing why Lucinda seemed so flustered at the picnic. Someone might offer the suggestion that the reason for her behavior was that *Lucinda was kissed by Oscar*. The ability to highlight particular sentence information by using different sentence types is very helpful for maintaining a coherent discourse, but it means that knowledge of both structural position (e.g., subject) and sentence type (e.g., active vs. passive) are needed to determine who did what to whom.

■ Four Debates Concerning the Development of Morphosyntax

As already noted, morphosyntactic development is the domain in which theories of language development most strongly conflict. Chapter 8 presents four of these conflicts, which are outlined below. Two of the debates pit Associative Learning theories against the other three theories presented in Chapter 1, and two others pit Triggering and Linguistic Hypothesis Testing theories against the other two.

How Far Do Children Generalize from Morphosyntactic Input?

In Chapter 1, we observed that the ability to generalize beyond the specific input encountered is a central focus of theories of language development. Therefore, most researchers working in the field of human language assume that language development ultimately results in ability to produce and comprehend sentences that the person has never encountered. However, we can ask whether this ability to generalize beyond the input is characteristic of language learners of all ages, or whether generalization is one of the aspects of linguistic ability that must develop. This debate generally pits researchers who are sympathetic to Associative Learning theories against those who are more inclined toward hypothesis testing or Triggering theories. That is, the divide generally is between theories in which generalization is the product of associations among experiences without a separate grammar and theories proposing that generalization reflects a grammar. In Associative Learning theories, early stages of learning are characterized by learners having access primarily to the specific experiences that they have had. Only later, as the number of associations among experiences grows, do they begin to generalize. Therefore, these accounts predict that early abilities are based on specific experiences and do not reflect generalization. Chapter 8 explores this debate with respect to whether children use new verbs in sentence types that were not part of their input.

Can Associative Learning Models Account for Generalization?

The second debate, like the one outlined above, pits Associative Learning theories against hypothesis testing and Triggering theories. The debate concerns the adequacy of Associative Learning theories as they are implemented by connectionist models for accounting for different sorts of linguistic generalization observed in infants and children. If the models demonstrate patterns of learning like that of humans, we will have some evidence that a mental grammar is not necessary to account for language development. In contrast, if the models are inadequate in some ways, these inadequacies can give us information about necessary components of a language learning mechanism. Chapter 8 examines this debate with respect to children's past tense overgeneralization errors (e.g., *goed*) and with respect to infants ability to learn abstract patterns from syllable strings.

Do Children Make Generalizations That Are Not Supported by the Input?

Recall from Chapter 1 that one rationale for highly constrained language learning mechanisms such as the one proposed by Triggering and Linguistic Hypothesis Testing theories is the **poverty of the stimulus** argument. The input to language learners is said to be impoverished if relevant data are not available for the learner to make a generalization. The debate concerning poverty of the stimulus has sparked two types of research: First, can we find evidence that learners have made those generalizations that have been deemed to be based on impoverished input? Second, is the input truly impoverished, such that a learning model without the generalization already built in fails to make the generalization? Chapter 8 examines these two approaches to the poverty of the stimulus question with respect to children's knowledge that sentences have a hierarchical structure and to their knowledge of how to interpret the word *one* in sentences like, *See the blue bottle? Where's another one?*

Do Children's Morphosyntactic Errors Reflect Possible Human Grammars?

Recall from Chapter 1 that a unique prediction of Triggering theories is that children's errors should reflect possible human grammars. This prediction is based on the proposal that children are born with all possible grammars available to them in the form of syntactic parameters, such as the parameter that allows or prohibits subjectless sentences. On this view, language development is the process of selecting the correct grammar for the target language by ruling out incorrect parameter settings. A related prediction is made by Linguistic Hypothesis Testing: children's errors should reflect only linguistic units and relations. A number of errors in children's early sentence forms have been treated as evidence either for Triggering or Linguistic Hypothesis Testing. Chapter 8 reviews two of these errors and evaluates the available evidence. The two error types are English-speaking children's subjectless sentences and their pronoun case errors.

■ Summary

Chapter 6 outlined four components of morphosyntax that are important in discussions of morphosyntactic development: syntactic constituents, syntactic categories, structural positions, and thematic roles. The chapter also outlined four current debates in research on morphosyntactic development. These debates align in different ways with the theories that were introduced in Chapter 1. You will see as you read the next two chapters that interpreting the data on children's morphosyntactic development is not easy. For almost every study, multiple interpretations consistent with opposing theories are possible. As you read about the studies, ask yourself if the data convincingly support a particular point of view, and if not, what additional data you might want to have.

■ References

Baker, M. C. (2001). *The atoms of language.* New York: Basic Books.

Mintz, T. H. (2003). Frequent frames as a cue for grammatical categories in child directed speech. *Cognition, 90,* 91–117.

7 | Children's Sensitivity to Sentence Forms

In Chapter 6, we discussed four components of morphosyntax: (1) syntactic constituents, (2) syntactic categories, (3) structural positions, and (4) thematic roles. Chapter 7 presents data on infants' and children's sensitivity to morphosyntactic form, without regard to sentence interpretation. The chapter focuses on syntactic constituents, syntactic categories, and structural positions insofar as the latter are reflected in word and phrase order.

■ Syntactic Constituents

We discussed in Chapter 6 that there are at least three cues to syntactic constituents: prosody, function morphemes, and cross-sentence comparisons. The majority of the work on language learners' knowledge of syntactic constituents has focused on infants' sensitivity to prosody. Although Chapter 5 presented research demonstrating young learners' sensitivity to function morphemes, no studies have specifically asked whether function morphemes can be used to locate syntactic constituents. Similarly, no studies have asked whether cross-sentence comparisons might help young language learners find constituents. Therefore, this section reviews four studies suggesting that infants in the first year of life are sensitive to the types of prosodic cues that might be helpful in locating syntactic constituents.

The degree of prosodic marking of morphosyntactic constituents varies greatly depending on the style of speech being used. Prosodic boundaries are more clearly marked in slow, careful, formal speech than in fast, informal speech (Cooper & Paccia-Cooper, 1980). Many parents use a particular speech style when speaking to their infants and children, and this style, which is referred to as "infant-directed speech" or "motherese," is characterized by a higher pitch and a wider pitch range than adult-directed speech (Fernald & Kuhl, 1987). Even newborns prefer to listen to infant-directed speech over adult-directed speech (Cooper, 1993), and older infants show increased brain activity to infant-directed versus adult-directed speech (Zangl & Mills, 2007). Importantly, this speech style tends to highlight prosodic cues to syntactic constituents (Jusczyk et al., 1992). Can infants use prosody to locate syntactic constituents? Although we do not have a firm answer to that question, we do have good evidence that infants are sensitive to the set of correlated cues that mark the edges of many syntactic constituents and that they remember strings of words that are prosodically grouped.

Thought Question

If infant-directed speech was found in every culture, what might you conclude about the cause of this speech style?

Prosodic marking to syntactic constituents often comprises the correlated cues of pausing, pitch change, and lengthening of the syllable at the right edge of the prosodic boundary, although the specific configurations of cues, especially for phrase boundaries, may differ across languages (Gussenhoven, 2004). Two studies asked whether infants are able to detect violations of this cue correlation. One study asked about clauses, which tend to be prosodically well marked in most speech styles and to be marked in similar ways across languages. In the study, researchers presented 6-month-olds with two types of passages: passages with normal prosody or passages in which the normal correlation of prosodic cues was disrupted by moving the pause from the edge of the clause to a position either before or after the end of the clause (Hirsh-Pasek et al., 1987). Examples of sentences from these two types of passages appear in 7a and 7b, with slashes indicating pauses. Infants listened significantly longer in the HPP to passages with normal pausing, as in 7a, than passages in which the normal correlation of prosodic cues was disrupted, as in 7b. Subsequent studies showed that even 4.5-month-olds could discriminate the two types of pausing (Jusczyk & Kemler Nelson, 1996) and that they are sensitive to similar correlated cues to edges of musical passages (Krumhansl & Jusczyk, 1990). These studies suggest that the cues that mark clausal constituents are available to infants very early and may mark edges of acoustic stimuli generally, as evident by the fact that they are also effective for music.

7a. Her wicked stepmother told Cinderella / that she couldn't go to the ball.
7b. Her wicked stepmother told Cinderella that she / couldn't go to the ball.

A similar study asked whether infants could also detect violations of correlated prosodic cues to phrasal constituents (Jusczyk et al., 1992). This study not only compared infants' listening times for passages with normal versus disrupted prosody (see sentences 7c and 7d), but it also asked if infants were better able to detect a difference for infant-directed speech than for adult-directed speech. The results showed that 9-month-olds, but not 6-month-olds, listened longer to passages containing the normal correlation of prosodic cues. Interestingly, when the 6-month-olds were brought back to the laboratory and tested at 9 months of age, they demonstrated a significant preference for normal prosody. The longer listening times for the normal versus disrupted prosody held for both infant-directed and adult-directed speech. However, it is important to note that the only adult-directed samples used in the study were read from storybooks and not spontaneous speech, whereas infant-directed speech was of both types. Therefore, we cannot be sure what prosodic information might be available in spontaneous adult-directed speech. Taken together with the previous study showing that even 4.5-month-olds are sensitive to the prosody of clausal constituents, this study suggests that cues to phrases may be subtler and require infants to have more exposure before they are able to detect the particular cue correlation used in their language.

7c. Many different kinds of animals / live in the zoo.
7d. Many different kinds / of animals live in the zoo.

Before leaving the topic of infants' sensitivity to the cue correlations that often mark syntactic constituents, it is important to note that, although the relation of prosodic cues and syntactic constituents is quite good, it is far from perfect (Nespor & Vogel, 1986). One domain in which the relation is not good is for sentences with pronoun subjects. Whereas infant-directed speech provides good information that the subject NP in 7e and 7f is a separate constituent from the VP, the pronoun subject in 7g and 7h is unlikely to be prosodically marked as a separate constituent. If infants are presented with natural and unnatural prosodic versions of 7e versus 7f and 7g versus 7h, do they listen longer when the pause is after the subject in both sets of stimuli? To ask this question, researchers used the same method described for the previous studies (Gerken, Jusczyk, & Mandel, 1994). They found that infants listened longer to the natural prosody version of the stimuli only when the subject NP was a multiword phrase (7e) and not a pronoun (7g). This study demonstrates the limits on prosody as a cue to syntactic constituents. Infants and young children almost certainly need to supplement prosody with other information if they are to locate the important syntactic constituents of all of the sentences they hear.

7e. The caterpillar / became a beautiful butterfly.
7f. The caterpillar became / a beautiful butterfly.
7g. He / became a beautiful butterfly.
7h. He became / a beautiful butterfly.

The three studies discussed so far in this section tell us only that infants are sensitive to prosodic cue correlations that might help them to locate syntactic constituents under some circumstances. Is there any evidence that infants treat prosodically marked syntactic constituents as units? One study addressed this question by asking if 6-month-old infants are better able to remember sets of words that occur together within a single clause than the same words that occur in sequence but not within the same clause (Soderstrom, Nelson, & Jusczyk, 2005). Using the HPP, they familiarized infants with one of two passages, one that contained the clause *Rabbits eat leafy vegetables*, and the other that contained *Leafy vegetables taste so good*. The design of the study is shown in Table 7–1. Note that the passage that contained *Rabbits eat leafy vegetables* also contains the words *leafy vegetables taste so good*, but straddling a clause boundary. The same is true of the other passage. Thus, the researchers wanted to know two things: (1) do infants better remember information contained within a single clause? and (2) do infants better remember strings of

Table 7–1. Design of Experiment by Soderstrom et al. (2005). Infants were familiarized with only one target clause, but were tested on all four test passages.

Target Clause	Rabbits eat leafy vegetables.	Leafy vegetables taste so good.
Familiarization	Many animals prefer green things. *Rabbits eat leafy vegetables.* Taste so good is rarely encountered.	John doesn't know what rabbits eat. *Leafy vegetables taste so good.* They don't cost much either.
Same clause test	Squirrels often feed on acorns. *Rabbits eat leafy vegetables.* Their favorites are not the same.	Children need to have healthy foods. *Leafy vegetables taste so good.* Salad is best with dressing.
Clause-straddling test	Students like to watch how *rabbits eat. Leafy vegetables* make them chew. They finish the whole bunch.	Mothers sometimes do the shopping. They must buy *leafy vegetables. Taste so good* helps their families.

words when the prosody is the same from familiarization to test? At test, infants heard all four passages shown in Table 7–1. The results are displayed in Figure 7–1. The largest effect was that infants listened longest to test passages that contained the same clause they had heard during familiarization (the two white bars are taller than the two dark bars). However, there was also some hint that maintaining the same prosody between familiarization and test was beneficial for memory, regardless of whether the words were contained in the same clause or straddled a clause (the two left bars are taller than the two right bars). These data suggest that infants remember both words and prosody and, importantly, best remember sets of words that form a prosodic unit. Because many prosodic units are also syntactic constituents, we tentatively conclude that infants best remember sets of words that form syntactic constituents.

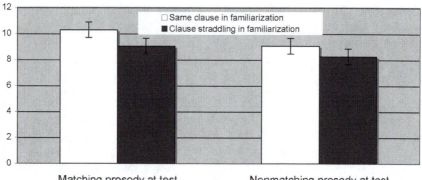

Figure 7-1. Data from Soderstrom et al. (2005) demonstrating that infants best remember information contained within a single clause.

■ Syntactic Categories

As discussed in the overview of morphosyntax in Chapter 6, sentences are composed of constituents of different types. These types include lexical categories like determiner, auxiliary verb, noun, and verb, as well as phrasal categories like noun phrase (NP), verb phrase (VP), and prepositional phrase (PP). We also discussed in Chapter 6 that, although there is a correlation between what a word or phrase refers to and its syntactic category, that relation is imperfect. For example, *think* and *idea* are a verb and noun, respectively, but they seem to refer to similar events. The word for *lightning* in English is a noun, but it refers to an event. Indeed, the word referring to *lightning* in Hopi is used as a verb. Furthermore, as noted in Chapter 6, many words like *brush* can be used as either a noun or a verb, and determining what the word refers to in a particular sentence requires you to first determine the syntactic category. Therefore, we concluded in Chapter 6 that it is the distribution of sentence contexts in which a word or phrase occurs, and not what the word or phrase refers to, that allows learners to determine its syntactic category.

Below, we explore three questions concerning syntactic categories. First, is there any evidence that children have knowledge of syntactic categories? One way to demonstrate such knowledge would be for them to use words in adultlike ways. Second, is there any evidence that children can use distributional information to segregate words into categories? Third, are the categories that children might discover using distributional cues consistent with theories of language development that propose innate constraints specific to language?

Children's Early Utterances as Evidence for Syntactic Categories

When children first begin combining words, do they show evidence of using syntactic categories? What might constitute evidence that they do? One type of evidence would be that children use words in the correct syntactic contexts and that particular categories should appear in all of their forms. A list of criteria for several syntactic categories that was proposed by Virgina Valian (1986) is given in Table 7-2. In addition to these criteria, we might expect children to use particular words in all or most of the appropriate contexts. For example, if a child uses the word *dog* in a subject NP, does she also use *dog* in NP's in other structural positions, such as direct object, indirect object, or object of a preposition? Three studies published over a 20-year period have attempted to address these two criteria.

In the first study, Valian (1986) examined the early multiword productions of six children ranging in age from 2;0 to 2;5 (2 years, 0 months to 2 years, 5 months). The children had mean lengths of utterance (MLU's) ranging from 2.93 to 4.14 morphemes per utterance (instructions for calculating MLU are given in Table 7-3). She found that children showed evidence of all of the syntactic constituents given in Table 7-2. Typical errors were failure to include determiners (see Chapter 5) and failure to use the mass/count distinction appropriately (e.g., *I see a bears*). Valian concluded that children showed firm evidence of syntactic category usage by the time they had an MLU of three morphemes per utterance. She further suggests the children are born expecting to encounter a set of syntactic categories. That is, she takes children's apparently early use of syntactic categories to support innate linguistic constraints.

In contrast to Valian's conclusion, a number of researchers have suggested that children do not generalize their word use in a way consistent with having mature syntactic categories. Rather, they suggest that

Table 7–2. Distributional Criteria for Six Different Syntactic Constituents.

Determiner Must appear, if present in NP, pre-Adj or pre-Noun or pre-both. Must not stand alone as sole content of an utterance or phrase. Must not be sequenced (exceptions: certain quantifiers).
Adjective Must appear, if present in NP, post-Det, and pre-Noun. Can form acceptable but not grammatical utterance as sole content of utterance or phrase. Can be sequenced: repetitions of same Adj, or different Adjs. Can appear as predicate Adj.
Noun Singular/plural distinction (via restriction of Det to subclass). Count/mass distinction. N/ProN distinction. Single Det used with all N subclasses.
Noun Phrase Substitution by it for full NP. Appearance of all NP subtypes in all legal positions.
Preposition Takes NP objects but does not inflect for Tense. Must appear, if present, pre-Det, pre-Adj, pre-N, or pre-NP.
Prepositional Phrase Occurs after NP, Adj, or Adverb within a Verb Phrase. Occurs in construction with Ns or Verbs.

From Valian, V. V. (1986). Syntactic categories in the speech of young children. *Developmental Psychology, 22,* 562–579. Copyright 1986. American Psychological Association. Reprinted with permission.

children learn to use words in the ways that they have heard them used, and only very gradually broaden their usage to forms that they have not yet heard (Tomasello, 2000). Recall from Chapter 6 that this view is entailed by Associative Learning theories of language development.

Table 7-3. Instructions for Calculating MLU.

For each of the first 100 utterances that satisfy the following criteria, count the number of morphemes (e.g., *The dog* = 2, *My dogs* = 3, *Doggy* = 1). Add up the total number of morphemes over the 100 utterances and divide by 100 to get the mean. Miller and Chapman (Miller & Chapman, 1981) provide MLU norms by age.

Don't count as part of the 100 utterances:
- any utterance that contains even a single unintelligible word (e.g., *I want ? for dinner*)
- any utterance that contains a list of Individual letters of the alphabet (e.g., ABC's) and counting (one, two, three).

Don't count as a morpheme, even though the utterance can be included in the 100 utterances:
- repetitions within an utterance as the results of stuttering or false starts are not assigned morphemes, but the utterance itself can be used as one of the 100 utterances. For example, the utterance *my dad dad is big* should be assigned a morpheme count of 4 morphemes. The second production of *dad* isn't counted.
- fillers such as *um*, *well*, and *oh* are not counted as morphemes. For example, the utterance *Um, dog* should be assigned a morpheme count of 1.

Count as one morpheme:
- social words like *hi*, *yeah*, and *no*
- *thank you*
- proper names, compound words, and reduplications (e.g., *Spider Man*, *birthday*, *quack-quack*, *night-night*)
- single number words (*I have two dog* = 4 morphemes)
- all full auxiliaries (*is*, *have*, *can*, *must*, *would*)
- all inflections (possessive - 's), plural -s, third singular -s on verbs, regular past tense -ed, progressive -ing)
- irregular past tense morphemes (e.g., *got*, *did*, *went*, *saw*)
- indefinite pronouns (i.e., *anybody*, *anyone*, *somebody*, *someone*, *everybody*, *everyone*)

Count as two morphemes:
- negative contractions, contractions and catenatives (e.g., *can't*, *don't*, *won't*, *he's*, *that's*, *gonna*, *wanna*, *hafta*), but only where there is evidence within the transcript that the child uses one part of the contraction separately (e.g., *can*, *do*, *will*, *not*, *he*, *that*, *is*, *going*, *want*, *have*, *to*). If no evidence is available, count these as one morpheme.

Adapted from Brown, R. (1973). *A First Language*. Cambridge, MA: Harvard University Press. Reprinted with permission.

To determine if children use particular words in all/most of the possible syntactic contexts, Pine and Martindale (1996) examined the spontaneous speech of seven children with MLU's ranging for 2.20 to 3.31. They looked at the number of contexts in which children used *the* and *a* and found that they used these determiners in some contexts but not others. For example, in sentences containing verbs, children used determiners in direct objects, but not in subjects. Children also used *the* versus *a* in different contexts. Furthermore, the researchers found that children used determiners in significantly fewer contexts than their mothers did. They concluded that children showed evidence of using determiners in limited ways, rather than as a fully generalizable syntactic category.

Valian and colleagues (Valian, Solt, & Stewart, 2008) responded to Pine and Martindale by looking at the full range of determiners that children produce, not just *a* and *the*. Some additional determiners included in their examination were *this/that, these/those, another, one, two, some, more, many, all, my, your*, and *her*. They found that children used these determiners in the full range of possible contexts and that children used determiners in about as many overlapping contexts (e.g., *the juice* and *some juice*) as their mothers did. Importantly, they found that the number of overlapping contexts increased as children used a particular word multiple times. For example, there is obviously no overlap in the determiner contexts in which a noun like *juice* appears if a particular child is recorded saying that word only once. However, if the child is recorded saying *juice* six times, the chances to observe overlapping contexts increases, assuming that the child is able to combine *juice* with the full set of determiners. Valian and colleagues found that children used particular nouns with at least two different determiners at a rate of about 90% if the child produced that noun with a determiner six times. This finding suggests that we need to take into account not only the extent to which children appear to generalize, but also the number of opportunities we have to observe generalization in the language sample that we have collected.

Thought Question

How might you increase the number of opportunities you have to observe potential generalization in children's utterances?

Note that the debate about whether or not children's early utterances provide evidence for their knowledge of syntactic categories centers on whether children are conservative or whether they are willing to generalize beyond the input that they have been given. It is difficult to be sure of the specific input that children have encountered and, therefore, how conservative they are. One way to address this question is to create a language-learning situation in the laboratory and ask if children are willing to generalize beyond the input that we *know* they have been given. Two such studies are described below.

Children's Use of Distributional Cues to Discover Syntactic Categories

Imagine that you didn't know English, and you noticed the pattern of word use shown in Table 7–4. What kind of information might you get from such a pattern? One possibility is that you could create two groups of words: those that co-occur with *the* and *a* (gray cells) and those that co-occur with *can* and *is* _____*ing* (white cells). In addition, you could probably determine that *a ball* and *is tickling* are possible phrases in the language, even though these phases are not part of the input.

Thought Question

What might you conclude if you heard the phrases *the paint* and *can paint*? How might your conclusion be a problem for distributional cues for syntactic categories?

Table 7–4. Illustration of Some Distributional Cues for Nouns and Verbs in English

the dog	the tree	the cat	the kiss	the shoe	the ball
a dog	a tree	a cat	a kiss	a shoe	**???**
can chase	can catch	can eat	can throw	can wash	can tickle
is chasing	is catching	is eating	is throwing	is washing	**???**

One study used the HPP to ask whether young language learners can extract such information from linguistic patterns. The researchers exposed 17-month-old American children to a pattern like that in Table 7-4, but the pattern involved Russian masculine and feminine nouns, which occur with different case endings (Gerken, Wilson, & Lewis, 2005). The stimuli that were used are shown in Table 7-5. Children were familiarized for two minutes with the non-bolded words in Table 7-5. Note that if children were able to detect that the case endings *u* and *oj* occurred on one set of words and *ya* and *yem* occurred on another set, they might be able to predict the withheld bolded words. An ability to predict the bolded words in Table 7-5 is the equivalent of predicting that *a ball* and *is tickling* are possible phrases of English from the input in Table 7-4.

During test, children heard on separate trials the grammatical bolded words and ungrammatical words created by combining masculine nouns with feminine case endings and vice versa. Children were able to discriminate the grammatical from ungrammatical items, suggesting that they had discerned the pattern. In contrast to the 17-month-olds, 12-month-olds showed no evidence of learning the Russian gender pattern shown in Table 7-5, suggesting that the ability to track distributional cues and group words into syntactic categories is one that somehow unfolds over development (but see the study by Saffran et al, 2008, below).

Other researchers have investigated children's sensitivity to morphosyntactic distributions in their native language (Höhle, Weissen-

Table 7–5. Russian Feminine and Masculine Nouns, Each with Two Case Endings

Feminine Nouns					
polkoj	rubashkoj	ruchkoj	**vannoj**	knigoj	korovoj
polku	rubashku	ruchku	vannu	knigu	**korovu**
Masculine Nouns					
uchitel'ya	stroitel'ya	zhitel'ya	**medved'ya**	korn'ya	pisar'ya
uchitel'yem	stroitel'yem	zhitel'yem	medved'yem	korn'yem	**pisar'yem**

Note: Bolded words were withheld during familiarization and comprised the grammatical test items. An apostrophe after a consonant indicates that the consonant is palatalized in Russian. Ungrammatical words were *vannya, korovyem, medevedoj, pisaru.*

born, Kiefer, Schulz, & Schmitz, 2004). Researchers used the HPP to familiarize 14- to 16-month-old German learners with two nonsense words in either a noun context (preceded by a determiner) or a verb context (preceded by a pronoun). Some sample stimuli are shown in Table 7-6. During test, children heard passages in which the new words were used as nouns or verbs. Children who were familiarized with phrases in which the novel word was used as a noun listened longer to test passages in which it was used as a verb (a novelty preference). These results suggest that children track the morphosyntactic contexts that occur with particular nouns. When they hear a new word in a noun context, they expect that the new word will also appear in other noun contexts.

Are Syntactic Categories Innate?

The sections above suggest that children in the second and third years of life treat syntactic constituents as though they can be segregated into different groups that appear to correspond roughly to adult syntactic categories. However, as noted in Chapter 6, it is important to realize that these groups of words are not necessarily identical to the syntactic categories that are proposed by Triggering and Linguistic Hypothesis Testing theories of language development. Distributionally cued groups are entities like "words that can occur after *the* and *a.*" Recall from Chapter 6 that proposed innate linguistic constraints (see Table 6-1) assume that children are able to label words and phrases

Table 7–6. Sample Familiarization Phrases and Test Passages Used by Hohle et al. (2004)

	Noun Context	*Verb Context*
Familiarization phrases	Ein Glamm (A glamm)	Sie glamm (She glamms)
Test passages	Das Glamm lag schon lange unter dem alten Bett. *(The glamm laid already long under the old bed.)*	Der Junge glamm immer auf dem Weg zur Schule. *(The boy glammed always on his way to school.)*

with syntactic categories like "noun," "adjective," "noun phrase," and so forth. Even if the word groups identified by distributional cues are perfectly aligned with these syntactic categories, the groups would not be labeled. How might children attach an innate label like "noun" to distributionally cued categories?

The dominant answer to that question since the early 1980s has been the **Semantic Bootstrapping** hypothesis (Grimshaw, 1981; Pinker, 1984). In this view, children are born with innate linking rules that say something like "words for objects are nouns," "words for actions are verbs," and so forth. Children apply this rule to the first words that they learn, thereby both separating words of different types from each other and labeling the types with the assumed innate labels. However, as already discussed, reference is not sufficient to divide words like *idea* or *think* into categories. Therefore, in the Semantic Bootstrapping proposal, children move on to a second stage of learning syntactic categories in which they notice that many of the words that fall into the "noun" category also share other properties, such as being preceded by *the* or *a* and occurring in particular locations with respect to words that fall into the "verb" category. Therefore, after children use what words refer to (hence, the "semantic" in "Semantic Bootstrapping") to get them started, they switch to using distributional cues to assign the rest of the syntactic constituents they encounter to syntactic categories.

What is the evidence for Semantic Bootstrapping? One type of evidence might be that children correctly use words that can be categorized via reference earlier than words that do not fit the innate linking rules. For example, *ball* refers to an object, whereas *idea* does not. Is there any evidence that children know the syntactic category of words like *ball* before words like *idea*? Contrary to Semantic Bootstrapping, the data suggest that as soon as children produce a particular word, they appear to use it in the correct syntactic contexts (Maratsos, 1982). A second type of evidence for Semantic Bootstrapping might be that children do not appear to use distributional cues to learn categories until about 14 months (Höhle et al., 2004), or perhaps 12 months (Saffran et al., 2008) (see discussion below). Recall from Chapter 5 that children begin associating words like *mommy* and *daddy* with the appropriate referent by age 6 months and producing first words by about 1 year. Perhaps children need to learn the referents for a few words and categorize these using Semantic Bootstrapping before they can use distributional cues for syntactic categorization. So far, no researcher has looked for this type of evidence for the Semantic Bootstrapping hypothesis. In short, although there is good evidence that children are able to sort words from the input into different groups, there is no evidence as to whether these groups are consistent with the innate categories proposed by Triggering and Linguistic Hypothesis Testing theories.

Thought Question

How might you go about testing the hypothesis that children must learn the meaning of a few words of a language before using distributional cues for syntactic categorization?

■ Word Order

Recall from Chapter 6 that word order is an important cue to structural position (e.g., subject, direct object, etc.) and ultimately to "who did what to whom" in languages like English. We discuss whether young learners can use word order to interpret sentences in Chapter 8. We start, however, by asking whether children are sensitive to word order without regard to meaning. As with the development of syntactic categories, we can ask whether children show sensitivity to word order in their early productions as well as in perception.

Word Order in Child Production

To some extent, we have already established that children learning English demonstrate sensitivity to word order in their early utterances because all of the tests of syntactic categories are also tests of word order. For example, one test of determiners is that they precede nouns. In virtually none of the tests of syntactic categories did children appear to produce two words in the wrong order. However, there are at least two types of frequent word order errors in young children's productions. One of these errors in word order probably actually reflects **omissions**. For example, English-speaking children often fail to produce **copular verbs** (e.g., *is*, *are*, etc.), which can lead to productions like the first two child utterances in Table 7-7. There is some

Table 7–7. Some Word Order Errors by Young Children Involving Omission and Co-mission.

Child Form	Likely Adult Form	Error Type
That bear big	That bear is big	copula omission
What he doing?	What is he doing?	copula omission
Why he can go?	Why can he go?	failure to invert subject and auxiliary verb
What can he can do?	What can he do?	duplicate auxiliary verb

debate about whether omission errors reflect a mismatch between the child's grammar and the grammar of her community (Becker, 2004), or whether such errors simply reflect the child's immature ability to plan and produce strings of words as long as those produced by adults (e.g., Gerken, 1996). Perhaps an even greater mystery surrounds children's errors of **co-mission**, instances in which children produce words in the wrong order or insert an extra word, which can be seen in the second two child utterances of Table 7-7. Note that these errors are particularly likely in questions. Like errors of omission, these word order errors of co-mission have been given different interpretations by researchers from different theoretical perspectives (Rowland, 2007; Santelmann, Berk, Austin, Somashekar, & Lust, 2002). A discussion of the particular hypotheses researchers have created to account for children's word order errors would take us too far away from our question—are children sensitive to word order? However, it is important to note that children do make some errors in word order production, suggesting that, insofar as they are sensitive to word order, they are not simply memorizing the word orders in their input. Rather, they are making generalizations based on the entire pattern of utterances in their input.

Word Order in Infant Perception

As in the studies of infants' sensitivity to the order of segments in a syllable (Chapter 3), the first studies examining infants' sensitivity to word order began with the language the infant was already learning.

Shady, Gerken, and Jusczyk (1995) used the HPP and presented 10.5-month-olds with normal English sentences as well as sentences in which determiners and nouns were reversed, resulting in phrases like *kitten the*. The stimuli were recorded using a speech synthesizer to avoid disruptions in prosody that are likely to occur when a human talker produces ungrammatical sentences. Infants listened longer to sentences with normal word order, suggesting that they were able to tell the difference between the two types of stimuli. Because it is unlikely that infants of the age tested were able to understand the sentences and base their judgment of good versus bad word order on meaning, what information did they use? The answer is that many of the reversed word order sentences contained two function morphemes in sequence (e.g., *a that*). Such sequences are virtually non-existent in English, and infants were probably responding to this and similar aspects of the stimuli. Nevertheless, this study suggests that infants were able to keep track of the frequent word order patterns in their language many months before they begin combining words themselves.

Other evidence that children attend to word order can be seen in studies where one word in a sequence predicts another. Santelmann and Jusczyk (1998) used the HPP and presented 18-month-olds with passages that contained sentences with verbs ending in the inflection *-ing*. The sentences were either grammatical, such that the VP began with the auxiliary verb *is* (e.g., *Grandma is singing*) or ungrammatical, such that the VP began with the auxiliary verb *can* (e.g., *Grandma can singing*). In English, *is* but not *can* predicts the subsequent appearance of *-ing*. Children listened longer to the grammatical sentences demonstrating that they were sensitive to the English **nonadjacent dependency** between *is* and *-ing*.

In a similar study that looked at children's ability to learn new non-adjacent dependencies between words, Rebecca Gómez (2002) familiarized 18-month-olds with an artificial language in which sentences had the form AXB and CXD. That is, A words predicted B words and C words predicted D words (like *is* predicted *-ing* in the study using English). She found that when there was a large number of X words (24 of them), children were able to ignore the word that occurred in the X position and learn the A_B and C_D order.

Studies with younger learners demonstrate that they are able to rapidly learn the order of adjacent words in an artificial language. In one such study, Gómez and Gerken (1999) presented 12-month-olds with a subset of strings produced by one of two artificial languages.

The two languages began and ended in the same CVC nonsense words, with the only difference being the sentence-internal sequences of words allowed. Half of the infants were familiarized with sentences from Grammar 1 and half with sentences from Grammar 2. For example, *vot pel* was a legal sequence in sentences of Grammar 1, but not Grammar 2. During test, both groups of infants heard new sentences from the two grammars. Infants familiarized with Grammar 1 listened longer to Grammar 1 test sentences, and infants familiarized with Grammar 2 listened longer to Grammar 2 test sentences (a familiarity preference). This study showed that infants rapidly learned about the orders of adjacent words in their familiarization language and applied this knowledge to new sentences during test.

Phrase Order in Infant Perception

So far, we have been talking about syntactic categories and word order separately. However, recall from Chapter 6 that real sentences are made up of ordered *phrases* (see Table 6-1). Can human infants also learn an artificial language that uses phrase structure rules, in which utterances in the language are made up of ordered phrases that are in turn made up of lexical categories? One study that asked this question took the interesting approach of comparing human 12-month-olds' ability to learn such an artificial language with the ability of cotton-top tamarins (Saffran et al., 2008). Infants and tamarins learned one of two kinds of languages. The rules of one language just entailed the correct ordering of words, as in the Gómez and Gerken (1999) experiment described above. The other language entailed learning that words belonged to categories and that the categories were ordered with respect to each other. That is, the second language used phrase structure rules. Table 7-8 shows the rules of the phrase structure language, words in each lexical category, sample familiarization stimuli, and the grammatical and ungrammatical test sentences.

Infants were tested using the HPP. Tamarins were tested using the following procedure: The evening before testing, the tamarins were presented with the familiarization (either word-order or phrase-order) language for two hours in their enclosure. The next day, each animal heard 2 minutes of refamiliarization followed immediately by testing in which grammatical and ungrammatical test stimuli were played from a concealed loudspeaker on different trials.

Table 7–8. Rules and Words Used in Artificial Language Learning Experiment with 12-month-old human infants and cotton-top tamarins by Saffran et al. (2008)

Phrase structure rules	Words used in phrase structure rules
S → AP + BP + (CP) AP → A + (D) BP → CP + F CP → C + (G)	A words: *biff hep mib rud* C words: *cav lum neb sig* D words: *klor pell* F words: *dupp loke jux vot* G words: *tiz pilk*

Sample familiarization stimuli	
rud pell cav pilk dupp[1] *hep klor neb tiz loke*[2] *mib klor sig jux*[3] *rud pell neb pilk dupp*[4] *hep pell neb loke* *rud pell cav vot* *hep lum pilk loke* *rud sig pilk vot* *mib lum tiz loke* *biff cav pilk jux* *rud pell neb pilk dupp* *biff sig dupp cav* *hep cav loke neb*	*hep sig loke neb* *mib klor cav vot sig* *rud pell lum loke neb* *hep klor sig dupp lum* *biff pell neb jux cav* *hep lum pilk vot sig* *mib sig pilk dupp cav* *rud neb tiz loke lum* *biff neb jux lum tiz* *hep cav loke neb pilk* *mib sig dupp cav pilk* *mib neb tiz jux* *rud cav jux lum*

Sample grammatical test sentences for phrase structure rules	Sample ungrammatical test sentences for phrase structure rules
hep pell cav pilk dupp[1] *hep klor cav tiz vot*[2] *mib klor cav jux*[3] *rud pell neb pilk loke*[4]	*hep pilk cav pell dupp* *rud pilk lum klor vot* *hep klor cav tiz* *biff pilk lum klor jux*

For a real language equivalent to the rules, see Table 6–1. Note that phrasal constituents in parentheses are optional. Superscripts show close matches between familiarization and grammatical test items.

Animals were scored as responding to the test stimulus if they turned to look toward the speaker either during the presentation of the test stimulus or within 2 seconds afterward. The results showed that, although both infants and tamarins were able to learn the word-order language, only infants were able to learn the phrase-order language.

These results are very interesting, because they suggest that human infants are capable of learning a complex languagelike pattern that is not as easily learnable by cotton-top tamarins. However, the study is inconsistent with the results of Gerken et al. (2005), who found that 12-month-olds were unable to use distributional cues to learn Russian gender categories. Furthermore, it is possible that infants in the Saffran et al. (2008) study were using word order as a cue even in the phrase structure language, because no test sentence was made up of a sequence of words that was entirely different from sequences heard during familiarization. For example, all four grammatical test sentences share at least three syllables in the correct sentence positions with a familiarization sentence, whereas none of the ungrammatical test items have as great an overlap (see superscripts in Table 7–8). Therefore, infants could distinguish grammatical from ungrammatical test items and never treat *biff* and *hep* or *cav* and *lum* as members of two different categories. Interpreting the results from the phrase structure language in this way suggests that infants and tamarins might differ in the overall complexity of information that they can process. The results do not necessarily suggest that human infants have a set of linguistic constraints that guide their generalizations. Nevertheless, research comparing human abilities to learn languagelike systems with those of nonhuman animals potentially is very helpful in identifying possible learning mechanisms and their biological underpinnings. We discuss another such study in Chapter 8.

■ Summary

Chapter 7 presented some of the available data on three aspects of morphosyntactic development that apply to sentence form without respect to sentence meaning: (1) syntactic constituents, (2) syntactic categories, and (3) structural positions as they are reflected in word and phrase order. With respect to syntactic constituents, there is good evidence that language learners can use prosody to divide the streams of words that they hear into smaller chunks that largely correspond to syntactic constituents. There is also growing evidence suggesting that words contained within a prosodic unit are better remembered.

With respect to syntactic categories, there is still some debate about whether very young children form such categories and whether any categories that they do form are as abstract and widely generalizable as syntactic categories proposed for adult language. Data from children in their second year suggest that they are able to form very simple categories based on distributional information. A largely unanswered question at this point is whether or not learners have innate categories that they expect to encounter, and if they do, how they might link these innate categories with the words and phrases they encounter in their input.

Word order is a cue to structural positions such as sentence subject, direct object, and so forth in languages like English that do not use morphologic cues (i.e., case morphemes). In English, children generally appear to produce consistent word orders, and these orders appear to mirror ones that occur in the input language. However, there are notable exceptions, especially in children's question formation, suggesting that sensitivity to word order may interact in complex ways with other types of information in the child's input. Sensitivity to word order is also quite clear in studies with infants, as shown by studies of infants listening to their own language as well as learning new languages in the laboratory. In these situations, infants appear to be able to detect the order of both adjacent and nonadjacent words. Finally, we considered whether infants can learn the order of phrases, which are themselves made up of lexical categories. One study suggests that they can, while a nonhuman species cannot. Given the potential importance of this work, further research is needed to replicate and elaborate on the findings.

The studies reported in Chapter 7 pave the way to ask what many researchers would take to be the ultimate question: How do language learners come to express and understand meaningful sentences that they have never heard before? We address these questions in Chapter 8.

■ References

Becker, M. (2004). Copula omission is a grammatical reflex. *Language Acquisition: A Journal of Developmental Linguistics, 12*(2), 157–167.

Brown, R. (1973). *A first language*. Cambridge, MA: Harvard University Press.

Cooper, R. P. (1993). The effect of prosody on young infants' speech perception. *Advances in Infancy Research, 8,* 137-167.

Cooper, W., & Paccia-Cooper, J. (1980). *Syntax and speech.* Cambridge, MA: Harvard University Press.

Fernald, A., & Kuhl, P. K. (1987). Acoustic determinants of infant preference for motherese speech. *Infant Behavior and Development, 10,* 279-293.

Gerken, L. A. (1996). Prosodic structure in young children's language production. *Language, 72,* 683-712.

Gerken, L. A., Jusczyk, P. W., & Mandel, D. R. (1994). When prosody fails to cue syntactic structure: Nine-month-olds' sensitivity to phonological versus syntactic phrases. *Cognition, 51*(3), 237-265.

Gerken, L. A., Wilson, R., & Lewis, W. (2005). Seventeen-month-olds can use distributional cues to form syntactic categories. *Journal of Child Language, 32,* 249-268.

Gómez, R. L. (2002). Variability and detection of invariant structure. *Psychological Science, 13*(5), 431-436.

Gómez, R. L., & Gerken, L. A. (1999). Artificial grammar learning by 1-year-olds leads to specific and abstract knowledge. *Cognition, 70*(2), 109-135.

Grimshaw, J. (1981). Form, function, and the language acquisition device. In C. L. Baker & J. J. McCarthy (Eds.), *The logical problem of language acquisition.* Cambridge, MA: MIT Press.

Gussenhoven, C. (2004). *The phonology of tone and intonation.* Cambridge: Cambridge University Press.

Hirsh-Pasek, K., Kemler Nelson, D., Jusczyk, P. W., Wright Cassidy, K., Druss, B., & Kennedy, L. (1987). Clauses are perceptual units for prelinguistic infants. *Cognition, 26,* 269-286.

Höhle, B., Weissenborn, J., Kiefer, D., Schulz, A., & Schmitz, M. (2004). Functional elements in infants' speech processing: The role of determiners in segmentation and categorization of lexical elements. *Infancy, 5*(3), 341-353.

Jusczyk, P. W., Hirsh-Pasek, K., Kemler Nelson, D. G., Kennedy, L. J., Woodward, A., & Piwoz, J. (1992). Perception of acoustic correlates of major phrasal units by young infants. *Cognitive Psychology, 24*(2), 252-293.

Jusczyk, P. W., & Kemler Nelson, D. (1996). Syntactic units, prosody, and psychological reality during infancy. In J. Morgan & K. Demuth (Eds.), *Signal to syntax: Bootstrapping from speech to grammar in early acquisition* (pp. 389-410). Cambridge, MA: MIT Press.

Krumhansl, C. L., & Jusczyk, P. W. (1990). Infants' perception of phrase structure in music. *Psychological Science, 1*(1), 70-73.

Maratsos, M. (1982). The child's construction of grammatical categories. In E. Wanner & L. Gleitman (Eds.), *Language acquisition: The state of the art.* Cambridge: Cambridge University Press.

Miller, J. F., & Chapman, R. S. (1981). The relation between age and mean length of utterance in morphemes. *Journal of Speech and Hearing Research, 24*(2), 154-161.

Nespor, M., & Vogel, I. (1986). *Prosodic phonology*. Dordrecht: Foris.

Pine, J. M., & Martindale, H. (1996). Syntactic categories in the speech of young children: The case of the determiner. *Journal of Child Language, 23*, 369-395.

Pinker, S. (1984). *Language learnability and language development*. Cambridge, MA: Harvard University Press.

Rowland, C. F. (2007). Explaining errors in children's questions. *Cognition, 104*(1), 106-134.

Saffran, J. R., Hauser, M., Seibel, R., Kapfhamer, J., Tsao, F., & Cushman, F. (2008). Grammatical pattern learning by human infants and cotton-top tamarin monkeys. *Cognition, 107*, 479-500.

Santelmann, L. M., Berk, S., Austin, J., Somashekar, S., & Lust, B. (2002). Continuity and development in the acquisition of inversion in yes/no questions: Dissociating movement and inflection. *Journal of Child Language, 29*, 813-842.

Santelmann, L. M., & Jusczyk, P. W. (1998). Sensitivity to discontinuous dependencies in language learners: Evidence for limitations in processing space. *Cognition, 69*(2), 105-134.

Shady, M. E., Gerken, L. A., & Jusczyk, P. W. (1995). Some evidence of sensitivity to prosody and word order in ten-month-olds. In D. MacLaughlin & S. McEwan (Eds.), *Proceedings of the 19th Boston University Conference on Language Development* (Vol. 2). Sommerville, MA: Cascadilla Press.

Soderstrom, M., Nelson, D. G. K., & Jusczyk, P. W. (2005). Six-month-olds recognize clauses embedded in different passages of fluent speech. *Infant Behavior and Development, 28*(1), 87-94.

Tomasello, M. (2000). First steps toward a usage-based theory of language acquisition. *Cognitive Linguistics Special Issue: Language Acquisition, 11*(1-2), 61-82.

Valian, V. V. (1986). Syntactic categories in the speech of young children. *Developmental Psychology, 22*, 562-579.

Valian, V. V., Solt, S., & Stewart, J. (2008). Abstract categories or limited-scope formulae? The case of children's determiners. *Journal of Child Language, 35*, 1-36.

Zangl, R., & Mills, D. L. (2007). Increased brain activity to infant-directed speech in 6-and 13-month-old infants. *Infancy, 11*(1), 31-62.

8 Assigning Meaning to Sentence Forms and Four Debates About Morphosyntactic Development

As noted in Chapter 6, Chapter 8 presents data on how infants and children use sentence form to assign meaning. It also presents illustrations of four debates in the study of morphosyntactic development. The first section focuses on how children assign thematic roles, such as agent, theme, and so forth to the structural positions subject, direct object, and so forth, and asks about children's use of word order, sentence type, morphologic case marking, and particular verbs in the assignment of thematic roles. With Chapter 7, this discussion provides a basic look at the development of morphosyntax, which, as noted in Chapter 6, is the area of language development that sparks the most theoretical controversy. The flavor of this controversy is presented as four ongoing debates. First we ask how far children generalize beyond their input in using verbs to express meaning. As noted in Chapter 6, this debate pits Associative Learning theories against the other three theories discussed in Chapter 1. Then we ask whether Associative Learning models can account for morphosyntactic generalization. This debate also pits Associative Learning theories against the other three. Next, we ask whether children make generalizations that are not supported by the input. This debate pits Triggering and Linguistic Hypothesis Testing theories against General Purpose Hypothesis Testing and Associative Learning. And, finally, we ask if children's morphosyntactic errors reflect possible human grammars. This debate also pits Triggering and Linguistic Hypothesis Testing theories against the other two.

■ Assigning Thematic Roles

Recall that thematic roles, such as agent, theme, and so forth, indicate the role of an NP in sentence interpretation (deciding who did what to whom). When do learners begin to correctly interpret sentences, indicating that they are able to assign thematic roles? What information do they use? The information that figures most heavily in fixed word order languages like English is word order, which is explored below. In addition to word order, at least three factors determine the correct assignment of thematic roles to structural positions. One of these is sentence type. The subject of active sentences is often the agent, but the subject of passive sentences like, *The dog was chased by the cat* is usually the theme. Following the discussion of word order, we discuss how children distinguish different sentence types. Another factor influencing thematic role assignment is case marking. Recall from Chapter 6 that many languages indicate case, which determines thematic role, on NP's, eliminating the need to mark the same information with word order. We next discuss what children know about case marking. Finally, the particular verb used in the sentence influences thematic role assignment. For example, in the active form, the subject of verbs like *push* is an agent, whereas the subject of verbs like *saw* is an experiencer, and we discuss how children learn about particular verbs.

Using Word Order to Assign Thematic Roles

We saw in Chapter 7 that children are very sensitive to the order of words in sentences, as evidenced both by production and perception data. But are they able to use word order to mark meaning relations? Three studies suggest that children are able to use word order to assign thematic roles in active sentences, and particularly transitives (e.g., *The dog chased the cat*) from an early age. In the publication that introduced the field of language development to the Intermodal Preferential Looking procedure (IPLP), researchers asked whether young children show evidence of using word order to understand sentences (Golinkoff, Hirsh-Pasek, Cauley, & Gordon, 1987). Note that the children in this study were 28-month-olds, and at least some of them may have been marking thematic roles with word order in their own productions. The children were seated in front of two video displays showing different scenes. Between the displays was a speaker that played auditory stimuli and a camera that recorded the infant's face. For example, one scene might be of Big Bird tickling Cookie Monster, and the other might be of Cookie Monster tickling Big Bird. From the speaker might come sentences like *Big Bird is tickling Cookie Monster. Where? Big Bird is tickling Cookie Monster.* The measure of interest was how long infants looked at the display that matched the sentence versus the nonmatching display. If infants did not use word order to determine meaning, they should have looked equally long at each display because both characters and the act of tickling were depicted in both. However, the researchers found that children looked reliably longer at the matching display, suggesting that they can use word order information to determine who the agent of an action is.

Another study asked whether young children could use word order to interpret the meaning of *new* verbs in sentences with different word orders (Naigles, 1990). The study began with two groups of 25-month-olds being presented with a video of a duck pushing a rabbit up and down, while both did arm circles (Table 8-1). Half of the children (Transitive Group) heard the sentence *The duck is gorping the bunny*, while the other half (Intransitive Group) heard *The duck and the bunny are gorping.* Notice that there is no direct object after the verb in the latter sentence. Naigles then tested the children to determine what meaning they had assigned to the nonsense verb *gorping*. Children from both groups heard the neutral question, *Where's gorping?* while being presented with two videos, one with only the duck pushing the rabbit up and down and the other with only the animals doing arm circles. If children were able to use the arrangements of words in the two familiarization sentences to infer the meaning of *gorping*, children in the Transitive Group should think that *gorping* means *to push up and down*. In contrast, children in the Intransitive Group should think that *gorping* means *to do arm circles*. Naigles found that, as predicted, children in the Transitive Group looked longer at the video of the duck pushing the rabbit up and down than at the other video. Children in the Intransitive Group looked longer at the two animals circling their arms.

Fisher (2002a) was also interested in whether young children could use the word order cues to thematic role in verb learning. (This study was also discussed with respect to syntactic cues to word

Table 8–1. Schematic of Experiment.

Training	Transitive Group		Intransitive Group	
	Sees	Hears	Sees	Hears
	A duck pushes a rabbit up and down, while both do arm circles.	The duck is gorping the bunny.	A duck pushes a rabbit up and down, while both do arm circles.	The duck and the bunny are gorping.
Test	**Transitive Group**		**Intransitive Group**	
	Sees	Hears	Sees	Hears
	A duck pushes a rabbit up and down.	Where's gorping?	A duck pushes a rabbit up and down.	Where's gorping?
	A duck and a rabbit do arm circles.		A duck and a rabbit do arm circles.	

From: Naigles, L. R. (1990). Children use syntax to learn verb meanings. *Journal of Child Language, 17, 357–374.* Copyright 1990 Cambridge University Press. Reprinted with permission.

meaning in Chapter 5.) To ensure that children in previous studies could not use any information about the specific nouns in the sentence (e.g., *duck* or *bunny*) as clues, Fisher used pronouns, resulting in transitive sentences like, *She pilks her back and forth* and intransitive sentences like, *She pilks back and forth.* A possible scene might be one in which Participant A pulls Participant B along the floor by Participant B's backpack. At test, the video was frozen on a still frame, and the experimenter asked, *Which one pilked the other one? Point!* or *Which one pilked? Point!* Both 30- and 40-month-olds, as well as adults, were more likely to point to the agent when they had heard the verb in a transitive sentence. For example, adults who heard, *She pilks her back and forth* chose the agent 100% of the time, but they chose the agent only 31% of the time when they heard, *She pilks back and forth.* The reason for this asymmetry is that a transitive verb makes it clear what role each noun (or pronoun) is playing, whereas an intransitive verb used to describe a scene with two possible actors does not definitively indicate which actor is being described.

Thought Question

Naigles (1990) found that children interpreted the subject as the agent for both transitive and intransitive sentences, whereas Fisher (2002 a) found that they only interpreted the subject as agent for transitive sentences. What factor(s) might have led to the differences in findings in these two studies?

These three studies indicate that, by the third year of life, children are able to assign the thematic role 'agent' to the first noun of an active transitive sentence. Can children use information other than word order to assign thematic roles? We examine this question below.

Using Sentence Type to Assign Thematic Roles

Recall from Chapter 6 that the first NP in a sentence is not always the agent. For example, in passive sentences like 8a and 8b, below, the first noun is typically the theme. Thus, word order is not always a good cue to the thematic role of a NP. How do you know that *the milk* and *the dog* are the themes of 8a and 8b, respectively? In 8a, you might rely on who the likely agent is—*milk* is an unlikely agent of the act of spilling. But that approach won't help you in 8b—dogs are at least as likely to chase cats as cats are to chase dogs. Whether you realize it consciously or not, you use the morphology of the sentences to indicate that 8a and 8b are not active sentences. That is, you use the morphemes *was, -ed,* and *by,* combined with word order, to tell you who did what to whom. When do language learners determine that sentence type (e.g., active, passive, etc.) is an important factor to consider when assigning thematic roles?

8a. The milk was spilled by the cat.
8b. The dog was chased by the cat.

The first studies to ask this question of young children were reported by Bever (1970) and Maratsos (1974). These researchers used the **Act-Out** procedure to determine how 2- to 5-year-olds interpreted reversible active and passive sentences. Reversible sentences are ones like 8b and its active counterpart, in which either NP could logically perform the action. Children generally showed an increase over age in the number of passives they acted out correctly (Figure 8-1). However, many children showed a brief drop in their performance just before age 4 years. Bever interpreted this drop in performance to indicate that children at the end of their 3rd year were overusing word order as a cue to thematic role assignment, perhaps due to the high frequency of sentences in which the subject is indeed the agent. That is, they briefly overgeneralized their use of a "first noun = agent" strategy to passives, where such an approach consistently yields an incorrect interpretation. Finally, they began to use morphological information to distinguish actives from passives, which allowed them to assign the proper thematic roles to the NP's in passive sentences. We will see several other examples in this chapter of children apparently becoming worse and then better in their linguistic abilities.

Using Morphological Case Markers to Assign Thematic Roles

As noted in Chapter 6, English makes little use of case marking as compared with many languages. In this section, we describe how children acquire more richly case-marked languages like Polish and Turkish. We discussed in Chapter 7 that even infants are highly sensitive to

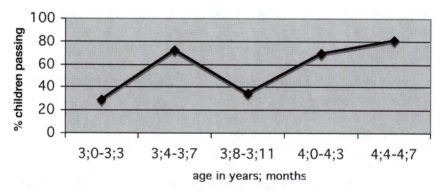

Figure 8–1. Data from Maratsos (1974) Table 1. Passing was defined as acting out two or three out of three passive sentences correctly. Note the dip in performance occurring at 3;8 to 3;11.

the order in which words typically occur. In this chapter, we have seen that 2-year-olds are able to use word order to determine the thematic roles of novel verbs. Does young learners' relative sensitivity to word order mean that languages relying primarily on case marking are more difficult to learn than languages relying primarily on word order? We can address that question by determining when children learning a richly case-marked language are able to use case to assign thematic roles.

One language that has a much richer case marking system than English is Polish. Weist (1983) used the Act-Out procedure to test comprehension of reversible sentences by 2- and 3-year-old children learning Polish. For example, children might hear sentences like those in 8c and 8d, which are the Polish equivalents of two Russian sentences that you saw in Chapter 6. Note that the first noun is the agent (nominative case) in 8c, whereas the second noun is the agent in 8d. Children attended to the case marking, treating nouns marked with a nominative case as the agent for a large majority of sentences. In a similar study, Slobin and Bever (1982) found that children learning Turkish, another richly case marked language, also used case marking to interpret sentences, even before the age of 2 years. An important observation made by Slobin and Bever (1982) is that the rate at which children learn to use word order and/or case marking as cues to thematic roles depends on the regularity of that cue in their language. In Turkish, word order plays almost no role, and case marking is very regular. In contrast, Serbo-Croatian has a more complex case marking system, such that the same form can be used to mark more than one case. Because of the ambiguity that such a system can introduce, case marking is backed up with word order information, with the agent appearing before the theme. Young children learning Serbo-Croation performed less well on a sentence comprehension task than children learning Turkish, suggesting that understanding the relative contribution to thematic role assignment of two cues is harder than using just one. The notion that each language offers a set of sometimes competing cues to thematic roles, including animacy, word order, and case marking, and the likelihood of particular verbs being used in particular sentence types has been fruitfully explored by a number of researchers, both with respect to language development and adult sentence comprehension (Bates & MacWhinney, 1987; MacDonald, Pearlmutter, & Seidenberg, 1994; McRae, Hare, Elman, & Ferretti, 2005). The studies suggest strong continuity of cue use between childhood and adulthood, with major changes being knowledge of particular verbs and efficiency of cue use.

8c. Dziewczynka obudzila chlopca.
     girl+nominative woke up boy+accusative
     The girl woke up the boy.

8d. Pania uderzyl chlopiec.
     lady+accusative hit boy+nominative
     The boy hit the lady.

Learning the Thematic Role Requirements of Particular Verbs

Determining the thematic roles of the NP's in a sentence not only depends on word order, sentence type, and case marking, but assigning the right thematic roles also depends on the particular verb being used. For example, the subject of an active sentence containing some verbs is an experiencer, not an agent (e.g., 8e). Similarly, some verbs, like *fill* in 8f require a direct object that is a location and allow an optional theme to be added in a prepositional phrase. Other verbs, like *pour* in 8g require a direct object that is a theme and allow an optional location to be added in a prepositional phrase.

8e. Arielle loves her pug.
8f. Oscar filled the sink with water.
     agent V location with theme
8g. Oscar poured water into the sink.
     agent V theme into location

Although children appear to learn early in language development to assign the thematic roles agent and theme to the subject and object of active sentences, they appear to take longer to learn to assign thematic roles to verbs that do not fit this pattern. One way that we can see the protracted development of thematic role assignment is in children's production errors. Melissa Bowerman (1982) described some errors produced by her daughters between the ages of 3 and 6 years. Two examples are given in 8h and 8i. In 8h, the child is using a thematic role arrangement more appropriate for the verb *pour* than the semantically similar verb *fill*. In 8i, she has incorrectly placed the location *you* as the direct object of the verb *pour*. Interestingly, the child had used the verbs *fill* and *pour* correctly at earlier ages, again demonstrating a kind of regression in development. Bowerman suggests that her daughter was beginning to note the semantic similarity between verbs like *fill* and *pour*. This new insight caused her to temporarily confuse the thematic role requirements of the semantically similar verbs.

8h. Can I fill some salt into the bear? (Can I fill the bear with salt?)
8i. Mommy, I poured you. Yeah, with water. (Mommy, I poured water on you.)

Children appear to make similar errors involving thematic roles in their sentence *comprehension*. Looking at verbs like *fill* and *pour*, Gropen and his colleagues (Gropen, Pinker, Hollander, & Goldberg, 1991) used the **Picture Selection** procedure and presented 3- to 5-year-old children with pairs of cartoon panels and asked them to choose which panel depicted a particular verb. For example, one panel showed a woman pouring water into a glass but spilling it so that the glass ended up empty. The other panel of the pair showed the same woman putting the glass under a dripping faucet with the result that it ended up full. For this pair of pictures, a child might be asked *which one of these shows filling?* or *which one of these shows pouring?*

For an adult, the panel in which the glass ends up empty is an example of pouring, and the panel in which the glass ends up full is an example of filling. Nearly all children at all ages selected the appropriate panel when asked about pouring. However, children up to the age of 4.5 years appeared to behave at chance (choosing the two panels about equally often) when asked which panel depicted filling. Thus, the younger children in this study ignored a critical aspect of the meaning of verbs like *fill* (i.e., the end state of the action). This aspect of the meaning is expressed in the required versus optional thematic roles (location and theme, respectively).

Thought Question

Monitor the situations in which you use the word *fill*. Is there anything you can find about those situations to explain why children might not fully encode all of the aspects of its meaning?

Summary of Assigning Thematic Roles to Structural Positions

One of the main problems faced by children learning the syntax of their language is to determine how the language expresses "who did what to whom." Solving this problem entails linking structural positions, such as subject NP, direct object, object of the preposition, and so forth with thematic roles, such as agent, theme, location, and so forth. Children from as young as age 2 years appear to behave as though there is some regularity in how thematic roles are marked, at least for basic sentence types. Both comprehension and production studies suggest some mastery of word order and/or case marking in thematic role assignment. However, children continue to struggle with how to meld meaning and structure into the late preschool years. We can see this struggle in children's difficulties with assigning the correct thematic roles to passive sentence and with semantically related but structurally different verbs like *fill* and *pour*. As in the other domains of language that we have discussed, children appear to have the rudiments of the linguistic abilities required for the adult system. However, using these abilities flexibly and in real-life situations with multiple cognitive and communicative demands takes considerable time. With the basics of morphosyntactic development in hand, we are ready to discuss four debates in this area of language development.

■ How Far Do Children Generalize from Morphosyntactic Input?

The first debate about morphosyntactic development that we will discuss concerns generalization, which since Chapter 1, we have taken as the focus of research on language development. If children learned only to produce the sentences that they heard others produce, there would clearly be no generalization. Although children ultimately go beyond the forms that they have encountered, we can nevertheless ask if they do so from the very beginning of language development, or whether generalization develops through experience with language.

One group of researchers who support the latter view, that generalization develops, is Tomasello and his colleagues. They have suggested that children's early verb use is formulaic (Tomasello, 2003). For example, Akhtar and Tomasello (1997) presented children with a novel action with Bert and Ernie dolls. They might say, *Look at what Ernie's doing to Bert. It's called dacking.* They then asked children to describe what was happening, with the expected target being, *Ernie is dacking Bert.* They found that young children were not able to combine the information that they had been given about the verb's thematic role assignment to produce their own transitive sentence. Such findings might be taken to contradict research presented above that demonstrates that 2-year-olds are able to infer the meaning of novel verbs (Fisher, 2002a; Naigles, 1990). Tomasello and Fisher have written an enlightening exchange on how to interpret the 2-year-old comprehension data (Fisher, 2002b; Tomasello, 2000; Tomasello & Abbot-Smith, 2002).

Note that the Akhtar and Tomasello study required children to make a number of inferences about the types of sentences in which the novel verb could occur (Bert is doing something to Ernie; that something is called *dacking*; Bert should be the agent and Ernie the theme of *dacking*). Another approach to the question might be to determine if children know that, if a verb can be used in one sentence type, it can also be used in a related type. For example, if a child hears a verb used in a passive voice (e.g., *Bert was dacked by Ernie*) she should also know how to use it in an active voice (*Ernie dacked Bert*). However, given how long it appears to take children to under-stand the thematic role structure of passives, another pair of sentence types is needed to determine if children are able to generalize across sentence types at an earlier age.

Conwell and Demuth (2007) chose a pair of sentence types, dou-ble object datives and prepositional datives (8j and 8k), that are very often constructed with the same verbs. They reasoned that, if children understand that the recipient in sentences like 8j appears in the prepositional phrase of sentences like 8k, children hearing 8j with a new verb should be able to use that verb correctly in sentences like 8k. They introduced 3-year-olds to two new verbs, *pilk* and *gorp*. One verb was used in the double object dative form like 8j, and the other was used in the prepositional dative form like 8k. The question was whether and how often children who heard the new verb only in one form would generalize it to the other form. The data, which are shown in Figure 8–2, clearly indicate that 3-year-olds understood the thematic role relations between the two types of dative sentences. However,

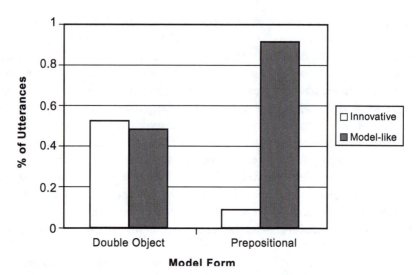

Figure 8–2. Percent of children's utterances in which they used a novel verb in a new sentence type (innovative) versus in the same sentence type in which they first heard the verb (model-like). Reprinted from *Cognition, 103*(2), Conwell, E., and Demuth, K., Early syntactic productivity: Evidence from dative shift, pp. 163-179, Copyright 2007, with permission from Elsevier. Reprinted from *The Lancet, 103*, Conwell, E., and Demuth, K., Early syntactic productivity: Evidence from dative shift, pp. 163-179, Copyright 2007, with permission from Elsevier.

the data also show that children are biased to produce the prepositional dative form, perhaps because all dative verbs can appear in this form, whereas a number of dative verbs can never occur in the double object form. For example, it grammatical to say, *Bert donated the ball to Ernie*, but not **Bert donated Ernie the ball*. The conflicting data from Akhtar and Tomasello (1997) and Conwell and Demuth (2007) suggest that the structure of the task and the particular generalization of interest each might play a role in children's ability to demonstrate morphosyntactic generalization.

8j.   Bert gave Ernie the ball (double object dative).
8k.   Bert gave the ball to Ernie (prepositional dative).

■ Can Associative Learning Models Account for Generalization?

We have already discussed in Chapters 1 and 6 that one of the important activities in language development research is the creation of computer models of language learning to test various learning theories. Connectionist models (e.g., Rumelhart & McClelland, 1986) are computer instantiations of Associative Learning theories. If these models can show learning behaviors similar to human infants and children, we will have some evidence that language learning does not require a grammar. This section outlines two areas in which the value of connectionist models of generalization have been debated. The first concerns past tense overgeneralization, and the second concerns abstraction over series of words that contain a repetition pattern.

Past Tense Overgeneralization

In Chapter 1, we encountered the famous example of children who say *goed* instead of *went*. This type of overgeneralization shows us that children generalize beyond the input that they have encountered, because they have presumably never heard *goed*. Traditional accounts of such overgeneralization errors entail the child forming a rule something like the following:

> For regular verbs, if the present tense form of the verb ends in a voiced consonant or a vowel, with the exception of /d/, make the past tense by adding /d/. If the present tense form of the verb ends in a voiceless consonant, with the exception of /t/, make the past tense by adding /t/. And if the present tense form of the verb ends in /d/ or /t/, make the past tense by adding /əd/.

In the view that children's generalizations reflect a grammar (either innate or learned), children's past tense errors reflect the overapplication of such a rule to irregular verbs like *go, have, take,* and so forth. In the early 1980s, a connectionist account of children's overgeneralization errors was published, and it set off a storm of claims and counterclaims about whether or not rulelike behavior was possible without the child actually learning rules (Rumelhart & McClelland, 1986).

There are three stages of learning in the model. In each stage, the model is given a present tense form for which it must generate a past tense version (Table 8-2). The connections in the model are strengthened or weakened, depending on whether the past tense form is correct or incorrect. Both present and past tense forms are represented as triplets of phonemes (triphones), which are then associated with the relevant articulatory features. Table 8-3 shows the regular verbs

Table 8-2. Illustration of Early Preponderance of Irregular Verbs in Stage 1 (unshaded rows) and Later Addition of Regulars in Stage 2 (shaded rows). In the model, triphones are further represented in terms of articulatory features (e.g., voiced, voiceless, etc.).

Word	IPA transcription	IPA transcription of past tense
go	/go/	/wɛnt/
take	/teik/	/tʊk/
have	/hæv/	/hæd/
eat	/it/	/eit/
give	/gɪv/	/geiv/
kiss	/kɪs/	/kɪst/
hug	/hʌg/	/hʌgd/
snow	/sno/	/snod/
bake	/beik/	/beikt/
like	/laik/	/laikt/
live	/lɪv/	/lɪvd/
save	/seiv/	/seivd/
want	/want/	/wantəd/
scratch	/skrætʃ/	/skrætʃt/

Table 8–3. Triphone Representation of Present and Past Tense Regular Verbs (# = word boundary)

Present tense	Present Tense in Triphones	Past Tense in Triphones
kiss	#kɪ, kɪs, ɪs#	#kɪ, kɪs, ɪst, st#
hug	#hʌ, hʌɢ?, ʌg#	#hʌ, hʌg, ʌgd, gd#
snow	#sn, sno, no#	#sn, sno, nod, od#
bake	#bei, beik, eik#	#bei, beik, eik, kt#
like	#lai, laik, aik#	#lai, laik, aik, kt#
live	#lɪ, lɪv, ɪv#	#lɪ, lɪv, ɪvd, vd#
save	#sei, seiv, eiv#	#sei, seiv, eivd, vd#
want	#wa, wan, ant, nt#	#wa, wan, ant, ntə, təd, əd#
scratch	#sk, kræ, rætʃ, ætʃ#	#sk, kræ, rætʃ, ætʃt, tʃt#

from Table 8-2 represented as triphones. In Stage 1, the model learns a large number of irregular verbs (e.g., *go-went*), as well as some regular verbs (e.g., *like-liked*), and stores associated present tense and past tense forms (unshaded rows of Table 8-2). In Stage 2, more regular verbs enter the lexicon, many of which share triphones and features with the existing irregulars (shaded rows of Table 8-2). For example, regular verbs like *snow, bake, like, live,* and *save* end in the same sounds are do irregular verbs like *go, take,* and *give.* There is even more similarity between irregular and regular forms at the level of features, such as voiced, voiceless, and so forth (Table 8-3). When the model applies these connections to all forms, the irregular forms that were initially correct now adapt to the very frequent present tense-past tense regularities found among the regular verbs. That is, the model overgeneralizes to irregular verbs the patterns that exist between present and past tense regular verbs. Finally, in Stage 3, children must relearn the irregulars and make individual connections between each irregular present form and the relevant past form.

Thought Question

If the connectionist past tense model included only triphones (as in Table 8–3), and not articulatory features, what might you predict about children's overregularizations (hint: imagine that a child knows a large number of regular verbs ending in /k/ and /v/).

What is so intriguing about this account of children's overgeneralization errors is that the child does need to form grammatical rules. Rather, overgeneralization arises out of the pattern of connections that exist among the set of regular present forms and their associated past tense forms. Shortly after the connectionist model of past tense learning was published, a number of criticisms were launched. We discuss just two of these here. One criticism is that, although the model does not embody grammatical rules of the sort proposed by Triggering and the two hypothesis testing theories, the account depends on the learner having access to articulatory features, which are a crucial component of the grammar-based generalization (Lachter & Bever, 1988). Lachter and Bever suggest that the connectionist model has been programmed with information that makes the task learnable. Furthermore, they suggest that, by using a single symbol to represent the end of the word, more information that is crucial to the grammar-based solution has been programmed into the model. For example, the triphones in Table 8–3 allow the generalization that s# in present tense becomes st# in past tense, v# in present tense becomes vd# in past tense, and so forth. Although any computational model must encode the input and output in some form, it is important to consider how much of the solution to the learning problem is dictated by encoding itself. A second criticism is that the model produces errors that seems unlike anything a human learner would ever produce (Pinker & Prince, 1988). For example, it produces the present tense–past tense pairing shown in Table 8–4. Such errors can be taken to suggest that the model is not learning in the same way that human children do. Despite the amount of time that has passed since these initial debates, researchers are still grappling with the question of whether we need to posit a grammar in order to account for children's language development, and if we do, whether key components

Table 8–4. Some "Odd" Present Tense–Past Tense Pairings Generated by the Rumelhart and McClelland (1986) Connectionist Model

Present Tense	Past Tense Generated by Model
squat	squakt
mail	membled
tour	toureder
mate	maded

of that grammar need to be innate. A more recent version of the debate is presented in the next section.

Children's Generalization of Abstract Patterns

The second version of the debate concerning whether Associative Learning theories, in the form of connectionist models, can capture the kinds of learning seen in human language development took the opposite approach from the one described above. Rather than showing that a model *can* behave like an infant or child, this approach noted a type of generalization that many connectionist models *cannot* make and asked if human infants can make the generalization. A very similar pair of studies was published in 1999 (Gómez & Gerken, 1999; Marcus, Vijayan, Rao, & Vishton, 1999); however, we focus on the study by Marcus and colleagues because it led to an extensive debate in the literature. Marcus and colleagues used the HPP and exposed 7-month-olds to three-syllable strings with AAB (e.g., *wi-wi-did, de-de-li*, etc.) or ABB (*wi-di-di, de-li-li*, etc.) patterns (Table 8–5). During test, infants heard strings with the same pattern they had heard during training as well as the other pattern, both instantiated in new vocabulary (e.g., *ba-ba-ko* vs. *ba-ko-ko*). Infants trained on AAB stimuli preferred ABB stimuli at test, whereas infants trained on ABB stimuli preferred AAB stimuli at test (a novelty preference). Marcus et al. (1999) argued that, because connectionist models can only keep track of what syllables or words occur next to each other and not whether

Table 8–5. AAB Familiarization Stimuli Used by Marcus et al. (1999)

A syllables	B syllables			
	di	je	li	we
le	leledi	leleje	leleli	lelewe
wi	wiwidi	wiwije	wiwili	wiwiwe
ji	jijidi	jijije	jijili	jijiwe
de	dededi	dedeje	dedeli	dedewe

those syllables or words are identical, these models cannot capture infants' generalization to new syllables that exhibit the same pattern of identity (first syllable repeats vs. second syllable repeats).

However, a number of connectionist models were developed to capture at least some aspects of the types of learning demonstrated in the Gómez and Gerken (1999) and Marcus et al. (1999) studies (Altmann & Dienes, 1999; Elman, 1999; McClelland & Plaut, 1999; Seidenberg & Elman, 1999; Shastri, 1999). The interesting aspect of the modeling enterprise in this debate is what components need to be included in the models to allow them to generalize. As noted with respect to past tense errors, grammar-based and Associative Learning models can look very much like each other if information that is crucial to the grammar is included as part of the Associative Learning model. Rather than focus on whether learning patterns like those in Table 8–5 requires a grammar or not, other researchers have asked whether such learning is specific to language or even specific to humans. Dawson and Gerken (2006) exposed 4-month-olds to AAB or ABA patterns instantiated in musical notes and found that they were able to generalize to new AAB and ABA note sequences. Studies with rats and cotton-top have shown that they can learn patterns like those in Table 8–5 when the patterns are instantiated in syllables or musical notes (Hauser, Weiss, & Marcus, 2002; Murphy, Mondragon, & Murphy, 2008). Therefore, whatever the learning mechanism required for generalization over such stimuli, it appears to be a general purpose mechanism and not one specific to language.

■ Do Children Make Generalizations That Are Not Supported by the Input?

As noted in Chapters 1 and 6, one of the main arguments for tightly constrained approaches to language development is the view that children make generalizations for which they have no evidence in the input (poverty of the stimulus). This section explores two of these, one classic and one relatively recent.

Hierarchical Structure in Question Formation

As an example of an innate constraint, Chomsky (1980) proposed that children consider linguistic generalizations based on hierarchical sentence structure, and never consider generalizations based on the linear order of words. For example, in making questions of the statements in Table 8–6, children should never consider moving the first verb to the front of the sentence (the starred ungrammatical question in the bottom row of the table). In addition, it has been claimed that two-clause questions are very rare in children's input and that children produce the correct sentence form without ever hearing such a sentence.

Table 8–6. Statement-Question Pairs That Illustrate the Importance of Hierarchical Structure in Linguistic Generalizations

Statement	Question
The man <u>is</u> nice.	Is the man nice?
The dogs <u>are</u> thirsty.	Are the dogs thirsty?
The dogs who are thirsty <u>are</u> nice.	Are the dogs who are thirsty nice?
The cats <u>are</u> chasing the dogs who are thirsty.	Are the cats chasing the dogs who are thirsty?
	*Are the cats are chasing the dog who thirsty?

There is a great deal of debate about whether or not young children are likely to hear sentences like, *Are the cats chasing the dogs who are thirsty?* If you are interested in reading more about this debate, read the article by Pullum and Scholz (2002) as well as the replies to that article by other researchers. Instead of pursuing this debate, however, we focus on children's early production of two clause questions like this one and the evidence that they have mastered such question forms. In the most widely cited study examining this issue, Crain and Nakayama (1987) asked 30 children in two age groups (3;2–4;7 and 4;7–5;11) to produce two-clause questions using the following procedure: The experimenter would tell the child a two-clause statement, such as, *The dog that is sleeping is on the blue bench.* Children would then be told to ask Jabba the Hut if that statement were true, thereby producing a question like, *Is the dog that is sleeping on the blue bench?* The younger group produced 62% ungrammatical questions, whereas the older group produced only 20%. On the face of it, the claim that children have early mastery over such question forms appears to be overstated. However, Crain and Nakayama noted that children never produced ungrammatical sentences like the starred question in Table 8–6. Rather, they produced errors containing an extra verb, such as, *Is the dog that is sleeping on the bench is blue.* The researchers suggested that these errors might reflect the following strategy: produce the verb *is* followed by a copy of the experimenter's statement. Note that this strategy does not bear the marks of an incorrect generalization like the starred example in Table 8–6. However, neither does it show unequivocal evidence that children are making a generalization based on hierarchical structure. Even if children do make the correct generalization without ever hearing a two-clause question, connectionist modelers have shown that a model can also make the correct generalization based on exposure to other two-clause utterances that are not questions (Lewis & Elman, 2001). Thus, the theme continues: It is difficult to formulate research questions about morphosyntactic development to definitively rule out grammarless approaches to generalization.

Anaphoric *One*

Another area of morphosyntax in which it has been claimed that children do not receive sufficient information in the input concerns anaphoric *one*, as shown in sentence 81. The appropriate interpretation of *one* 81 is *red ball*, that is, *one* refers to the adjective plus the noun. But how does the child know that the referent is *red ball*, and not just *ball?* Because every red ball is also a ball, every time the child encounters a situation in which it is clear that the referent is *red ball*, she will also have evidence that the referent is ball. Researchers used the IPLP to ask if 18-month-olds interpret *one* the way that adults do. Children saw a single picture presented on a screen and heard a description of it (e.g., Look! A yellow bottle; Lidz, Waxman, & Freedman, 2003). They were then shown two pictures (e.g., a yellow bottle and a blue bottle) and asked either a neutral question (*Now look. What do you see now?*) or an anaphoric *one* question (e.g., *Now look. Do you see another one?*). In the neutral question condition, children looked longer at the novel picture (e.g., the blue bottle), suggesting that when the sentence did not tell them what to look at, they preferred to see something new. In the anaphoric condition, children looked longer at the old picture (e.g., the yellow bottle), suggesting that they interpreted *one* in an adultlike manner. The researchers concluded that knowledge that anaphoric *one* needs to refer to the whole NP, complete with the adjective, is part of children's innate morphosyntactic knowledge.

81. I'll play with this red ball and you can play with that one.

Other researchers were able to create a computational model of learning anaphoric *one* that used a hypothesis testing approach to modeling, instead of an Associative Learning approach (Regier & Gahl, 2004). The rationale behind this approach is that if anaphoric *one* could refer to just the noun and not the whole NP, the child should have expected to encounter that situation some time in the set of situations in which anaphoric *one* was used. That is, in this version of hypothesis testing (called Bayesian hypothesis testing; Tenenbaum & Griffiths, 2001), the learner determines what she should expect to see based on different hypotheses. If she fails to see the predicted outcome of one of the hypotheses after encountering enough input, she is able to rule out the unsupported hypothesis. We discussed a similar example in Chapter 1: I give you a set of numbers that are all divisible by 4, but they are also all divisible by 2. This scenario is directly parallel to the red ball versus balls in general situation. In Chapter 1 you learned that if you encounter 10 numbers divisible by 4 and none that are divisible by 2 and not by 4, and if your input is unbiased, you can make a reasonably safe bet that "divisible by 4" is a better hypothesis than "divisible by 2." In Chapter 5, we discussed a similar example with respect to whether the nonsense word *fep* referred to dogs or Dalmations. Such versions of hypothesis testing combine properties of both Triggering and Associative Learning approaches: Like Triggering, they entail learning a grammar, and like Associative Learning, they are responsive to some aspects of input statistics.

■ Do Children's Morphosyntactic Errors Reflect Possible Human Grammars?

The final controversy addressed in this chapter concerns how we should interpret children's morphosyntactic errors. Recall from Chapters 1 and 6 that Triggering theories propose that children's errors should reflect incorrect parameter settings for the particular language that they are learning. However, the forms used in these errors should be grammatical in some other language. Linguistic Hypothesis Testing theories make a similar prediction: Children's incorrect hypotheses should be linguistically sensible, employing linguistic units and structures. Various morphosyntactic errors made by children have been taken as evidence for these claims. We examine two of these: English-speaking children's omission of sentence subjects and their incorrect production of pronoun case.

■ English-Speaking Children's Subjectless Sentences

Young children learning English produce sentences like, *Want ice cream* instead of *I want ice cream* or *Push him* instead of *He pushed him* (Hyams, 1986). The interest in this phenomenon stems from the fact that human languages appear to come in two versions with respect to the presence of overt subjects. Languages like English require that statements have subjects, whereas **pro-drop** languages like Spanish and Italian permit statements without subjects. Hyams suggested that English-speaking children's production of sentences without subjects is evidence that they are born with their **pro-drop parameter** set to allow pro-drop or subjectless sentences. On this view, what triggers children to change their parameter to disallow pro-drop? Non-pro-drop languages like English have special syntactic constructions with semantically empty subjects, such as *It is raining*. Notice, there is no *it* to point to in the world, suggesting that the syntax requires a subject, even when the sentence meaning does not. Hyams proposed that it is when English-learning children take note of semantically empty subjects that they reset the pro-drop parameter to disallow subjectless sentences. This hypothesis predicts that children should produce sentences like *It's raining* at the same time they begin to include subjects on all statements.

There have been a number of studies that suggest alternative explanations for English-speaking children's subjectless sentence. Valian (1991) reasoned that if English-speaking children initially have the same pro-drop setting as children learning a pro-drop language like Italian, both groups should produce pronoun subjects equally infrequently. She studied the spontaneous speech of children learning English and Italian and found that English-speaking children produce pronoun subjects 50% to 80% of the time. In stark contrast, Italian children produce pronoun subjects less than 5% of the time. This is evidence that English-speaking children don't have the same morphosyntax as Italian children.

What causes English-speakers' omissions? Bloom (1990) addressed that question by examining the spontaneous productions of Adam, Eve, and Sarah in the Brown corpus of the CHILDES database (Brown, 1973; MacWhinney, 2000). He found that children were less likely to produce subjects for sentences with longer VP's than sentences with shorter VP's. This finding suggests that children omit subjects due to constraints on the amount of material that they are able to produce in a single utterance. It is consistent with the observation that children omit many parts of words and sentences, not just subjects.

Why do children omit subjects and not objects? That is, why are children unlikely to solve the problem of production constraints by producing sentences like, *I like her*, with the final word *her* omitted? Gerken (1991) attempted to answer that question in terms of the rhythmic patterns in which sentence subjects versus objects occur. Subject pronouns are unstressed syllables in utterance-initial position. We know that children also omit initial unstressed syllables from words like *giraffe* (weak syllable omission, Chapter 4). Could subject omissions be the result of difficulty producing initial unstressed sylla-bles? If so, children should also omit initial determiners, like the *more* than determiners later in the sentence. To test this possibility, Gerken asked children between the ages of 23 and 30 months to imitate sentences like those in 8m through 8p below. It was predicted that stressed words, like *Jane* and *bear* would be produced frequently, regardless of whether they were in the subject or object of the sentence. As predicted by both the pro-drop and the production constraint views, children omitted pronoun subjects more than pronoun objects. The key prediction of the production constraint view was that the unstressed determiner *the* would be preserved less frequently when it was a subject, as in 8o than when it was an object, as in 8p. The pro-drop account has no basis for predicting differential production of subject versus object determiners. This production constraint prediction was borne out, providing some support for the view that constraints on production play a role in children's subjectless sentences.

8m.   He kissed Jane.
8n.   Jane kissed him.
8o.   The bear kissed Jane.
8p.   Jane kissed the bear.

Children's Pronoun Case Errors

Although English does not mark case on all nouns as many languages do, it does mark case on pronouns, as indicated in Table 8–7. Thus, it

Table 8–7. English Pronoun Case

Case	1st person singular	2nd person	3rd person singular	1st person plural	3rd person plural
Nominative	I	you	he/she	we	they
Objective	me	you	him/her	us	them
Genitive	my	your	his/her	our	their

is grammatical in English to say, *I like Sam* but not, *Me like Sam*. It has been observed for many years that English-speaking children under the age of about 3 years do not have full mastery over pronoun case in production, making errors like those in 8q through 8v, below (errors from Rispoli, 2005). The most frequently produced and discussed errors are like the ones in 8q through 8s, in which a pronoun that should be in nominative case is replaced by one with the same person and number, but in either objective or genitive case. However, it is also possible for pronouns that should be in genitive case to be produced in objective or nominative case (8t and 8u, respectively) or pronouns that should be in objective case to be produced with nominative case (8v).

8q. And her just goes.
8r. Pretend him is a cowboy.
8s. But them are all going to.
8t. This is him daddy.
8u. I find he mouth.
8v. This puppy goes on he.

Language development researchers have taken two general approaches to the errors. In one approach that is consistent with Triggering and Linguistic Hypothesis Testing, the errors reflect a component of the target (adult) grammar that is either missing or incorrect (e.g., Radford, 1990; Schütze & Wexler, 1996). For example, Shütze and Wexler proposed that children who make such errors have a grammar in which marking verb tense and agreement is optional. One advantage of this approach is that it attempts to link a set of children's errors together under a single grammatical principle. We return to this point in the discussion of Specific Language Impairment in Chapter 9. The alternative approach is most consistent with Associative Learning theories (Pine, Rowland, Lieven, & Theakston, 2005; Rispoli, 1998). For example, Rispoli (1998) notes the similarity of the phonological forms of objective and genitive cases for the first person singular (e.g., *me, my*) and suggests that the salience of those two similar forms makes it difficult for children to access the quite different nominative *I* form. One advantage of this approach is that it makes fine-grained predictions about the prevalence of particular pronoun case errors (see Thought Question, below).

Thought Question

Look at the 3rd person singular pronouns in Table 8–7. Does Rispoli's (1998) account make different predictions pronoun case errors involving masculine versus feminine pronouns? Why?

Summary of Children's Morphosyntactic Errors

What should be clear from the studies in this section is that children's errors can be taken as evidence for a variety of viewpoints about the nature of language development. Distinguishing among theories based solely on English-speaking children's spontaneously produced speech is likely to be impossible. Such studies need to be supplemented by studies of children learning other languages, elicited production and comprehension studies, and computer models that instantiate the theories under consideration.

■ Summary

Chapter 8 first examined how children assign meaning to sentences. The data presented at the beginning of the chapter suggest that when cues for assigning thematic roles are robust and applicable across a number of sentence types and particular verbs, children use these cues very early. However, children take longer to adapt to less typical sentence types (e.g., passive) and to sort out the relation between verbs that mean similar things but have different sentence structures (e.g., *fill* vs. *pour*). Children appear to be as able to use word order as well as case marking in assigning thematic roles, with the caveat that whatever the cue, it must be used consistently (e.g., Turkish vs. Serbo-Croation).

The remainder of Chapter 8 focused on four debates about morphosyntactic development that bear on the theories of language development outlined in Chapter 1. The evidence used in these debates comprises a mixture of behavioral data from infants and children as well as computational models of various types. The theoretical questions addressed concern whether or not we need to posit a grammar to account for children's behavior and whether we need to posit innate constraints that are specific to language. With respect to the need for a grammar, the data suggest that children are remarkable generalizers in at least some areas of morphosyntax and that computational models that do not include a grammar can generalize in ways unlike human learners. However, given the relative success that grammarless approaches have had suggest that, if there is a grammar, it might be closer to the data and less abstract than some linguistic grammars that have been proposed.

With respect to the need for innate constraints that are specific to language, the data supporting such constraints all appear to be amenable to some other explanation. However, we must keep in mind that the form of the constraints that have been posited (e.g., interpretation of anaphoric *one*, pro-drop, subject-verb agreement) might not be correct, but other forms of constraints are possible. Clearly, there is much more research to be done to understand the nature of morphosyntactic development. Chapter 9 focuses on the question of the biology of language by examining language learning in situations different from those discussed so far. Perhaps data from these alternative situations will shed some light on the mechanisms of language development.

■ References

Akhtar, N., & Tomasello, M. (1997). Young children's productivity with word order and verb morphology. *Developmental Psychology, 33*, 952–965.

Altmann, G., & Dienes, A. (1999). Rule learning by seven-month-olds and neural networks. *Science, 284*, 875.

Bates, E., & MacWhinney, B. (1987). Competition, variation, and language learning. In B. MacWhinney (Ed.), *Mechanisms of language acquisition* (pp. 157–193). Hillsdale, NJ: Lawrence Erlbaum.

Bever, T. (1970). The cognitive basis for linguistic structures. In J. Hayes (Ed.), *Cognition and the development of language* (pp. 279–362). New York: Wiley.

Bloom, P. (1990). Subjectless sentences in child language. *Linguistic Inquiry, 21*, 491–504.

Bowerman, M. (1982). Reorganizational processes in lexical and syntactic development. In E. Wanner & L. Gleitman (Eds.), *Language acquisition: The state of the art*. Cambridge: Cambridge University Press.

Brown, R. (1973). *A first language.* Cambridge, MA: Harvard University Press.

Chomsky, N. (1980). The linguistic approach. In M. Piattelli-Palmarini (Ed.), *Language and learning* (pp. 109–116). Cambridge, MA: Harvard University Press.

Conwell, E., & Demuth, K. (2007). Early syntactic productivity: Evidence from dative shift. *Cognition, 103*(2), 163–179.

Crain, S., & Nakayama, M. (1987). Structure dependence in grammar formation. *Language, 63,* 522–543.

Dawson, C., & Gerken, L. A. (2006). 4-month-olds discover algebraic patterns in music that 7.5-month-olds do not. In *Proceedings of the Twenty-Ninth Annual Conference of the Cognitive Science Society* (pp. 1198–1203). Mahwah, NJ: Erlbaum.

Elman, J. (1999). *Generalization, rules, and neural networks: A simulation of Marcus et al.* Unpublished manuscript, University of California, San Diego.

Fisher, C. (2002a). Structural limits on verb mapping: The role of abstract structure in 2.5-year-olds' interpretations of novel verbs. *Developmental Science, 5*(1), 55–64.

Fisher, C. (2002b). The role of abstract syntactic knowledge in language acquisition: A reply to Tomasello (2000). *Cognition, 82*(3), 259–278.

Gerken, L. A. (1991). The metrical basis for children's subjectless sentences. *Journal of Memory and Language, 30,* 431–451.

Golinkoff, R., Hirsh-Pasek, K., Cauley, K., & Gordon, L. (1987). The eyes have it: Lexical and syntactic comprehension in a new paradigm. *Journal of Child Language, 14,* 23–45.

Gómez, R. L., & Gerken, L. A. (1999). Artificial grammar learning by 1-year-olds leads to specific and abstract knowledge. *Cognition, 70*(2), 109–135.

Gropen, J., Pinker, S., Hollander, M., & Goldberg, R. (1991). Affectedness and direct objects: The role of lexical semantics in the acquisition of verb argument structure. *Cognition Special Issue: Lexical and Conceptual Semantics, 41*(1–3), 153–195.

Hauser, M. D., Weiss, D., & Marcus, G. F. (2002). Rule learning by cotton-top tamarins. *Cognition, 86*(1), B15–B22.

Hyams, N. (1986). *Language acquisition and the theory of parameters.* Dordrecht, Holland: Reidel.

Lachter, J., & Bever, T. G. (1988). The relation between linguistic structure and associative theories of language learning: A constructive critique of some connectionist learning models. *Cognition, 28*(1), 195–247.

Lewis, J. D., & Elman, J. L. (2001). A connectionist investigation of linguistic arguments from the poverty of the stimulus: Learning the unlearnable. In J. D. Moore & K. Stenning (Eds.), *Proceedings of the Twenty-Third Annual Conference of the Cognitive Science Society* (pp. 552–557). Mahwah, NJ: Erlbaum.

Lidz, J., Waxman, S., & Freedman, J. (2003). What infants know about syntax but couldn't have learned: Experimental evidence for syntactic structure at 18 months. *Cognition, 89*(3), B65-B73.

MacDonald, M., Pearlmutter, N., & Seidenberg, M. S. (1994). The lexical nature of syntactic ambiguity resolution. *Psychological Review, 101*, 676-703.

MacWhinney, B. (2000). *The CHILDES project: Tools for analyzing talk* (3rd ed.). Mahwah, NJ: Lawrence Erlbaum Associates.

Maratsos, M. (1974). Children who get worse at understanding the passive: A replication of Bever. *Journal of Psycholinguistic Research, 31*(1), 65-74.

Marcus, G. F., Vijayan, S., Rao, S. B., & Vishton, P. M. (1999). Rule learning by seven-month-old infants. *Science, 283*, 77-80.

McClelland, J. L., & Plaut, D. C. (1999). Does generalization in infant learning implicate abstract algebraic rules? *Trends in Cognitive Sciences, 3*, 166-168.

McRae, K., Hare, M., Elman, J. L., & Ferretti, T. (2005). A basis for generating expectancies for verbs from nouns. *Memory and Cognition, 33*(7), 1174-1184.

Murphy, R. A., Mondragon, E., & Murphy, V. A. (2008). Rule learning by rats. *Science, 319*(5871), 1849-1851.

Naigles, L. R. (1990). Children use syntax to learn verb meanings. *Journal of Child Language, 17*, 357-374.

Pine, J. M., Rowland, C. F., Lieven, E. V. M., & Theakston, A. L. (2005). Testing the Agreement/Tense Omission Model: Why the data on children's use of non-nominative 3psg subjects count against the ATOM. *Journal of Child Language, 32*(2), 269-289.

Pinker, S., & Prince, A. (1988). On language and connectionism: Analysis of a parallel distributed processing model of language acquisition. *Cognition, 28*(1), 73-193.

Pullum, G. K., & Scholz., B. C. (2002). Empirical assessment of stimulus poverty arguments. *Linguistic Review, 19*, 9-50.

Radford, A. (1990). Genitive subjects in child English. *Lingua, 106*, 113-131.

Regier, T., & Gahl, S. (2004). Learning the unlearnable: The role of missing evidence. *Cognition, 93*, 147-155.

Rispoli, M. (1998). Me or my: Two different patterns of pronoun case. *Journal of Speech, Language, and Hearing Research, 41*(2), 385-393.

Rispoli, M. (2005). When children reach beyond their grasp: Why some. *Journal of Child Language, 32*(1), 93-116.

Rumelhart, D. E., & McClelland, J. L. (1986). *Parallel distributed processing: Explorations in the microstructure of cognition.* Cambridge, MA: MIT Press.

Schütze, C. T., & Wexler, K. (1996). Subject case licensing and English root infinitives. In A. Stringfellow, D. Cahma-Amitay, E. Hughes, & A. Zukowski (Eds.), *Proceedings of the 20th Annual Boston University Conference on Language Development.* Somerville, MA: Cascadilla Press.

Seidenberg, M. S., & Elman, J. (1999). Do infants learn grammar with algebra or statistics? *Science, 284,* 435–436.

Shastri, L. (1999). Infants learning algebraic rules. *Science, 285*(5434), 1673–1674.

Slobin, D. I., & Bever, T. G. (1982). Children use canonical sentence schemas: A crosslinguistic study of word order and inflections. *Cognition, 12*(3), 229–265.

Tenenbaum, J. B., & Griffiths, T. L. (2001). Generalization, similarity, and Bayesian inference. *Behavioral and Brain Sciences, 24,* 629–640.

Tomasello, M. (2000). Do young children have adult syntactic competence? *Cognition, 74*(3), 209–253.

Tomasello, M. (2003). *Constructing a language: A usage-based theory of language acquisition.* Cambridge, MA: Harvard University Press.

Tomasello, M., & Abbot-Smith, K. (2002). A tale of two theories: Response to Fisher. *Cognition, 83*(2), 207–214.

Valian, V. V. (1991). Syntactic subjects in the early speech of American and Italian children. *Cognition, 40,* 21–82.

Weist, R. M. (1983). The word order myth. *Journal of Child Language, 10*(1), 97–106.

9 Issues in the Biology of Language

■ We Need More Data

We began this book with an introduction of a central question of language development: How do learners generalize beyond the linguistic input to which they are exposed in order to comprehend and produce new utterances that are consistent with the language of their community? The theories about how language learners generalize that were outlined in Chapter 1 and carried throughout the intervening seven chapters focus on how strongly constrained by their biology learners are, and whether the constraints that guide language development are specific to language or more general constraints on human thought and information processing. In the next section, we review the highlights of the preceding chapters as they pertain to questions about the biology of language.

However, what should be clear by now is that the results of many existing studies of normal language development are equivocal with respect to the relative contributions of human biology and language input. Although researchers continue to refine their predictions and use an ever increasing set of tools to address this question, studying normal language development alone may be insufficient. That is because normal language development reflects the near-perfect symbiosis of nature and nurture—the genetically typical learner is being exposed to the rich language environment of her community. Given that language development is almost certainly a swirling dance of biology and environment (see Chapter 1), it's no wonder that we don't have a clear look at the individual dance partners. However, as noted in Chapter 1, trying to identify the specific contributions of biology and environment in language development contributes to a broader enterprise of understanding whether the environment selects among genetically prespecified alternatives, or whether minds are actually constructed from the interaction of environment and biology.

If we can agree on the value of answering that question, it appears that we need another window onto the language development process. One such window is afforded by studies of language development in less typical situations. These situations include language learning under conditions of genetic impairment, learning a language later in life, and creating language from very incomplete input or even from no input. These issues are discussed in the remainder of the chapter. The specific questions that we can try to answer from these alternative views of language development include:

1. Can linguistic ability be dissociated from general intelligence?
2. Can specific proposed linguistic constraints (e.g., parameters) be affected by a genetic disorder?
3. Is there a critical or sensitive period for learning language?
4. Do children learning language without rich input make up for the lack of input in their generalizations?

■ What Do We Know So Far?

Before we examine language learning in less typical situations, let's try to summarize the data from Chapters 1 through 8, which focus largely on language development in normally developing children learning a single spoken language.

The Raw Materials for Language

First, human infants appear to be born with the requisite auditory sensitivity to perceive most of the sound differences used in human languages (Chapter 3) and to match at least some auditory input with the oral-motor activity that could be used to produce it (Chapter 4). These observations tell us that the raw materials of spoken language are readily available to humans. We cannot know from these data whether the skills we see in newborns are present specifically for learning spoken language or whether human language takes advantage of pre-existing sensory-motor abilities. However, other data suggest that, at least on the perception side, the abilities that we see in human infants are shared by some nonhuman species (Chapter 3). For example, human infants and rats are sensitive to similar aspects of language prosody. Dogs and chinchillas, like human infants, are able to demonstrate categorical perception of a variety of speech sound contrasts. Altogether, the data on early abilities suggest that the raw materials for language development are not specific to language, but rather that humans might break into the language system using general purpose perceptual (and perhaps motor) abilities shared with other species.

Learning About the Form of the Input

The raw materials discussed above are quickly shaped by the particular linguistic environment of the learner. Within the first year of life, infants narrow their sensitivity to the speech contrasts used in their target language (Chapter 3). They narrow their generalizations from those not part of human language to only linguistically possible generalizations, perhaps as a function of their increased knowledge of the patterns in their target language. They also come to recognize typical properties of their target language, including stress patterns and sequences of phonemes. They use their growing sensitivity to likely sound patterns to identify word-sized units in the input, and their abilities to recognize and remember word forms become increasingly robust (Chapter 5). During the second year of life, children are able to find and remember more complex patterns in their input, many of which relate to how words combine into sentences (Chapter 7). Infants' and children's productions are also shaped by their input during the first and second years of life. Sounds and sound sequences that are frequent in the target language are increasingly seen in both babble and early words (Chapter 4). A growing body of evidence suggests that general purpose mechanisms that can compute some range of statistical calculations on the input can go a long way toward explaining children's ability to generalize based on the form of their target language.

Mapping Forms to Meanings

Not only are infants and children learning about the typical forms that can be found in their input, they are also learning about the ways in which word and sentence forms are mapped to meanings (Chapters 5 and 8). It is in the domain of form-meaning mapping that many of the major clashes among theoretical positions can be seen. With respect to words, a variety of innate constraints specific to solving this mapping relation have been proposed, although nearly all of them have been challenged by a combination of child word-learning data and computational modeling data (Chapter 5). Perhaps, as researchers explore children's abilities to make form-meaning mappings of words that do not refer to observable objects, actions, and qualities of the environment, but rather that refer to purely mental concepts, we will gain a better understanding of the relative contributions of innate expectations about what words can mean, general purpose statistical computation abilities, and expectations about the thoughts and intentions of our fellow humans.

It is with respect to mapping forms to meanings in sentences, or morphosyntax, where we find the most obvious stalemate between more constrained theories that posit innate language-specific abilities and less constrained theories that rely on general-purpose learning mechanisms applied to rich input. The data themselves are often equivocal even with respect to children's ability to generalize about sentence form-meaning mapping (Chapter 8). Are failures to demonstrate generalization by young children due to insensitive measures, or do they reflect the true state of affairs? And, insofar as generalization relies on knowledge of particular words (e.g., *pour* vs. *fill*), should we be surprised if children haven't fully untangled all of the components of word meaning? In short, young children do not show completely mature abilities to map sentence forms to meanings, either in comprehension or production. But it's an open question whether we should interpret their abilities as reflecting an incomplete mastery of a domain, just as we might see in children learning math or other skills, or whether we should interpret their abilities as an intact (possibly innate) grammar coupled with immature memory or processing abilities.

Part of the frustration in interpreting data on children's development of morphosyntax is that there may be more disagreement among linguists about how to characterize adult morphosyntactic ability than there is about adult abilities in other domains of language. Without substantial agreement about where the path is headed, it is very difficult to pick out subtle markers along the way. Perhaps by examining language emerge in less typical situations, we will not only gain a better understanding of the dance of biology and environment involved in language development, but also about how to understand the adult linguistic system. The following three sections explore this possibility.

■ The Development of Language in Two Atypical Populations

Recall from Chapter 1 and throughout this book that theories of language development can be divided into those that propose a learning mechanism specific to language (Triggering and Linguistic Hypothesis Testing) and those that propose a general purpose learning mechanism (General Purpose Hypothesis Testing and Associative Learning). One prediction made by the former theories is that the ability to learn language can be dissociated from the ability to learn other skills. Put another way, a child might show poor language ability and normal abilities in other domains or, conversely, normal language ability and poor abilities in other domains. Two groups of children have been identified as possibly meeting these predictions: children with Specific Language Impairment and children with Williams syndrome. The language abilities of these two groups of children are discussed below.

Specific Language Impairment

Specific Language Impairment, or **SLI** is a disorder of language that is usually identified in the late preschool/early school years. The main diagnostic criteria are: (1) significantly deviant language for their age, (2) absence of obvious neurologic deficits, (3) normal hearing, and (4) intelligence within the normal range. Estimates about the number of children affected by SLI range from 3% to 7% (e.g., Tomblin et al., 1997). Although the cause of SLI is unknown, researchers have long noted an aggregation of language-related disorders in families (e.g., Stromswold, 1998). For example, in one study, 13% of the siblings of children with SLI were diagnosed with SLI themselves if no parent was also diagnosed with a language disorder, 40% if one parent was diagnosed, and 71.4% if both parents were diagnosed as language impaired (Tallal, Hirsch, & Realpe-Bonilla, 2001). Twin studies further confirm the family aggregation, but add the important observation that an identical (monozygotic) twin of an affected child is more likely to also be affected than is a fraternal (digzyotic) twin (Figure 9–1). Brain structure abnormalities have also been found in children with SLI and members of their families (e.g., Plante, 1991). These findings, along with recent DNA evidence, have been taken to suggest that there

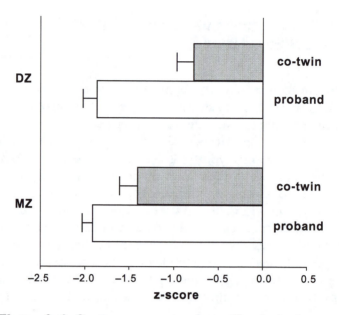

Figure 9–1. Scores on a nonword repetition task of children with SLI (proband) and their fraternal (dizygotic) or identical (monozygotic) twin. From Bishop, D. V. M. (2006). What causes specific language impairment in children? *Current Trends in Psychological Science, 15,* 217–221.

is a substantial genetic component underlying SLI. However, whether the genetic effect is specific to language is under debate.

Characteristics of children with Specific Language Impairment can include: (1) a late onset for language production, (2) shorter Mean Lengths of Utterance (MLU's) than normally developing peers (see Chapter 7 for more information about MLU), (3) deficits in rapid word learning, and (4) deficits in the production of grammatical morphemes (Rice, 2007). It is the latter deficit that has generated the greatest debate about the underlying cause of SLI, and we discuss it in more detail below.

Thought Question

What do the studies of twins contribute that studies of affected family members who are not twins cannot tell us?

However, a variety of nonlinguistic deficits have also been found to have a higher incidence among children with SLI than in children with normally developing language, including: (1) problems with working memory, (2) speech perception, (3) visual imagery, and (4) analogical reasoning (for reviews, see Joanisse & Seidenberg, 2003; van der Lely, 2005). The question is whether the linguistic and nonlinguistic deficits seen in children with SLI stem from a central cause, and therefore are not specific to language, or whether children with SLI tend to have multiple genetically based deficits, some, but not all of which, are specific to language. Although there are a number of hypotheses of both types (language-specific, nonspecific) about the cause of SLI, the remainder of this section focuses on two of these.

One of the areas of notable deficit in children with SLI is in the production of verbal morphology (see 9a and 9b, below). For example, although a normally developing 3-year-old might use past tense *-ed* in an average of 53% of required contexts, a 5-year-old with SLI might use this inflection in only 23% of required contexts (Rice, Wexler, & Cleave, 1995). One proposed cause of this sort of omission that is not specific to language is that children with SLI have deficits in the ability to perceive, process, and remember auditory input, including speech (e.g., Joanisse & Seidenberg, 2003; Leonard, 1998). In this view, English grammatical morphemes are often less than a syllable (e.g., /d/), and when they are a full syllable, they tend to contain *schwa*, which may be perceptually indistinct. Due to the low perceptual quality of English function morphemes, children might form less robust representations of them and therefore be less able to access them rapidly in constructing sentences. There are several types of evidence in favor of this view. First, as noted in Chapter 4, children with SLI do not omit function morphemes from different sentence positions equally frequently. Rather, they omit morphemes that comprise unfooted syllables more often than morphemes that belong to a trochaic foot (e.g., McGregor & Leonard, 1994). This omission pattern suggests that phonology plays a role in children's omissions. Second, children learning different languages omit different function morphemes, and the particular morphemes that they omit appear to be related to the phonological properties of the morphemes (Leonard & Bortolini, 1998). For example, Italian-speaking children with SLI have difficulty producing pronounlike clitics, like *lo* in 9c. English-speaking children with normal language and with SLI have little trouble with the corresponding *him*. Leonard and Bortolini suggest that the Italian clitic is often unfooted, which makes is vulnerable to omission. A third piece of evidence that phonology plays a role in the productions of children with SLI is that they are less likely to produce past tense morphemes on nonsense verbs with lower phonotactic probabilities than higher probabilities (Leonard, Davis, & Deevy, 2007, see Chapters 2 through 4 for discussions of phonotactics). This result suggests that at least part of the problem in producing verbal morphology experienced by children with SLI is affected by how typical in their language is the phonological form that they are trying to produce.

9a. *He play yesterday.
9b. *She run to the store.
9c. Gina lo vede.
    Gina him sees
    Gina sees him.

There is also some evidence against the view that the perceptual and phonological properties of language are responsible for the deficits seen in SLI (van der Lely, 2005). For example, inflections that produce an extra syllable (e.g., *pushes, wanted*) are more perceptually salient than their nonsyllabic counterparts, but are nevertheless more problematic for children with SLI. Cross-linguistic studies also suggest some problems with the perceptual/phonological view. For example, in French the form *le* can be either a determiner (*the*, 9d) or a clitic (*him*, 9e). French children with SLI have difficulty with the clitic, but not the determiner.

9d. Donnez-moi le livre.
    Give me the book.
9e. Anne le chasse.
    Anne him chases
    Anne chases him.

An alternative account of SLI, and the production of verbal morphology in particular, is that this disorder reflects a genetic deficit specific to language. One hypothesis within this framework is that children with SLI experience an extended period in which marking verb tense and agreement is optional in their grammar (see the discussion of pronoun case errors in Chapter 8). This view makes three predictions (Rice, 2007): First, verb tense errors should be dissociable from other parts of language. Second, verb tense errors should be dissociable from other aspects of syntax. And, finally, all morphemes relating to tense within the grammar proposed for adults should be equally affected. The first two predictions have been partially supported, in the sense that some children who show few or no other errors in language production have deficits in the production of verb morphology. However, many children show additional linguistic problems, even groups of children who show no other nonlinguistic problems. For example, a group of children studied by Heather van der Lely, whose disorder she names "Grammatical SLI," have difficulties interpreting which noun in a sentence a pronoun refers to. This problem does not appear to be related to verbal morphology. With respect to the third prediction, a number of researchers have suggested that incorrect pronoun use (*Her like it*) by children with SLI is predicted by the same component of the grammar that is responsible for the production of verbal morphology. Since producing an incorrect pronoun is an error of co-mission, rather than of omission, the finding that these errors may be correlated in the same children supports the view that verbal morphology is a particular problem for children with SLI.

Thought Question

How might the view of pronoun case errors proposed by Rispoli in Chapter 8 be incorporated with the perceptual/phonological account of SLI presented in this chapter?

Finally, one very interesting observation made by Bishop (2006) makes it clear that it will be almost impossible to trace the diagnosis called "SLI" to a single cause. She found that monozygotic twins showed much more similar production of verbal morphology than dizygotic twins. Recall from Figure 9-1 that monozygotic twins also showed greater deficits in nonword repetition. The interesting twist is that there was no relation between the production of verbal morphology and nonword repetition performance. As Bishop notes, "Both impairments were found in SLI, and both were heritable, yet they were only weakly correlated, and genetic analysis suggested that different genes were implicated in the two deficits." Bishop further cautions researchers and clinicians against thinking that identifying a disorder as "genetic" means that it will run the same course regardless of environment.

Thought Question

Can you determine from Bishops's words of caution which view of the interaction of genetics and environment she thinks is most likely?

Williams Syndrome

Williams syndrome (WS) might be thought of as the mirror-image of SLI, in that children with Williams syndrome are claimed to have better language skills than would be expected based on their nonverbal intelligence. WS is a rare genetic disorder, with estimates of its prevalence ranging from 1 in 20,000 live births to 1 in 7,500 (Brock, 2007). WS has sometimes been referred to as "pixie syndrome," because those affected have pixielike or elfin faces. People with WS are often described as being extremely friendly. Most people with WS exhibit mild to moderate mental retardation, with particularly poor spatial skills.

Researchers have examined a number of different areas of language in people with WS. Here, we focus on complex syntax and vocabulary. With respect to complex syntax, the data suggest that, although children with WS perform more poorly than typically developing peers, the structures that they finder harder are the same structures that younger normally developing children find more difficult. That is, their syntactic development appears to be delayed, although it may never fully catch up with that of normally developing children (Brock, 2007). Interestingly, one area of particular difficulty for children with WS is in using syntax to describe spatial situations, precisely the domain that causes them the most difficulty in tests of general cognition (Landau & Zukowski, 2003). This finding may be taken to suggest a strong relation between general cognition and language development, rather than supporting the view that the two domains are dissociable (Brock, 2007).

With respect to vocabulary, younger children with WS are delayed with the acquisition of their first words and have been reported to perform much lower than expected for their chronologic age on tests of vocabulary (Thal, Bates, & Bellugi, 1989; Volterra, Caselli, Capirci,

Tonucci, & Vicari, 2003). However, their vocabulary in the early years is consistent with their mental age. In contrast, teenagers and young adults with WS have been observed to have vocabulary scores on standardized tests that are better than their mental age (Bellugi, Marks, Bihrle, & Sabo, 1988). Indeed, a number of studies have found that adolescents and adults with WS have better receptive vocabulary knowledge than predicted by their *chronologic age*; that is, they outperformed age-matched normally developing peers. Furthermore, their utterances appear to contain relatively rare words or words that are unusual for the context. For example, Bellugi and colleagues (Bellugi, Bihrle, Neville, Jernigan, & Doherty, 1992) reported a person with WS using the phrase *evacuate the glass* when the expected phrase might have been *empty the glass*. Nevertheless, people with WS perform worse than even mental age matched controls on naming (producing a word when shown a picture, Brock, 2007). There is also evidence that children with WS approach word learning differently than normally developing children, obeying the mutual exclusivity constraint, but not the whole object or taxonomic constraints (Stevens & Karmiloff-Smith, 1997). In summary, people with Williams syndrome show an atypical mixture of language skills, with receptive vocabulary being one area in which they have spared linguistic ability in the face of deficits in general intelligence.

Summary of Two Atypical Populations

The data on SLI and WS present a somewhat confusing picture. On the one hand, it is quite clear that neither population exhibits completely normal abilities in one domain and uniformly poor abilities in another. Children with SLI have deficits in addition to language, and children with WS have poor skills in some language domains. Therefore, if the question we want answered is whether language and other cognitive domains are completely dissociable, the answer is *no*. However, if we ask whether the particular patterns of strengths and weaknesses seen in children with SLI and WS might tell us something about the components that make up language ability, the answer is more positive. Determining why verbal morphology is particularly affected in children with SLI and why receptive vocabulary is relatively spared in adolescents with WS is a tricky problem, and one that will occupy language researchers for many years to come. Nevertheless, the clues we gain from studying these atypical populations may help us to understand language in a new way, and, importantly, provide possible approaches for clinical intervention.

Age Effects on Language Learning

It has long been observed that it is harder to learn a second language when you are older than when you are younger. Eric Lenneberg (1967) incorporated this observation into the debate about the relative contributions of environment versus biology in language development. Lenneberg and others at the time hypothesized that language development was constrained by a **critical period** in which the human brain was prepared to take advantage of linguistic input. After that period (perhaps ending at puberty), some learning might occur, but it would not have the advantage of special language-learning mechanisms available during the critical period. Support for this claim could also be taken as support for the view that language is strongly constrained by biology. Since that early claim, researchers have considered the predictions of Lenneberg's view, as well as other interpretations of age effects in language learning. The research examines language learning in two populations: people who have learned a second language at different ages, and people who were not exposed to any normal language at the usual time, but rather learned a *first* language at different ages. We discuss examples of both types of studies of age effects on language learning.

Age Effects in Second Language Learning

More people in the world are bilingual or multilingual than monolingual. Because the situations under which people become bilingual are different, people can learn a second language at a variety of ages. The studies of age effects in second language learning have examined phonology, morphosyntax, and lexical semantics. The general approach for all three types of studies is to test immigrants who arrived in their new country at different ages. There is a potential confounding issue between age of arrival and number of years exposure to the language. For example, if you test a group of 20-year-old college students who arrived in the United States between the ages of 2 and 18 years, the students who arrived at age 2 will have had 18 years experience with

English, whereas those arriving at age 18 will have had 2 years experience. Therefore, most studies test people with a range of ages, so that all participants have had a reasonably long period of exposure to the second language.

With respect to phonology, nearly all of us know at least one person with a "foreign accent," or phonological production that is inconsistent with that of the person's current linguistic community. The data from a number of studies make clear what most of us have observed: People who learned their second language in adolescence or adulthood are much more likely to have an "accent" than people who learned as children (Oyama, 1976; Scovel, 2000). Despite the extreme robustness of the age effect, it does not support the view that there is a critical period, in that there does not appear to be a sharp cutoff in people's ability to learn the phonology of a second language. Rather, there appears to be a gradual decline in the likelihood that a second language learner will sound like a native speaker of his or her new language.

A similar, but perhaps more nuanced, picture emerges from the study of morphosyntax in second language learners. Johnson and Newport (1989) tested Chinese and Korean adults, who had immigrated to the United States at different ages, on their ability to make grammaticality judgments of English. The ungrammatical sentences reflected different types of morphosyntactic violations. For example, some ungrammatical sentences had incorrect word order for English (9f) whereas others omitted determiners (9g) or exhibited other violations. Two aspects of the data are of interest. First, as shown in Figures 9–2A and 9–2B, learning decreases steadily as age of arrival increases, up until about age 14, at which point learners are extremely variable in their performance, perhaps suggesting the use of different learning mechanisms. Second, performance on the grammaticality judgment test varied as to the type of morphosyntactic violation, with performance on word order being very good regardless of age of arrival, and performance on determiner omissions being strongly affected by age of arrival. Thus, just as in language development in children, word order appears to be easy to learn for second language learners, regardless of age. In contrast, elements of morphosyntax that cause problems for children with normal language and those with language disorders also prove more difficult for second language learners.

9f. *The boy the girl chased
9g. *I went to store

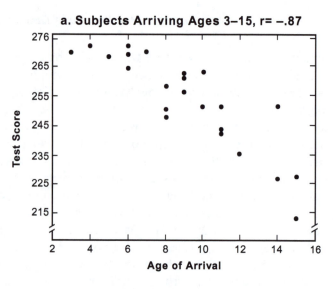

a. Subjects Arriving Ages 3–15, r= −.87

Test Score (y-axis)
Age of Arrival (x-axis)

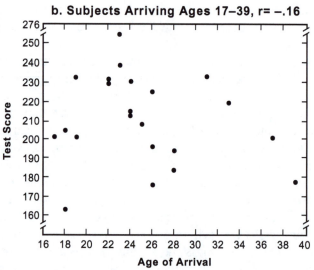

b. Subjects Arriving Ages 17–39, r= −.16

Test Score (y-axis)
Age of Arrival (x-axis)

*Note: The Y-axes are on different scales.

Figures 9–2. Scatterplot of scores on test of morphosyntactic judgments based on age of arrival to the U.S. Reprinted from *Cognitive Pyschology*, *21*, Johnson, J. S., and Newport, E. L. Critical period effects in second language learning; The influence of maturational state on the acquisition of English as a second language, pp. 60–99, Copyright 1989, with permission from Elsevier. Reprinted from *The Lancet, 21*, Johnson, J. S., and Newport, E. L., Critical period effects in second language learning; The influence of maturational state on the acquisition of English as a second language, pp. 60–99, Copyright 1989, with permission from Elsevier.

Compared with phonology and morphosyntax, lexical semantics (knowledge of word meanings) does not appear to be affected by age of arrival. Adult second language learners show brain responses that are different from native speakers for sentences with morphosyntactic violations, but not for sentences with incorrect word use (e.g., Weber-Fox & Neville, 1996). In summary, the results on second language learning suggest that not all components of language are affected equally and that when there is age-related decline in learning, performance drops off gradually, with even young arrivals performing less well than people who learned English from birth.

How should we explain this pattern of results in second language learning? At least two types of mechanisms have been suggested. One is that age itself (or maturation) is the underlying cause. Lenneberg's original proposal about critical periods relies on maturation. Other more recent suggestions are based on the notion that younger learners are fundamentally different from older learners, but this difference isn't in their ability to learn language per se. Rather, general purpose mechanisms such as memory and processing speed that affect all learning also affect language, serendipitously making it easier for younger humans to learn language (Elman, 1993; Newport, 1990). A second possibility is that learning a second language beyond childhood is harder because of interference from the first language. Although there are well-documented interference effects, interference is probably an incomplete explanation. That is because, as we discuss below, very similar age-related effects on language learning can be seen in children and adults who had no real first language at all (Newport, Bavelier, & Neville, 2001).

Age Effects in First Language Learning

A very small number of cases have been documented of children who were not exposed to a human language until well beyond the age that language is normally learned. One problem with these studies is that at least some of the children may have had pre-existing neuropsychological disorders that would have made language learning difficult even in the best of circumstances. Nevertheless, the studies suggest that there is an age effect in first language learning. Table 9–1 briefly summarizes the results from several studies. The data in the table show that the two older learners (both about 13 years) had poor out-

Table 9–1. Summary of Data from Four Studies of Children Deprived of Early Language Exposure

Child (Researcher)	Age	Input	Pre-existing condition?	Outcome
Victor (Itard, 1932)	approx. 13	?, not recent	some evidence	no speech
Genie (Curtiss, 1977)	13;6	very little	some evidence	little speech
Isabelle (Davis, 1947; Mason, 1942)	6;6	gesture	no evidence	normal language
Mary (Skuse, 1984)	2;4	some	probably	some speech, little language
Louise (Skuse, 1984)	3;6	some	no evidence	normal speech and language

comes with regard to spoken language, while two of the three younger learners achieved normal language. The one exception among the younger learners is likely to have had a neuropsychological disorder independent of language.

> **Thought Question**
>
> What one type of data would be most helpful for being able to draw the conclusion that age, and not a pre-existing neurologic condition, is responsible for the pattern of language outcomes seen in Table 9-1?

Another less rare population of people who learn their first language at different ages can be found among deaf adults whose exposure to American Sign Language (ASL) came at different points in their childhood or adolescence. These adults show effects of age of exposure on their morphosyntactic skills in ASL as much as 50 years later (Emmorey & Carina, 1990; Mayberry & Fischer, 1989; Newport, 1990). In summary, the data on age of exposure to first language are remarkably consistent with data from the more typical second language learning situation. The data suggest that there are effects of age and/or of nonlinguistic experience that prevent older learners from achieving the same outcomes as younger learners. We will see similar age effects when we look at people who must create language in order to communicate in the absence of a pre-existing target language.

■ Creating Language Structure

The studies presented above examined people who were not given a language model until after the normal age of exposure. However, these people were generally linguistically isolated, either because they were indeed alone, or because the people around them did not want to or could not communicate with them. In this section we contrast that situation with one in which a person or people without a full language model either augment a rudimentary input language or create a new language in order to communicate. One such study involves deaf children who are learning ASL from hearing parents who themselves learned sign language in adulthood to communicate with their deaf infant. These parents have been shown to make very inconsistent use of the morphosyntactic markers of ASL. Their children, however, regularize the inconsistent forms, thereby looking more like native signers than their parents (Ross & Newport, 1996; Singleton & Newport, 2004).

A similar situation can be seen in the fascinating emergence of Nicaraguan Sign Language (NSL; Kegl, 2002). NSL was created in the 1970s and 1980s when two schools for the deaf were begun in Nicaragua. Prior to the creation of the schools, deaf children stayed in their home villages, communicating as best they could with the hearing community. When the schools were begun, formal instruction emphasized spoken Spanish, lip-reading, and finger-spelling. However, in order to communicate with each other, the students developed their own sign system that became increasingly standardized across signers. Once the schools had been in operation for a sufficient number of years, new students did not need to create a language, but could learn the system that the previous students (the first cohort) had created. One interesting line of research has followed the change in NSL as the second cohort of students has begun using the language (Senghas, 2003; Senghas & Coppola, 2001). One study focused on a morpheme that modifies a basic verb (e.g., *pay*) to indicate the object of the verb. For example, a referent *man* might have been indicated as an arbitrary location in space (e.g., to the left of the signer), and to indicate that someone was paying the man, the verb *pay* would be made in the direction of the previously established referent (note that such a system is also used in other independently created signed languages). Members of the first cohort showed little use of this spatial verb marker. Adult members of the second cohort also showed little use of the marker. However, children of the second cohort substantially increased the use of the marker, but only in a set of contexts that were linguistically appropriate. Thus, like children learning ASL from an inconsistent model, children in the second cohort made the language more regular.

Another approach to understanding age effects on learning from inconsistent input can be seen in studies comparing adults' and children's ability to learn an artificial language in the laboratory. Hudson and Newport (1999; Hudson Kam & Newport, 2005) explored the conditions under which language learners are most likely to make changes to their input. They exposed adults and children to an artificial language system in which nonsense nouns and verbs referred to objects and actions in an artificial world presented on a video display. The language contained four types of sentences: intransitive, transitive, negative intransitive, and negative transitive. The sentences were presented with an optional negative marker followed by verb, subject, and an optional object. There were two determiners, and nouns were randomly assigned to occur with just one of them. Participants were assigned to one of four conditions, with consistency of determiner use in the input varying across conditions. Determiners were used either 45%, 60%, 75%, or 100% of the time. In a sentence completion task, adults matched their production of determiners to the condition that they were in. For example, adults in the 45% determiner use condition-produced determiners about 45% of the time, whereas adults in the 60% determiner use condition-produced determiners about 60% of the time. In contrast, 5- to 7-year-old children, when faced with sentences in which a determiner was presented 60% of the time, regularized determiner use, producing determiners on almost all utterances.

These results, like the results from the NSL study, suggest that children are more likely than adults to create a language system that is more regular than their input.

The studies described above all have in common the fact that learners take elements from their input that are not used systematically and make them systematic in ways consistent with existing languages. Other researchers have examined the situation when a deaf child has no language input at all and creates a gestural communication system called "home sign" (e.g., Feldman, Goldin-Meadow, & Gleitman, 1978; Goldin-Meadow & Mylander, 1998). Goldin-Meadow and Mylander (1998) report that four American and four Chinese deaf children, who were never exposed to a signed language, each showed a set of linguistic properties in their utterances that the authors convincingly argue cannot easily be attributed to the gestural input of their parents. First, they produced sequences expressing sentencelike content, as well as gestures for single words. Second, they produced multiclause sentences. Third, all eight children showed a pattern of production that is consistent with a particular grammatical system (ergative) that is found in human languages, such as Inuit. At the very least, the studies of home sign suggest that human children are biased to express themselves in predicates and arguments that have a regular form. That is, unlike the various nonhuman primates described in Chapter 1, children with no language input do not appear to be inclined to produce utterances that simply refer.

■ Summary

We began Chapter 9 with the hope that studies of language development in atypical populations or situations might augment the studies discussed in Chapters 2 through 8, with the result that we would have a better understanding of the relative contributions of biology, linguistic input, and their interaction. Although the studies presented in this chapter raise at least as many questions as they answer, they combine with the information that we already have to allow us to make several tentative conclusions about the nature of language development.

First, infants and children, regardless of whether they are genetically intact and learning language in a typical situation or not, are keen observers and impressive generalizers. We began the book with the assumption that generalization is the central question in studies of language development, and study after study demonstrated that infants and children notice and generalize over a vast variety of patterns in their environment. Studies of artificial language learning demonstrate that they even generalize patterns that do not occur in real human languages. Such studies suggest that our human ability to generalize from input may initially extend beyond patterns that we actually put to use in the service of communication. A related point is that the types of generalizations that we make most readily change as we gain experience with our world. We saw in Chapter 3 that older learners fail to make some phonological generalizations that younger learners make. And we saw in Chapter 5 that the shape bias in word learning seems to emerge through experience with many shape-based categories. Thus, whatever propensities to generalize we are born with may quickly be replaced with new ones that are more in keeping with the particular environment we inhabit.

Second, infants and children overgeneralize. The famous example of children producing *goed* instead of *went* has been the subject of at least 50 years of theorizing. Grammarless computational models of overgeneralization are important because they demonstrate that the young child's almost obsessive cleanup of messy input may have its origins in a fairly simple mechanism. Whether such models ultimately can account for the types of overgeneralization we see in real learners has yet to be determined. A number of studies presented in Chapter 9 demonstrate that, although children have a propensity to overgeneralize, adults do not. This observation may in fact lie at the heart of age-related differences in the ability to learn a language. As seen in the studies of Nicaraguan Sign Language, children's propensity to overgeneralize is largely responsible for language change. One question we must now ask is whether children's overgeneralization stems from general cognitive abilities (e.g., the inability to remember the specifics of the input as well as adults can) or whether they show a particular propensity to overgeneralize *languagelike* input.

Third, humans seem to want their communication structured in certain ways. The studies of deaf children's creation of home sign clearly show that what we want to communicate to our fellow humans is predicative, not merely referential. However, the fascinating data on home sign must be seen in the context of the data on Nicaraguan Sign Language. The relation between a human predisposition for predicative communication and the stable communicative system (language) that is the ultimate result is expressed nicely by Ann Senghas (2003), writing about the second cohort of NSL users: " . . . this new version of the language is not unrelated to its model; it is derived from it. Forms that exist in free variation or with some other function in the language of the first cohort were available for the second cohort to use as raw materials for creating new form-function mappings. If the first stage were not necessary, all of NSL would have appeared in a single sweep, instead of being built cohort by cohort." Thus, one way of viewing these studies is that humans are biologically disposed to communicate certain aspects our mental lives: predicates and arguments, or thought of another way, events. The predicate-argument or event structure of our intended communication puts some constraints on the forms that language can take. But those constraints alone ultimately do not determine the grammars that each language settles on. Rather, child language learners, largely through a process of overgeneralization, reshape the input.

Alas, the notion that children reshape their input brings us back to our original question about the nature (and nurture) of language learners. Do the structures that children impose on messy input reflect an innate grammar that is elicited by certain types of environmental stimuli? Or are the linguistic structures that arise from the learning process simply good ways to communicate efficiently? The observation that human languages use a relatively limited set of forms to communicate might be taken as evidence for the view that input elicits pre-existing grammars. However, the data from Specific Language Impairment and Williams syndrome make clear that the entity we call 'language' does not reflect a single ability. Phonology, morphosyntax, and lexical knowledge are differentially affected by different genetic anomalies.

Furthermore, even within these larger linguistic domains, there is considerable variation: Verbal morphology may be affected in SLI differently than some other aspects of morphosyntax. Receptive vocabulary in WS is affected very differently from the ability to produce a label for a picture. In short, when language "breaks," it fractures along lines not easily predicted by either a general purpose learning mechanism or any currently proposed innate grammar. Those of us who care about the biological underpinnings of language and what they reveal about what it means to be human clearly have many years of work ahead of us. This book is an invitation to join us.

■ References

Bellugi, U., Bihrle, A., Neville, H., Jernigan, T., & Doherty, S. (1992). Language, cognition and brain organization in a neurodevelopmental disorder. In M. Gunnar & C. Nelson (Eds.), *Developmental behavioral neuroscience* (pp. 25-56). Hillsdale, NJ: Erlbaum.

Bellugi, U., Marks, S., Bihrle, A., & Sabo, H. (1988). Dissociations between language and cognitive functions in Williams syndrome. In D. Bishop & K. Mogford (Eds.), *Language development in exceptional circumstances* (pp. 177-189). Edinburgh, UK: Churchill Livingstone.

Bishop, D. V. M. (2006). What causes Specific Language Impairment in children? *Current Trends in Psychological Science, 15*, 217-221.

Brock, J. (2007). Language abilities in Williams syndrome: A critical review. *Development and Psychopathology, 19*, 97-127.

Curtiss, S. (1977). A psycholinguistic study of a modern-day "Wild Child" New York: Academic Press.

Davis, K. (1947). Final note on a case of extreme isolation. *American Journal of Sociology, 52*, 432-437.

Elman, J. L. (1993). Implicit learning in neural networks: The importance of starting small. *Cognition, 46*, 71-99.

Emmorey, K., & Carina, D. (1990). Lexical recognition in sign language, Effects of phonetic structure and morphology. *Perceptual and Motor Skills, 71*, 1227-1252.

Feldman, H., Goldin-Meadow, S., & Gleitman, L. (1978). Beyond Herotodus: The creation of language by linguistically deprived deaf children. In A. Lock (Ed.), *Action, symbol, and gesture: The emergence of language* (pp. 351-414). New York: Academic Press.

Goldin-Meadow, S., & Mylander, C. (1998). Spontaneous sign systems created by deaf children in two cultures. *Nature, 391*(6664), 279-281.

Hudson, C., & Newport, E. L. (1999). Creolization: Could adults really have done it all? In A. Greenhill, H. Littlefeld, & C. Tano (Eds.), *Proceedings of the 23rd Annual Boston University Conference on Language Development* (pp. 265-276). Somerville, MA: Cascadilla Press.

Hudson Kam, C., & Newport, E. L. (2005). Regularizing unpredictable variation in creole formation: The roles of adult and child learners. *Language Learning and Development, 1*, 151-195.

Itard, J. M. G. (1932). *The wild boy of Aveyron.* New York: Century.

Joanisse, M. F., & Seidenberg, M. S. (2003). Phonology and syntax in specific language impairment: Evidence from a connectionist model. *Brain and Language, 86*, 40-56.

Johnson, J. S., & Newport, E. L. (1989). Critical period effects in second language learning; the influence of maturational state on the acquisition of English as a second language. *Cognitive Psychology, 21*, 60-99.

Kegl, J. (2002). Language emergence in a language-ready brain: Acquisition issues. In G. Morgan & B. Woll (Eds.), *Language acquisition in signed languages* (pp. 207-254). Cambridge: Cambridge University Press.

Landau, B., & Zukowski, A. (2003). Objects, motions, and paths: Spatial language in children with Williams syndrome. *Developmental Neuropsychology, 23,* 105-137.

Lenneberg, E. (1967). *Biological foundations of language.* New York: Wiley.

Leonard, L. B. (1998). *Children with specific language impairment.* Cambridge, MA: MIT Press.

Leonard, L. B., & Bortolini, U. (1998). Grammatical morphology and the role of weak syllables in the speech of Italian-speaking children with specific language impairment. *Journal of Speech, Language, and Hearing Research, 41*(6), 1363-1374.

Leonard, L. B., Davis, J., & Deevy, P. (2007). Phonotactic probability and past tense use by children with specific language impairment and their typically developing peers. *Clinical Linguistics and Phonetics, 21,* 747-758.

Mason, M. K. (1942). Learning to speak after six and one-half years of silence. *Journal of Speech Disorders, 7,* 295-304.

Mayberry, R., & Fischer, S. D. (1989). Looking through phonological shape to lexical meaning; The bottleneck of non-native sign language processing. *Memory and Cognition, 17,* 740-754.

McGregor, K., & Leonard, L. B. (1994). Subject pronoun and article omissions in the speech of children with specific language impairment: A phonological interpretation. *Journal of Speech and Hearing Research, 37,* 171-181.

Newport, E. L. (1990). Maturational constraints on language-learning. *Cognitive Science, 14,* 11-28.

Newport, E. L., Bavelier, D., & Neville, H. J. (2001). Critical thinking about critical Periods: perspectives on a critical period for language acquisition. In E. Dupoux (Ed.), *Language, brain, and cognitive development: Essays in honor of Jacques Mehler* (pp. 481-502). Cambridge, MA: MIT Press.

Oyama, S. (1976). A sensitive period for the acquisition of a non-native phonological system. *Journal of Psycholinguistic Research, 5,* 261-283.

Plante, E. (1991). MRI findings in the parents and siblings of specifically language-impaired boys. *Brain and Language, 41*(1), 67-80.

Rice, M. L. (2007). Children with Specific Language Impairment: Bridging the genetic and developmental perspectives. In *Blackwell's handbook of language development.* (pp. 173-190). Malden, MA: Blackwell.

Rice, M. L., Wexler, K., & Cleave, P. L. (1995). Specific language impairment as a period of extended optional infinitive. *Journal of Speech and Hearing Research, 38,* 850-863.

Ross, D. S., & Newport, E. L. (1996). The development of language from non-native linguistic input. In A. Stringfellow, D. Cahana-Amitay, E. Hughes, & A. Zukowski (Eds.), *Proceedings of the 20th Annual Boston University*

Conference on Language Development: Vol. 2. (pp. 634–645). Somerville, MA: Cascadilla Press.

Scovel, T. (2000). A critical review of the Critical Period Hypothesis. *Annual Review of Applied Linguistics, 20,* 213–223.

Senghas, A. (2003). Intergenerational influence and ontogenetic development in the emergence of spatial grammar in Nicaraguan Sign Language. *Cognitive Development, 18,* 511–531.

Senghas, A., & Coppola, M. (2001). Children creating language: How Nicaraguan Sign Language acquired a spatial grammar. *Psychological Science, 12,* 323–328.

Singleton, J. L., & Newport, E. L. (2004). When learners surpass their models: The acquisition of American Sign Language from inconsistent input. *Cognitive Psychology, 49,* 370–407.

Skuse, D. (1984). Extreme deprivation in early childhood-ii. Theoretical issues and a comparative review. *Journal of Child Psychology and Psychiatry, 25,* 543–572.

Stevens, T., & Karmiloff-Smith, A. (1997). Word learning in a special population: Do individuals with Williams syndrome obey lexical constraints. *Journal of Child Language, 24,* 3737–3765.

Stromswold, K. (1998). Genetics of spoken language disorders. *Human Biology, 70,* 297–324.

Tallal, P., Hirsch, L. S., & Realpe-Bonilla, T. (2001). Familial aggregation in specific language impairment. *Journal of Speech, Language, and Hearing Research, 44,* 1172–1182.

Thal, D., Bates, E., & Bellugi, U. (1989). Language and cognition in two children with Williams syndrome. *Journal of Speech and Hearing Research, 32,* 489–500.

Tomblin, J. B., Records, N. L., Buckwalter, P., Zhang, X., Smith, E., & O'Brien, M. (1997). The prevalence of specific language impairment in kindergarten children. *Journal of Speech and Hearing Research, 40,* 1245–1260.

van der Lely, H. K. J. (2005). Domain-specific cognitive systems: Insight from Grammatical-SLI. *Trends in Cognitive Sciences, 9,* 53–59.

Volterra, V., Caselli, M. C., Capirci, O., Tonucci, L., & Vicari, S. (2003). Early linguistic abilities of Italian children with Williams syndrome. *Developmental Neuropsychology, 23,* 33–58.

Weber-Fox, C., & Neville, H. J. (1996). Maturational constraints on functional specializations for language processing: ERP and behavioral evidence in bilingual speakers. *Journal of Cognitive Neuroscience, 8,* 231–256.

10 Some Methods Used in Language Development Research

This chapter reviews some behavioral and brain activation methods used in language development research. For each method, the age range of use, the dependent variable (what is measured), and a reference for further information are given.

■ Some Behavioral Methods Focusing on Infant Form Discrimination

The methods in this section are used to ask if infants can discriminate two or more linguistic forms. Typically, the forms are syllables, the auditory forms of words or word lists, or the auditory forms of phrases, clauses, or sentences.

Contingent Sucking Rate Procedure

Age range: birth to 4 months

Dependent variable: sucking rate during test compared with baseline sucking rate

Reference for further information: DeCasper and Fifer (1980)

The Contingent Sucking Rate Procedure has two phases, a base rate phase and a test phase. In the base rate phase, infants are giver a pacifier that is connected to a pressure transducer to establish their median sucking rate. In the test phase, the stimulus that infants hear is contingent on their sucking rate relative to the base rate, with different groups of infants subject to different contingencies.] Generally, half of the infants hear Stimulus A if they suck above their baseline rate and Stimulus B if they suck below that rate. The other half of the infants hears Stimulus B for sucking above the baseline and Stimulus A for sucking above the baseline. If infants in the two groups show opposite patterns of sucking (e.g., A>B for group 1 and B>A for group 2), we can conclude that infants discriminate the two types of stimuli.

High Amplitude Sucking Procedure

Age range: birth to 4 months

Dependent variable: sucking rate during test compared with sucking rate at the end of habituation

Reference for further information: Jusczyk (1985)

The High Amplitude Sucking (HAS) Procedure uses the observation that infants can learn to control the presentation of an auditory stimulus by how hard they suck on a pacifier. The pacifier is attached to a pressure transducer, which measures the strength and frequency of the infant's sucking. The HAS Procedure has three phases: base rate, habituation, and test. The base rate phase is used to collect data about an individual infant's median sucking rate in the absence of any stimulus. During the habituation phase, infants are exposed to an auditory stimulus, and the presentation rate of the stimulus is contingent on how many sucks per second they make. As infants discover this contingency, their sucking rate at first increases. However, as they habituate to (lose interest in) the stimulus, their sucking rate decreases. When sucking rate falls to a predetermined criterion level, which is a function of the infant's baseline, the habituation phase ends. In some studies, a delay is introduced between habituation and test, whereas in other studies, the test phase immediately follows the habituation phase. During test, each infant is assigned to one of two (or more) conditions. Infants in the control group hear the same stimuli presented during habituation. Infants in the experimental condition(s) hear different stimuli from those heard during habituation. If infants in the experimental condition(s) show greater sucking rates in the test phase than habituation phase, while infants in the control group do not, we can conclude that infants are able to discriminate the habituation stimulus from the experimental stimulus presented at test.

Headturn Preference Procedure

Age range: 4 to 20 months

Dependent variable: amount of time infant orients toward source of sound on one type of test trial versus another

References for further information: Kemler Nelson, Jusczyk, Mandel, Myers, Turk, and Gerken (1995); Jusczyk and Aslin (1995)

The Headturn Preference Procedure (HPP) can be used in two different versions. In one version, infants are tested on the knowledge that they bring into the laboratory, and there is only a test phase. In the second version, infants are familiarized with some new auditory information and then tested. The test procedure for the two methods is identical (Figure 10–1). Both familiarization and test take place either in a sound-attenuated booth or other enclosure. The experimenter sits outside the structure and is prevented from hearing the auditory stimuli. The infant sits on the caregiver's lap in the booth, and there are lights and speakers on either side of the infant and a light in front of the infant. A video camera is focused on the infant's face. During the familiarization phase (which is only used in one version of the procedure), a central light flashes to get the infant's attention at center. The experimenter, upon seeing that the infant has looked to center, causes the computer that controls the procedure to begin familiarization. Sound comes out of both left and right speakers and continues to play throughout familiarization. In addition, so that infants become familiar with the contingencies of their looking and side lights flashing, one of the side lights begins to flash. When the infant looks away, the side light goes off, the center light goes on until the infant looks back to center, and a side light (randomly selected) flashes again. This sequence is repeated until the end of the familiarization stimulus, which usually plays for about two minutes. In the test phase, there are usually two to four types of test trials, half of which are consistent with some property of the infant's native language or with the familiarization stimuli and half that are similar but inconsistent. A test trial begins with the center light flashing. Upon seeing that the infant is looking at the center light, the experimenter initiates a trial on the computer. One of the side lights begins to flash, and when the infant looks to the appropriate side, the auditory stimulus plays out of the speaker over the light and continues to play until the infant looks away, at which point the trial ends. A new trial begins with the flashing

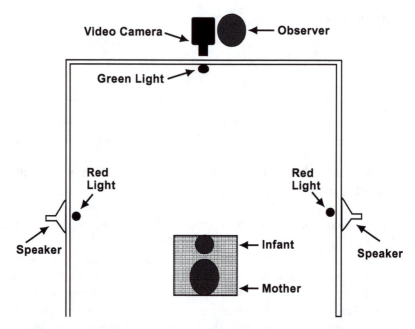

Figure 10–1. Schematic of Headturn Preference Procedure. From *Infant Behavior and Development*, *18*, Kemler Nelson, D., Jusczyk, P. W., Mandel, D. R., Myers, J., Turk, A. E., and Gerken, L. A., The headturn preference procedure for testing auditory perception, pp. 111–116, Copyright (1995), with permission from Elsevier. Reprinted from *The Lancet*, *18*, Kemler Nelson, D., Jusczyk, P. W., Mandel, D. R., Myers, J., Turk, A. E., and Gerken, L. A., The headturn preference procedure for testing auditory perception, pp. 111–116, Copyright (1995), with permission from Elsevier.

light, and proceeds as described. There are usually between 8 and 16 test trials per infant. If infants listen longer to one type of test stimulus than another, we can conclude that they are able to discriminate the two types of test stimuli.

Central Fixation Preferential Listening Procedure

Age range: 4 to 20 months

Dependent variable: amount of time infant toward a centrally presented visual display on one type of test trial versus another

Reference for further information: Maye, Werker, and Gerken (2002)

The Central Fixation Preference Procedure is almost identical to the HPP, described above, but instead of requiring infants to turn their heads, their looking time toward a centrally presented visual display (e.g., a bull's-eye or checkerboard) is measured. Auditory stimuli are presented from a single speaker that is usually below the visual display. As in the HPP, both test-only and familiarization-plus-test versions can be used.

Visual Habituation Procedure

Age range: 6 to 20 months

Dependent variable: amount of time that infants orient toward a centrally presented visual display (e.g., checkerboard) for one type of auditory stimulus versus another

Reference for further information: Horowitz (1975)

The Visual Habituation Procedure has two phases, a habituation phase and a test phase. In the habituation phase, infants hear some auditory stimulus as long as they look toward a centrally presented visual stimulus. When they look away, an attention-getting stimulus appears, and a new habituation trial begins. Infants participate in habituation trials for as long as their looking time per trial does not fall below a certain criterion, which is measured against the first few habituation trials. After habituation, infants are presented with two or more test trials of different types. If looking times at test increase over those at the end of habituation, we can conclude that infants discriminate the stimuli in the habituation phase from the stimuli in the test phase.

Conditioned Head Turn Procedure

Age range: 6 to 18 months

Dependent variable: how many correct head turns versus false alarms (turns when no change occurs) each infant makes

Reference for further information: Werker, Polka, and Pegg (1997)

Figure 10–2. A child being tested using the Conditioned Headturn Procedure. From *Early Development and Parenting, 6,* The conditioned head turn procedure as a method for testing infant speech perception, Werker, J. F., Polka, L., & Pegg, J. E., Copyright 1997, John Wiley & Sons Limited. Reproduced with permission.

The Conditioned Head Turn Procedure has a training phase and a testing phase (Figure 10–2). In the training phase, infants are taught that, if they turn their head when they detect a change in the auditory stimulus, they are rewarded with a mechanical toy becoming visible and moving (e.g., a toy monkey playing symbols). The changes in this phase should be ones that are readily detectable. In the test phase, the changes in the auditory stimulus can be of different types. If infants turn their head for a majority of stimulus changes, we can determine that they are able to detect that change. Note that this measure allows the researcher to make judgments about the abilities of individual infants and is therefore frequently used in clinical settings.

■ Behavioral Methods Focusing on Infants' Ability to Associate Form and Reference

The methods in this section are used to ask if infants are able to associate a linguistic form, usually a word or a sentence, with a referent, usually a static picture or video of an object or a scene.

Intermodal Preferential Looking Procedure

Age range: 6 months to 3 years

Dependent variables: the first picture that the infant looks at after hearing an auditory stimulus and the picture that the infant looks at the longest

Reference for further information: Golinkoff, Hirsh-Pasek, Cauley, and Gordon (1987)

The Intermodal Preferential Looking Procedure (IPLP) asks if infants are able to pair an auditory stimulus with the appropriate static picture or video (Figure 10–3). In it, the infant sits on a caregiver's lap or in a high chair. Two video screens or a single wide-screen is used to

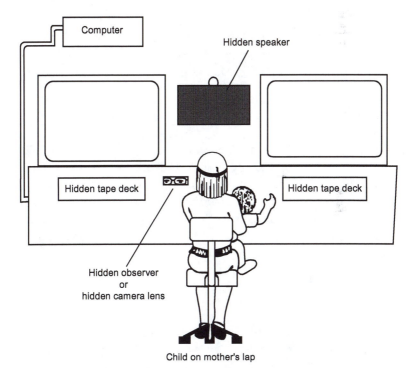

Child on mother's lap

Figure 10–3. Schematic of the Intermodal Preferential Looking Procedure. From Golinkoff, R., Chung, H. L., Hirsh-Pasek, K., Liu, J., Bertenthal, B. I., Brand, R., et al. Young children can extend motion verbs to point-light displays, *Developmental Psychology*, *38*(4), 604–614, 2002, American Psychological Association. Reprinted with permission.

present two pictures, one on the left and one on the right. A video camera is centered on the infant's face to allow an experimenter to determine where the infant is looking at each moment in time. An auditory stimulus is either spoken or presented from a centrally located speaker, and the stimulus refers to one or the other of the two pictures or videos (e.g., *Where's the baby?* presented when the infant can look at a picture or a baby or a shoe). The independent variable is the nature of the visual stimuli (e.g., pictures that represent two familiar objects versus one familiar and one unfamiliar), the auditory stimulus (e.g., a word that the child knows well versus one that she has just learned), or both. Often the dependent variables on test trials are compared to the comparable measures when no auditory stimulus is presented.

Looking While Listening Procedure

Age range: 6 months to 3 years

Dependent variables: a coder's judgment about where the infant is looking in a frame-by-frame coding of a video of the child or from an eye-tracker that is placed on the child's head

References for further information: Fernald, Swingley, and Pinto (2001), Aslin and McMurray (2004)

The Looking While Listening Procedure is very similar to the IPLP in the age of infants who can be tested, the equipment used, and the sorts of independent variables that can be manipulated. What differs is the dependent variable. The moment-to-moment looking data from the Looking While Listening Procedure can provide information about how a child processes auditory and visual information over time.

Switch Procedure

Age range: 14 to 20 months

Dependent variable: difference in looking time from the end of habituation to the switch trials

Reference for further information: Werker, Cohen, Lloyd, Casasola, and Stager (1998)

The Switch procedure involves two phases, habituation and test (Figure 10–4). In the habituation phase, the infant sees a picture and

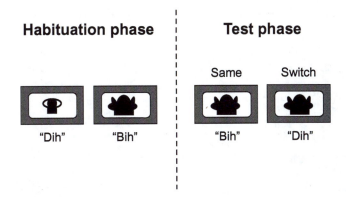

Figure 10–4. Schematic of one use of the Switch procedure.

hears an auditory stimulus (e.g., a word). When the infant's interest in the picture-word combination falls below a preset level, as evident by the length of looks at the picture, the habituation phase ends. In the test phase, the infant sees different combinations of pictures and words. The combination can either be the same as in habituation, a different word with a previously seen picture, or a different picture with a previously heard word. If infants show differential attention on test trials than at the end of habituation, we can conclude that they have noticed a difference in the picture-word pairing between habituation and test.

■ Methods Measuring Brain Activity

Four methods for measuring brain activity that can be used with infants and children are presented illustrated in Figure 10–5. For each method, a sample study is described.

Event-Related Potentials

Age range: newborn and older

Dependent variable: the time course of electrical activity from different brain in response to a stimulus, averaged over a large number of stimuli

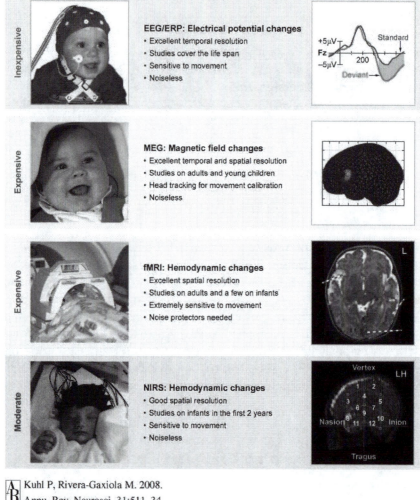

Neuroscience techniques used with infants

Inexpensive

EEG/ERP: Electrical potential changes
• Excellent temporal resolution
• Studies cover the life span
• Sensitive to movement
• Noiseless

Expensive

MEG: Magnetic field changes
• Excellent temporal and spatial resolution
• Studies on adults and young children
• Head tracking for movement calibration
• Noiseless

Expensive

fMRI: Hemodynamic changes
• Excellent spatial resolution
• Studies on adults and a few on infants
• Extremely sensitive to movement
• Noise protectors needed

Moderate

NIRS: Hemodynamic changes
• Good spatial resolution
• Studies on infants in the first 2 years
• Sensitive to movement
• Noiseless

Kuhl P, Rivera-Gaxiola M. 2008.
Annu. Rev. Neurosci. 31:511–34.

Figure 10–5. Four methods for measuring brain activity in infants and children. Reprinted, with permission, from the *Annual Review of Neuroscience*, Volume 31 ©2008 by Annual Reviews www.annualreview.org

Reference for further information: Kuhl and Rivera-Gaxiola (2008)

Event-Related Potentials (;ERPs) are measures of electrical activity in the brain in response to an environmental stimulus, such as a word. Small electrodes are attached to the listener's scalp, often by way of an electrode cap. Stimuli are presented, and the time course of the brain response is recorded. In one study using this method, 18- and 26-month-olds were presented with a gesture or a word, followed by a picture that either matched or didn't match the gesture or word (Sheehan, Namy, & Mills, 2007). Examples of gestures were the act of hammering or the act tooth-brushing. ERP's from the 18-month-olds showed a mismatch response (called an N400) when either the gesture or the word did not correspond to the picture, while the older children only showed the mismatch response when the word did not correspond with the picture.

Magnetoencephalography (MEG)

Age range: newborn and older

Dependent variable: the area(s) of the brain that are active while the participant is exposed to a particular stimulus and/or engaged in a particular task

Reference for further information: Kuhl and Rivera-Gaxiola (2008)

Magnetoencephalography (MEG) measures magnetic fields from electrical currents produced by the brain. In one recent study, sleeping infants were presented with normal speech and speech with the prosody removed (Sambeth, Ruohio, Alku, Fellman, & Huotilainen, 2008). Infants produced significantly stronger magnetic fields for the normal speech.

Functional Magnetic Resonance Imaging (fMRI)

Age range: newborn and older, although studies with fully awake children generally begin at age 3 or 4 years

Dependent variable: the area(s) of the brain that are active while the participant is exposed to a particular stimulus and/or engaged in a particular task

Reference for further information: Kuhl and Rivera-Gaxiola (2008)

Blood oxygen level-dependent (BOLD) fMRI measures changes in oxygen levels in the brain as a person is engaged in different types of mental activity (hearing language, hearing music, etc.). In one study with sleeping 2- and 3-year-olds who were presented with speech stimuli, the younger children showed activation in frontal, cerebellar, and occipital regions of the brain, in addition to the temporal regions that are normally active during speech processing (Redcay, Haist, & Courchesne, 2008). In contrast, 3-year-olds brain responses were more restricted to classic speech processing areas and were larger in those areas than were the responses of the younger children.

Near Infrared Spectroscopy (NIRS)

Age range: newborn and older

Dependent variable: the area(s) of the brain that are active while the participant is exposed to a particular stimulus and/or engaged in a particular task

Reference for further information: Kuhl and Rivera-Gaxiola (2008)

The Near Infrared Spectroscopy (NIRS) procedure takes advantage of the fact that infants' skulls are relatively thin. The procedure involves a headband or cap on the infant's head. The headband contains both emitters that emit near-infrared light onto the infant's skull, and detectors that collect the light refracted from the underlying brain tissue. Because near-infrared light is sensitive to changes in blood flow, and neural activity generally results in an increase in blood flow to the active area, NIRS is used as a neural activation. In one study, researchers presented 6- and 9-month-olds with speech stimuli either alone or accompanied by a visual stimulus (Bortfeld, Wruck, & Boas, 2007). In the speech alone condition, the left temporal regions of the brain were active, as we might expect them to be in adults. In the speech-plus-visual condition, both temporal and occipital (active for visual processing in adults) were active.

■ Methods for Testing Child Comprehension and Sensitivity to Morphosyntax

The methods in this section ask about children's ability to map a linguistic form onto meaning and to consciously evaluate the acceptability of linguistic forms, either as they relate to meaning, or just as forms.

Picture Selection Procedure

Age range: 20 months and older

Dependent variables: number of correct pictures selected or the time it takes to select a picture

Reference for further information: Gerken and Shady (1996)

In the Picture Selection Procedure, children hear a word or sentence and select the picture, usually out of a set of two-four pictures, that fits the word or sentence. In one version of the task, the independent variable is aspects of the word or sentence that would lead to selection of different pictures. For example, there might pictures of a pear and a bear with the accompanying word *pear*. Alternatively, at the sentence level, there might be a picture of a girl playing with one dog and another picture of a girl playing with two dogs, with the accompanying sentence, *The girl plays with the dogs*. In another version of the Picture Selection Procedure, only one of the pictures is related in any way to the auditory stimulus, but the auditory stimulus varies as to whether it is grammatical. For example, a child might hear *Find was dog for me* and be asked to choose among a dog, a shoe, a house, and a girl. The logic of this version of the procedure is that, if children notice the ungrammaticality of the sentence, they might be slower or less likely to choose the correct picture. The picture used in the task can either be presented as individual pages, in book form, or on a computer screen. If the latter form of presentation is used along with a touch-sensitive screen, the time that it takes children to respond can be measured.

Act-Out Procedure

Age range: 2 years and older

Dependent variable: number of sentences or sentence components correctly acted out

Reference for further information: Goodluck (1996)

In the Act-Out Procedure, children are given a set of toys and asked to act out a sentence with them. For example, a child might hear, *After he chased the pig, the cow took a nap*. The experimenter might note what the child did at the session itself. Often sessions are video-taped, and how the child acted out each sentence can be coded from the tape.

Grammaticality Judgments

Age range: 3 years and older

Dependent variable: the number of sentences children judge as grammatical

Reference for further information: McDaniel and Cairns (1996)

Children can be asked to say whether a particular sentence is grammatical. For example, an experimenter might ask, *"Is it ok to say 'I likes spinach?'"* Children can also be asked to say whether a particular sentence can have a particular interpretation. For example, the experimenter can show the child a dog puppet scratching itself and ask, *"Is it ok to say 'He scratched him?'"* One advantage of this task is that the experimenter can ask about multiple forms. For example, if the experimenter shows the child a dog puppet scratching a pig puppet, the experimenter can ask about the acceptability of both, *The dog scratched the pig* and *The pig was scratched by the dog.*

Truth-Value Judgments

Age range: 2 years and older

Dependent variable: the number of sentences of different types for which children accept as truthful a puppet's statement about an accompanying scene

Reference for further information: Gordon (1996)

The Truth-Value Judgment Procedure is something of a combination of Act-Out and Grammaticality Judgment Procedures. A scene is show to the child and a puppet. For example, the Smurf eats a hamburger inside a fenced area. The puppet then tries to describe the scene: *He ate the hamburger when the Smuf was inside the fence.* This sentence is not a truthful description of the scene because *he* cannot refer to the Smurf. If the child thinks that the told the truth, the puppet is fed a cookie, but if the puppet didn't tell the truth, the puppet is fed a rag.

■ Methods for Testing Language Production

The methods described in this section focus on methods for collecting children's speech and language production.

Spontaneous Speech

Age range: 6 months and older

Dependent variable: ways in which utterances are like and unlike the utterances of adult language

References for further information: de Boysson-Bardies et al. (1981), Chapter 4 of Snyder (2007)

Noting how children's utterances match and fail to match the utterances of the adult community is the origin of the study of language development. Researchers have studied children's spontaneously produced utterances at the level of babble, protowords, first words, first word combinations, sentence production, and discourse production. Spontaneous speech collected and coded by other researchers is available on the Child Language Data Exchange System (CHILDES; http://childes.psy.cmu.edu/). Collecting one's own spontaneous speech sample entails selecting a time that the child is likely to be talkative (or babbling), having the child engaged in an activity that is likely to generate speech, making sure that the environment is as quiet as possible to promote good recording, and setting up audio- and/or video-taping equipment so that it allows the child freedom but still results in a high-quality recording. Spontaneous speech data can be transcribed in a number of ways, depending on the research question. Phonetic transcription is best for young children who are still producing many phonologically deviant forms. Orthographic transcription is adequate for older children, with whom the linguistic area of interest is often word choice, sentence form, or discourse.

Imitative Speech

Age range: 18 months and older

Dependent variables: how children change the target utterance in their own imitation

Reference for further information: Lust, Flynn, and Foley (1996)

Imitative speech is often used when an experimenter wants to test hypotheses about the nature of a phenomenon that is first noticed in spontaneous speech. For example, is the child's omission of determiners like *the* affected by where in the sentence the determiner occurs, how long the sentence is, and so forth? Children who are asked to produce an utterance first produced by someone else often change the target utterance in ways that appear to be consistent with their own language development level. Therefore, imitation can be used to test hypotheses about the relation between an adult form and what the child is able to produce. Because children are sometimes reluctant to imitate an adult experimenter, having them imitate a puppet or computer is often a productive approach to eliciting imitated utterances.

Elicited Production

Age range: 18 months and older

Dependent variable: how many words, sentences, or sentence components the child produces correctly

Reference for further information: Thornton (1996)

Elicited productions are another useful and often time-saving supplement to children's spontaneous speech. Production can be elicited by simply asking children to name some pictures whose labels have specific properties of interest. For example, an experimenter might have a child produce the name for pictures of some soup and a shoe to determine if the productions of the first sounds were correct. The Elicited Production Procedure might also be used to get children to ask questions. For example, an experimenter might tell the child, *In this story, the crane is tickling one of the zebras. Ask the puppet which one.*

■ References

Aslin, R. N., & McMurray, B. (2004). Automated corneal-reflection eye tracking in infancy: Methodological developments and applications to cognition. *Infancy, 6*(2), 155–163.

Bortfeld, H., Wruck, E., & Boas, D. A. (2007). Assessing infants' cortical response to speech using near-infrared spectroscopy. *NeuroImage, 34*(1), 407–415.

de Boysson-Bardies, B., Sagart, L., & Bacri, N. (1981). Phonetic analysis of late babbling: A case study of a French child. *Journal of Child Language, 8*(3), 511–524.

DeCasper, A. J., & Fifer, W. P. (1980). Of human bonding: Newborns prefer their mothers' voices. *Science, 208*, 1174–1176.

Fernald, A., Swingley, D., & Pinto, J. P. (2001). When half a word is enough: Infants can recognize spoken words using partial phonetic information. *Child Development, 72*(4), 1003–1015.

Gerken, L. A., & Shady, M. E. (1996). The picture selection task. In D. McDaniel, C. McKee, & H. Cairns (Eds.), *Methods for assessing children's syntax* (pp. 125–146). Cambridge, MA: MIT Press.

Golinkoff, R., Chung, H. L., Hirsh-Pasek, K., Liu, J., Bertenthal, B. I., Brand, R., et al. (2002). Young children can extend motion verbs to point-light displays. *Developmental Psychology, 38*(4), 604–614.

Golinkoff, R., Hirsh-Pasek, K., Cauley, K., & Gordon, L. (1987). The eyes have it: Lexical and syntactic comprehension in a new paradigm. *Journal of Child Language, 14*, 23–45.

Goodluck, H. (1996). The act-out task. In D. McDaniel, C. McKee, & H. Cairns (Eds.), *Methods for assessing children's syntax* (pp. 147–162). Cambridge, MA: MIT Press.

Gordon, P. (1996). The truth-value judgment task. In D. McDaniel, C. McKee, & H. Cairns (Eds.), *Methods for assessing children's syntax* (pp. 211–232). Cambridge, MA: MIT Press.

Horowitz, F. D. (1975). Visual attention, auditory stimulation, and language. *Monographs of the Society for Research in Child, 39*(5), 1–140.

Jusczyk, P. W. (1985). The high-amplitude sucking technique as a methodological tool in speech perception research. In G. Gottlieb & N. A. Krasnegor (Eds.), *Measurement of audition and vision in the first year of postnatal life: A methodological overview* (pp. 195–222). Westport, CT: US Ablex.

Jusczyk, P. W., & Aslin, R. N. (1995). Infants' detection of the sound patterns of words in fluent speech. *Cognitive Psychology, 29*(1), 1–23.

Kemler Nelson, D., Jusczyk, P. W., Mandel, D. R., Myers, J., Turk, A. E., & Gerken, L. A. (1995). The headturn preference procedure for testing auditory perception. *Infant Behavior and Development, 18*, 111–116.

Kuhl, P. K., & Rivera-Gaxiola, M. (2008). Neural substrates of language acquisition. *Annual Review of Neuroscience, 31*, 511-534.

Lust, B., Flynn, S., & Foley, C. (1996). What children know about what they say: Elicited imitation as a research method for assessing children's syntax. In D. McDaniel, C. McKee, & H. Cairns (Eds.), *Methods for assessing children's syntax* (pp. 55-76). Cambridge, MA: MIT Press.

Maye, J., Werker, J. F., & Gerken, L. A. (2002). Infant sensitivity to distributional information can affect phonetic discrimination. *Cognition, 82*(3), B101-B111.

McDaniel, D., & Cairns, H. (1996). Eliciting judgments of grammaticality and reference. In C. M. D. McDaniel, & H. Cairns (Ed.), *Methods for assessing children's syntax* (pp. 233-254). Cambridge, MA: MIT Press.

Redcay, E., Haist, F., & Courchesne, E. (2008). Functional neuroimaging of speech perception during a pivotal period in language acquisition. *Developmental Science, 11*(2), 237-252.

Sambeth, A., Ruohio, K., Alku, P., Fellman, V., & Huotilainen, M. (2008). Sleeping newborns extract prosody from continuous speech. *Clinical Neurophysiology, 119*(2), 332-341.

Sheehan, E. A., Namy, L. L., & Mills, D. L. (2007). Developmental changes in neural activity to familiar words and gestures. *Brain and Language, 101*(3), 246-259.

Snyder, W. (2007). *Child language: The parametric approach*. Oxford: Oxford University Press.

Thorton, R. (1996). Elicited production. In D. McDaniel, C. McKee, & H. Cairns (Eds.), *Methods for assessing children's syntax* (pp. 77-102). Cambridge, MA: MIT Press.

Werker, J. F., Cohen, L. B., Lloyd, V. L., Casasola, M., & Stager, C. L. (1998). Acquisition of word-object associations by 14-month-old infants. *Developmental Psychology, 34*(6), 1289-1309.

Werker, J. F., Polka, L., & Pegg, J. E. (1997). The conditioned head turn procedure as a method for testing infant speech perception. *Early Development and Parenting, 6*, 171-178.

■ Index